IMAGES
of America

JOHNSTOWN

On the Cover: Harvey Jay Parish, the founder of Johnstown, is shown at the wheel of the first automobile in town, which Parish always jokingly referred to as his "One-lung Reo." He bought the car from the youngest automobile dealer in the state, Floyd Clymer of Berthoud, who was only 12 at the time. (Courtesy of Greeley History Museum.)

IMAGES
of America

JOHNSTOWN

Sandy Wailes Bennett and
the Johnstown Historical Society

ARCADIA
PUBLISHING

ISBN 978-0-7385-8119-4

Published by Arcadia Publishing
Charleston, South Carolina

Printed in the United States of America

Library of Congress Control Number: 2010922855

For all general information, please contact Arcadia Publishing:
Telephone 843-853-2070
Fax 843-853-0044
E-mail sales@arcadiapublishing.com
For customer service and orders:
Toll-Free 1-888-313-2665

Visit us on the Internet at www.arcadiapublishing.com

To those who have come before us, especially Clyde Miner Jr., whose memories preserving Johnstown's history have made all the difference

Contents

Acknowledgments

This book was compiled, written, and edited by Sandy Wailes Bennett. However, it would not have been possible without the research, photographs, and encouragement of the present and past members of the Johnstown Historical Society and museum. The author would especially like to thank Rebecca S. Healy, whose 1977 book, *A Tribute to Johnstown,* was essential in providing facts, information, and stories. Unless otherwise noted, all photographs were provided by the authors. The other images in this volume appear courtesy of the Greeley History Museum (GHM), the Denver Public Library Western History and Genealogy Department (DPL), and the Colorado Historical Society (CHS).

Devon Weston at Arcadia Publishing was indispensable in giving guidance and support. The following people are credited for their time, wisdom, information, and/or support in making this book possible: Candy Hamilton, Barbara Bowerman, Gregory Light, Peggy Ford Waldo, Ann Norman, Ann Schwalm, Gerri and Marvin Mellon, Doug Parish, the Albertson family, and Diane Brotemarkle. Finally thank you to my husband, Ken, my sons, Brad and Randy, and my sisters, Connie and Meg, for your support and love always, not just in writing this book.

Introduction

Johnstown is located on the plains of Colorado about 35 miles north of Denver, along the front range of the Rocky Mountains. It is a small Weld County community near the Fort Collins, Loveland, and Greeley triangle. Johnstown is growing rapidly, especially in land area. Now the town limits reach out to U.S. Highway 34, making it a short drive from downtown Johnstown to recreational facilities, medical services, entertainment, and shopping.

Even though it is ever changing and growing in population and land, Johnstown still retains that small town feel. Usually the reason you drive on one of the highways leading to Johnstown is that you intend to go there. People do not often just pass through. Therefore, it remains quiet. A person goes to Hays Market, intending to be there for only a few minutes, and ends up staying an hour and a half. People are still friendly there.

Harvey Jay Parish founded Johnstown. Parish realized that the Great Western Railway was going to be built just north of his homestead. He immediately purchased that land for $11 an acre and platted the town on that acreage. Johnstown was named after the founder's son. As Parish was planning the town in 1902, his son John was in the hospital in Denver suffering from a ruptured appendix. When Harvey was asked what he would call his new town, he replied, "It will be my son's town. Let's call it John's Town."

It is easy to imagine what the first settlers saw when they came to this area. There are remnants of the past everywhere a person looks. Dr. Glenn A. Jones walked from Windsor to Johnstown in the early 1920s. He reached the top of the hill north of town and called Johnstown "God's spot." He looked upon a beautiful valley, and to the west, a panoramic view of the Rockies. That view is still there.

One thing that is missing from the view of the plains is the abundant wildlife and the tribes of Native Americans who depended on the animals for their livelihood. Herds of buffalo and antelope brought the Arapaho and Cheyenne tribes to this area. They became friends with the early trappers and traders, until there were just too many white settlers coming into the area. When the gold seekers came in 1859 searching for their fortunes, it was the beginning of the end for the plains tribes. Many of the Arapaho and Cheyenne tribes were sent to Sand Creek and were never seen in the Johnstown area again. Sometimes someone finds an arrowhead in the freshly tilled soil. That is the only reminder that any of the plains tribes had been there.

Many who came looking for gold could not make a living from the treasure they sought. Many were "go backs" who turned away from mining and went home. Some, though, stayed and found the answer to the question "What else can we do?" The Brush brothers first became successful in the hay and freighting business near Johnstown and became suppliers to the miners. Bruce Johnson, a longtime friend of Jared Brush, described the freighting business from the Missouri River to Denver and the mining camps. They walked alongside five to six pairs of oxen hitched to wagons to make the 80-day round trip. They ate bread and water with a little syrup and sometimes bacon. There was not a tree, except along the river; nothing but barren prairie between where

Greeley and Golden now stand. In 1869, Jared Brush built a wooden barn in Johnstown, which was put together with wooden pegs. The barn is still used.

Although Stephen H. Long did not see the potential in the land for farming, Johnstown and Weld County have become one of the largest agricultural producers in the country. Three rivers, the Little Thompson and the Big Thompson as well as the South Platte, wind their way around Johnstown. First used by frontiersmen for travel and transport of goods, the rivers today continue to serve as the lifeblood of irrigation water for local agriculture. Although a large part of farmland began to be developed into residential housing in the mid-1990s, agricultural traditions continue today. Farms that have been worked in Johnstown for generations are still owned by the same family. They are still there.

The main industries of Johnstown were almost always agriculture related. The major industry in town for many years was the Great Western Sugar Factory. This barium-molasses refinery was known throughout the sugar world for its unique process. Foreign countries sent delegations throughout the years to view the operations.

Two groups of people who built the town but are hardly recognized are the female settlers and the Hispanic laborers in Johnstown. The women of the west needed to have that cowgirl spirit to survive the harsh conditions of the prairie. They established the moral and social values for the community. About one fourth of the population of Johnstown remains Hispanic. In the history of the community, people from Mexico were called on to perform the jobs that needed to be done. These people worked around feelings of prejudice many times, but they were the ones who, in large part, built the town of Johnstown. Many remained.

Echoes of the past and of the people who came before are still there. One need only look to see reminders. Some of the buildings that were originally built are still there. Most are not used for the same purpose as they once were, but they are still there. Some buildings, streets, and areas are named after Johnstown historical figures. These include Letford Elementary School, Glenn A. Jones Memorial Library, the Historic Parish House and Museum, Elwell Cemetery, Eddie Aragon Park, Hays Park, Parish Avenue, Becker Circle, and Maestas Street. The history of Johnstown is still visible everywhere.

One

The Land and People before Johnstown

Johnstown belies its looks. It may appear like any small town in the West, but underneath the facade is a town rich in the history of the 1800s. As with most stories of Colorado, the history of this area began with a river, the South Platte. Named for the French words meaning shallow, or flat, the South Platte breaks out of the mountains south of Denver and flows northeast past the vicinity of Johnstown and Weld County and finally out of Colorado. This river and this valley were the route of moving Indian tribes, explorers, trappers, traders, and gold seekers.

In 1820, the American explorer Stephen H. Long was sent to find the real worth of the Louisiana Purchase. He and his company followed the South Platte River all the way to the mountains. They found a landscape filled with animals of all kinds: herds of antelope, deer, buffalo, badgers, wolves, eagles, buzzards, ravens, owls, foxes, and rattlesnakes. The botanist of the expedition could not fathom how the barren land could support the amount of wildlife they found.

The Algonquin tribes of Cheyenne and Arapaho preceded the white men to the Platte River Valley by only 50 years. The Arapaho were especially good traders, and they welcomed the first white visitors to the area: the traders and trappers. The first dwellings of the white men along the river were trading posts, constructed for the purpose of purchasing beaver skins from the trappers and later buffalo skins from the Native Indian tribes. The white men and Indian tribes lived in peace and harmony until the miners came. The gold rush started in Colorado in 1859, and within 10 years, the plains Indians were either killed or relocated to the Indian Nation. Change came fast to the West. It did not take very long.

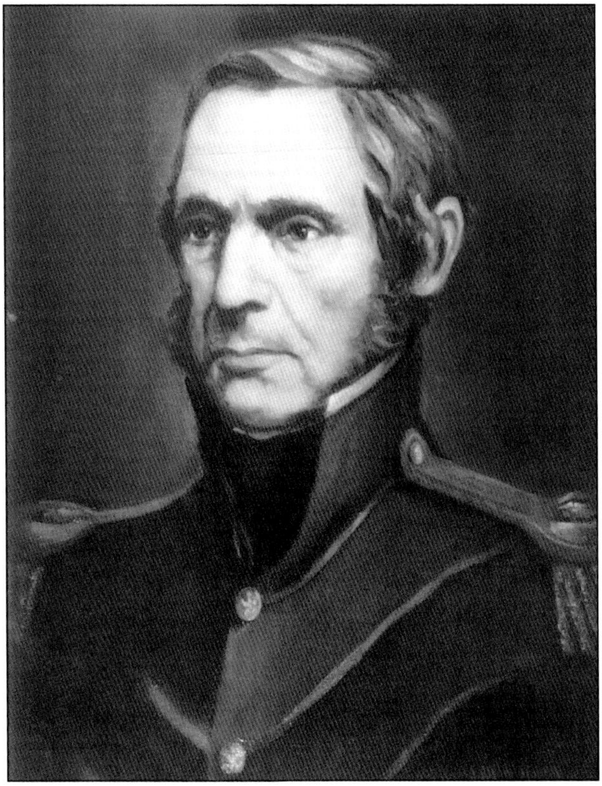

Almost 20 years after the Zebulon Pike Expedition was sent to explore this part of the United States, a second group, led by Maj. Stephen Harriman Long, followed the South Platte all the way to the mountains. Although Long found this region barren, the South Platte River has been the area's main lifeline. (CHS.)

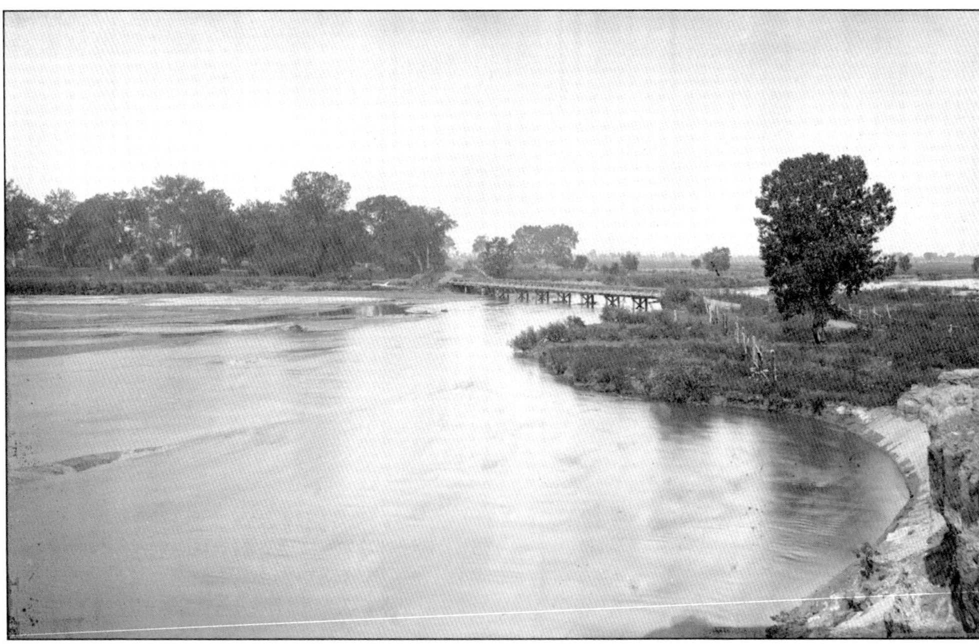

Travel was hampered because the South Platte River was found to be too shallow. In 1840, traders launched a boat, and soon it became stuck on the sandy bottom. Repeatedly the buffalo robes had to be unloaded to move it. The traders had to push the boat along most of the way for about 300 miles. Thereafter the long trip had to be made over land. (CHS.)

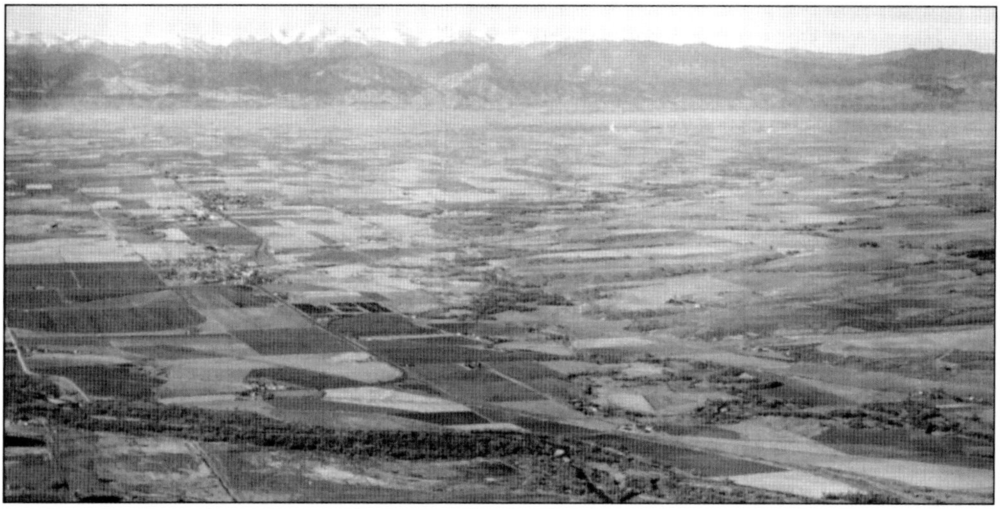

On June 30, 1820, the Long expedition saw the first landmark visible from far out on the Platte Trail; a distant view of the Rocky Mountains. Although they probably never got closer than 40 miles to them, one of the mountains was named Long's Peak. This more recent view of Johnstown in the foreground shows what the expedition may have seen during that time. (GHM.)

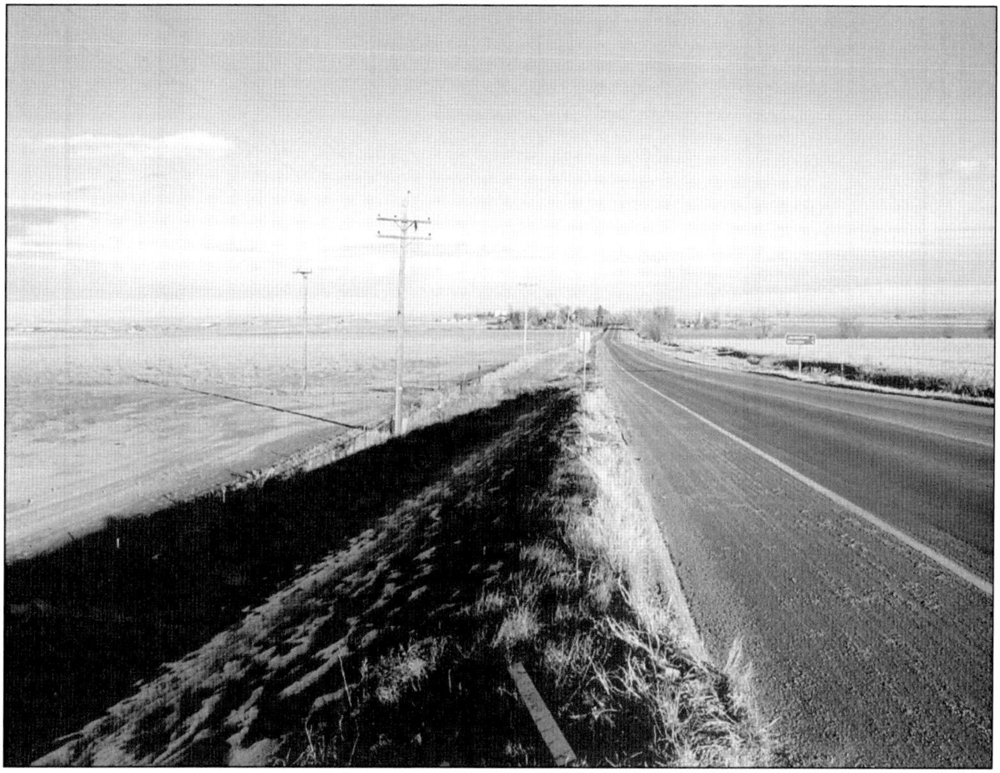

Although this photograph shows a barren view west of Johnstown, Long's estimate of northern Colorado proved to be shortsighted. He called this area "the Great American Desert," and stated that the land would be "uninhabitable by a people depending upon agriculture for their subsistence." Nothing could be grown here, he thought. So much for his opinion of what is now one of the largest agricultural counties in America.

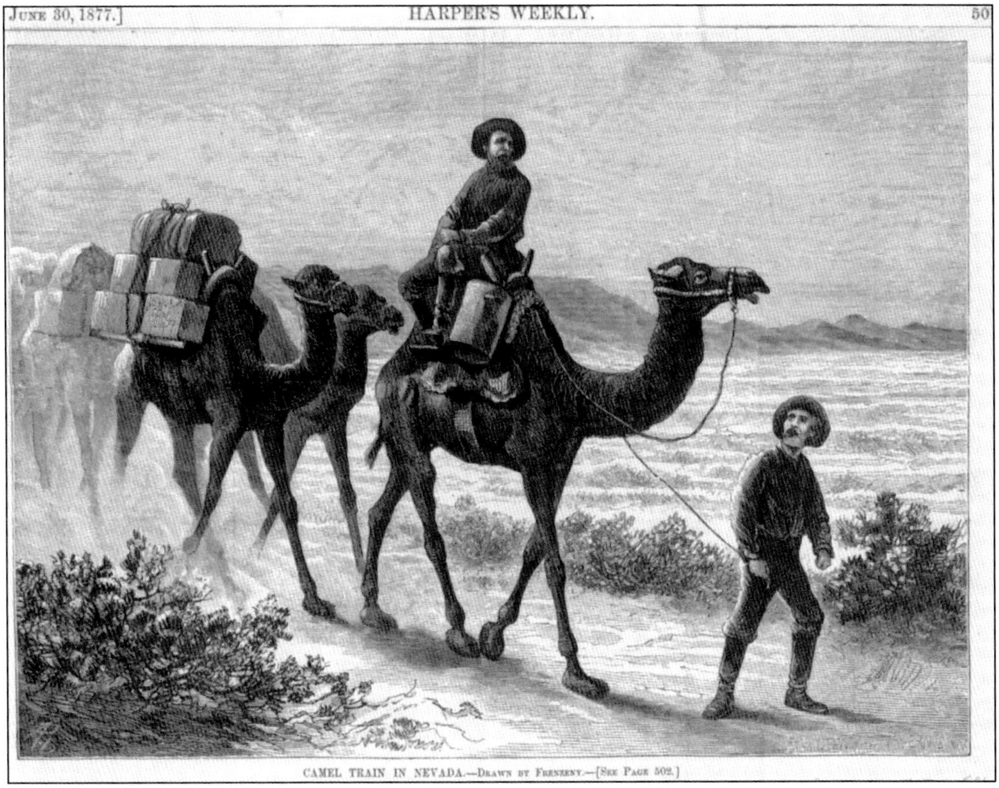

The U.S. government attempted to establish the "Rapid Transit Camel Express Company" in the mid-1860s. One of the trading forts, Fort Vasquez, was partially repaired and used for a stage station. The camels passed Vasquez on their trips from Missouri to Denver. The government must have believed that camels were the only way to cross this "Great American Desert." (DPL.)

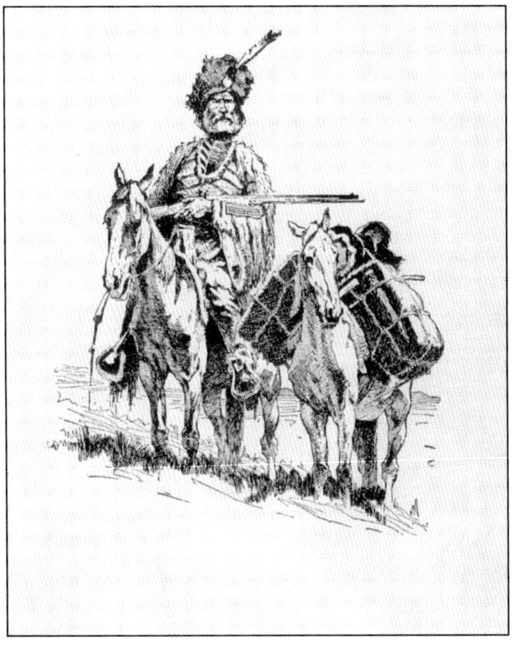

If Weld County ever needed a symbol to mark its early history, the form of a beaver would be very appropriate. These animals were the cause of the first white men in the area, the trappers. The trappers came to the Platte River for beaver pelts to address the need for beaver skin hats, popular among the elite in the East and in Europe. (DPL.)

James Beckwourth, the son of a slave and a white slave owner, came west in 1824 as a fur trapper. Beckwourth told many tall tales, including stories of being idolized by the trappers for his prowess in killing game. He was supposedly killed by Crow Indians, who preferred him dead rather than lose their chief to another tribe—a death dramatic enough to satisfy even Beckwourth, the great storyteller. (CHS.)

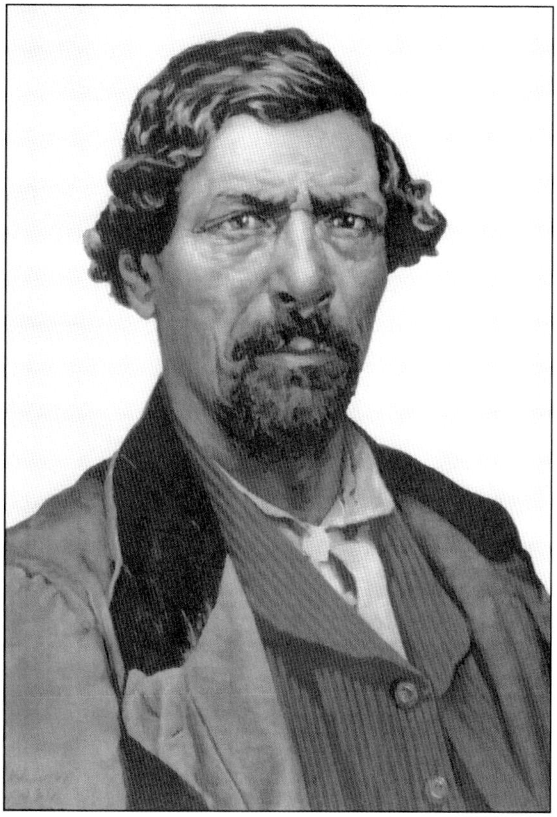

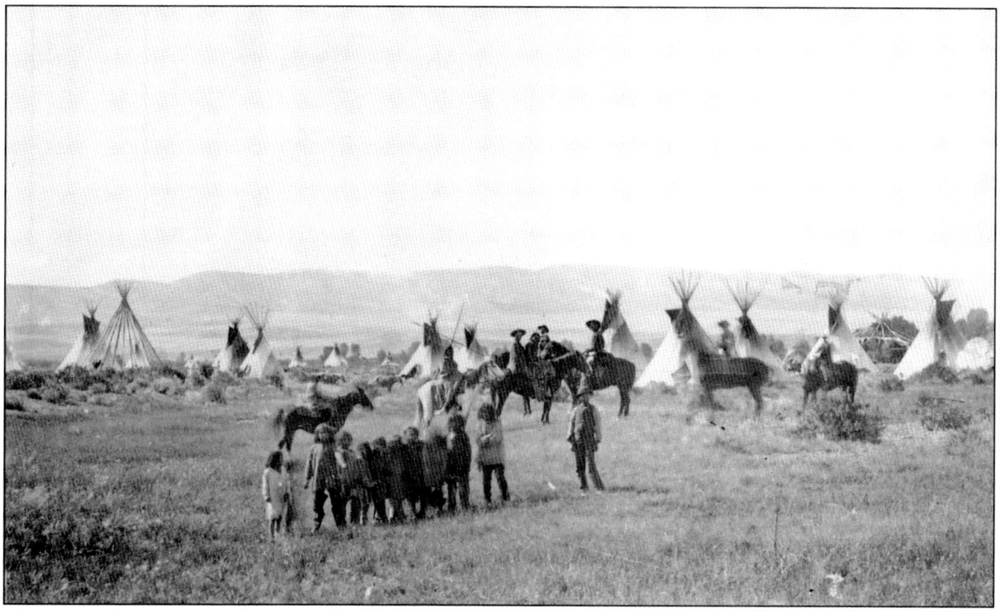

The Arapaho tribe was, for the most part, gentle and friendly. They had followed the buffalo to this part of Colorado and made it their home in the early 1800s. Although the Arapaho maintained a warrior society similar to that of other plains tribes, they were mainly interested in trading. They preferred peace and an uninterrupted flow of business to war. (DPL.)

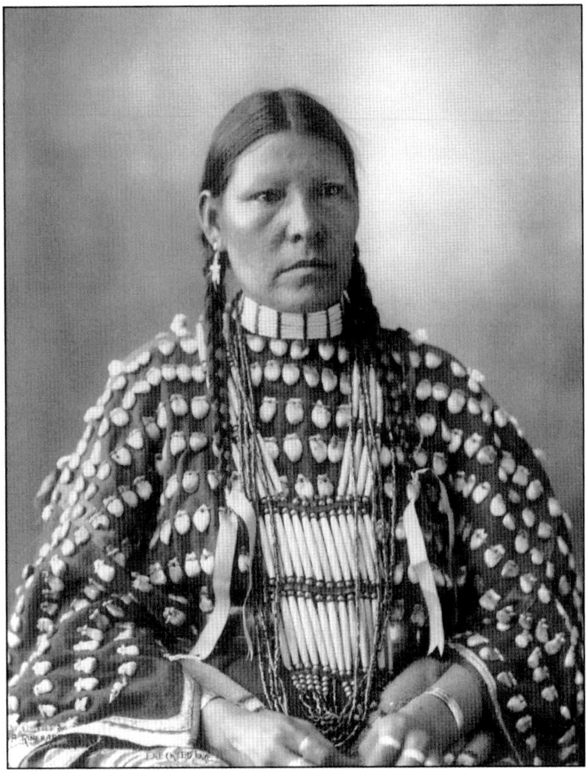

The Arapaho were a handsome people. They took pride in their appearance, bathing daily in the streams and combing and dressing their hair. They were aware of their good looks compared with other tribes. They suspected that the Utes wanted to marry the Arapaho women to improve their lineage. (DPL.)

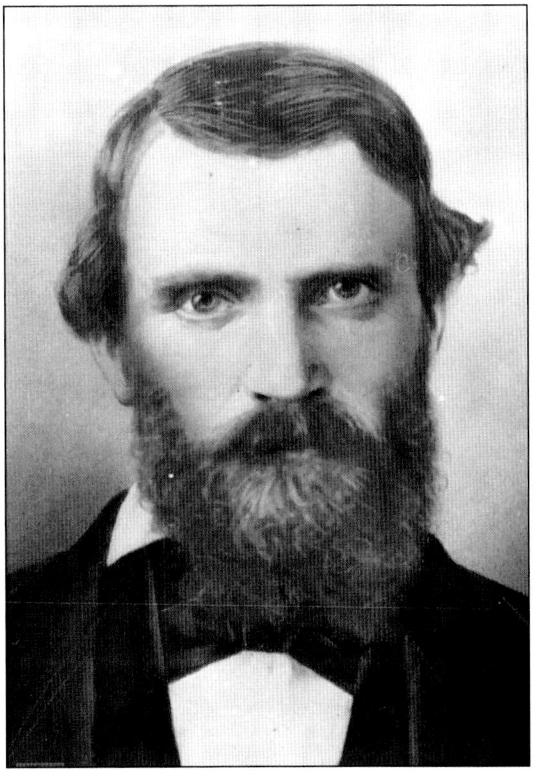

Eldbridge Gerry is reported to have been the first permanent white settler in Weld County. Gerry quit trapping about the time of the decline of the fur trade and settled on his fort-like ranch with his Indian wives. He was a good neighbor to the Indians, such as the Arapaho chief Left Hand, and to settlers on the Platte. (CHS.)

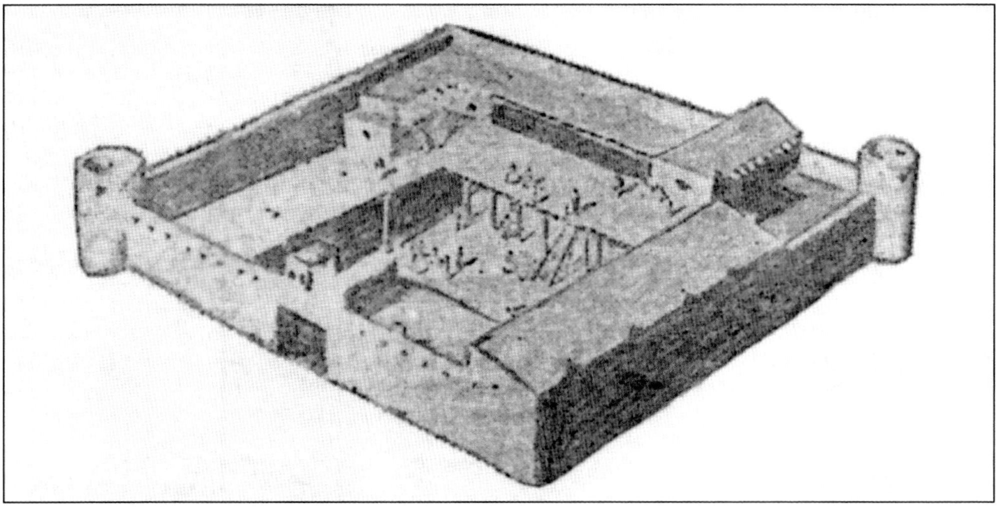

Four fur trading posts, including Fort St. Vrain, had been established on the South Platte River before 1840. About that time, the beaver fur market fell, so the forts started trading for buffalo hides. The Cheyenne and Arapaho Indians did most of the work, and the trappers became traders. They carried goods to the Indian camps to trade for buffalo robes and tongues. (DPL.)

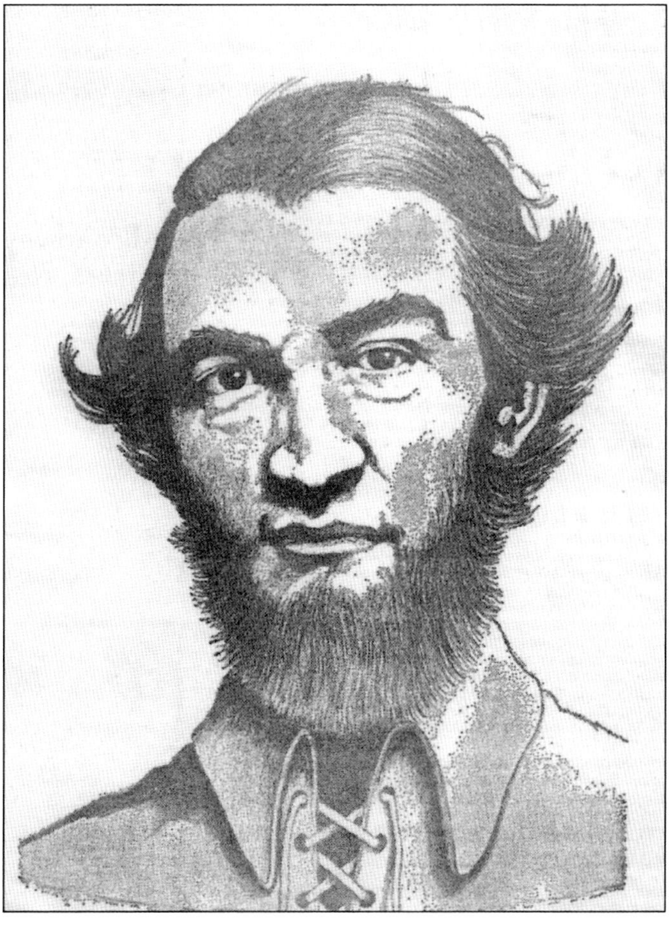

Marcellin St. Vrain was the youngest brother of Ceran, who was a partner to George Bent at Bent's Fort. Marcellin was the proprietor of Fort St. Vrain. He married a Sioux woman, with the hope of trading with them as well. This was the best way to gain the business of certain tribes and thereby compete with the other forts that were close by. (DPL.)

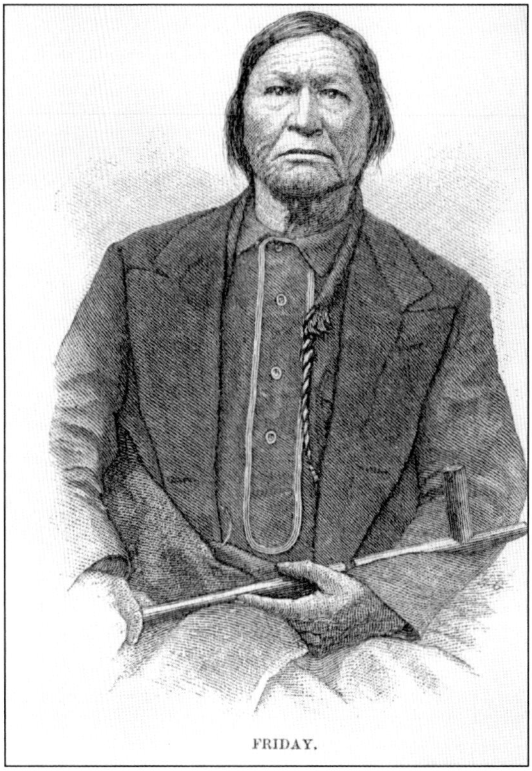

The Arapaho named Friday was adopted by an Indian agent Thomas Fitzpatrick and sent to school in St. Louis, where he learned to speak fluent English. He became an excellent translator, although he maintained close ties with his tribe. Whether using his bow or a gun, Friday was considered one of the best buffalo hunters, and the white traders learned from him. (DPL.)

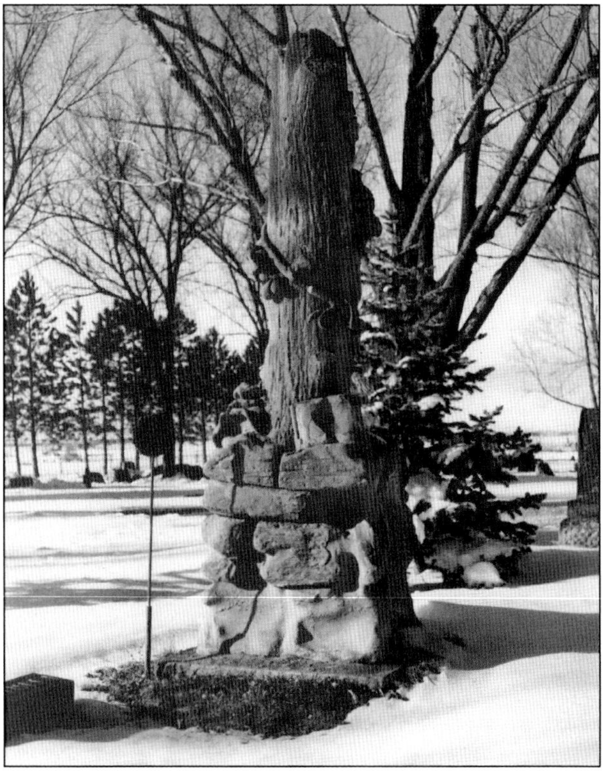

Friday supposedly made an annual visit to Fort St. Vrain, painting his face black, and sitting on the walls to mourn and cry. According to Marshall Cook, Marcellin St. Vrain had retaliated against a band of Arapaho, killing a large number, among whom were Friday's wife and children. This monument is a tribute to Cook, an early pioneer and father to Albina Clingenpeel of Johnstown. (GHM.)

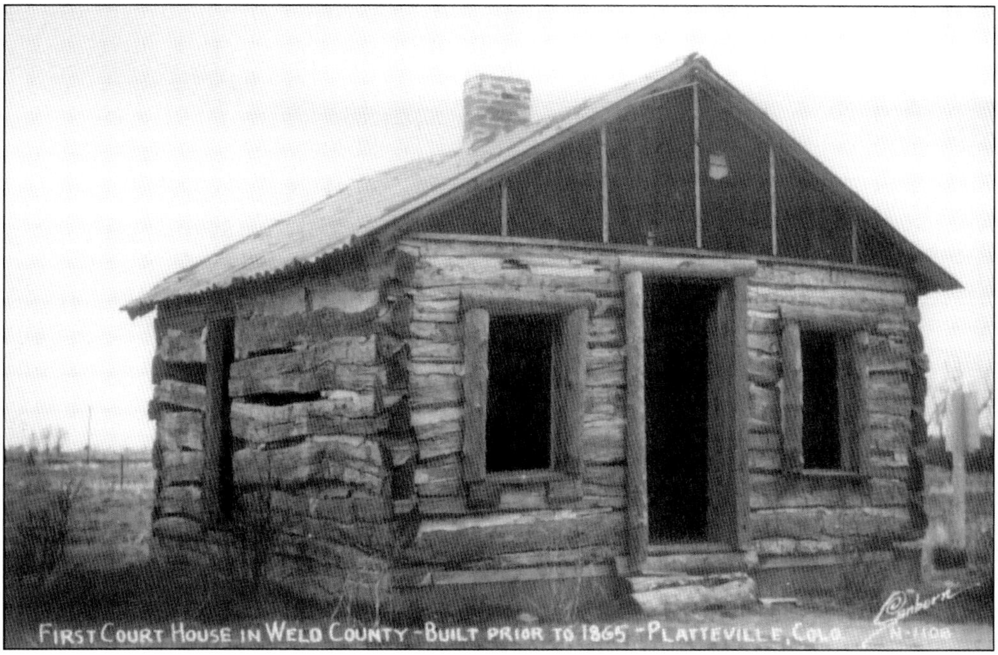

Weld County came into being in 1861 with the creation of Colorado Territory. St. Vrain became the county seat. Several sessions of the county commissioners were held at homes of various settlers. This cottonwood log cabin on the Andrew Lumry place served as a meeting place, as well as a courtroom. (GHM.)

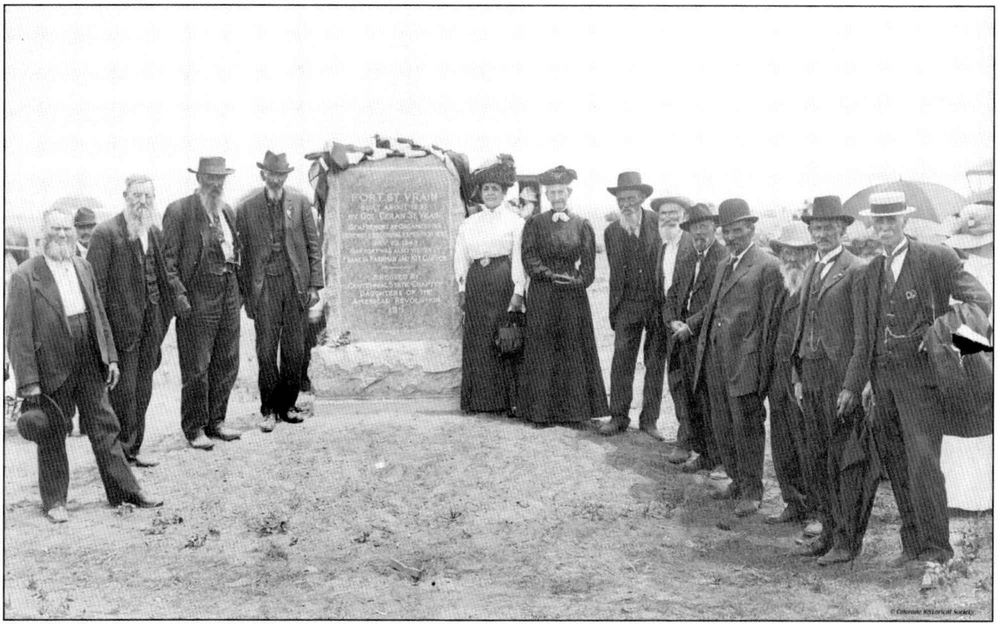

All that remains of Fort St. Vrain is this monument, shown at a dedication ceremony by the Daughters of the American Revolution in 1911. The first three people standing to the right of the monument are relatives of the St. Vrain family. The monument states that General Fremont reorganized his expedition at the fort, and it was visited by Francis Parkman and Kit Carson. (DPL.)

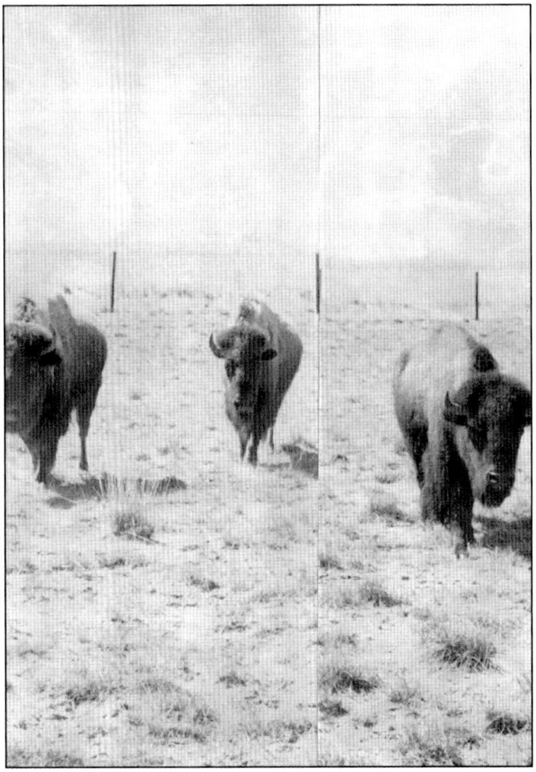

The discovery of gold at Cherry Creek, the present site of Denver, in 1858 prompted the newcomers to meet on December 21 to plan a Christmas feast. They went to great lengths to give themselves a feeling of home. The menu included buffalo tongue and "Taos Lightning," an early moonshine. Buffalo hides were prized for warm robes, and buffalo chips were burned for fuel. (GHM.)

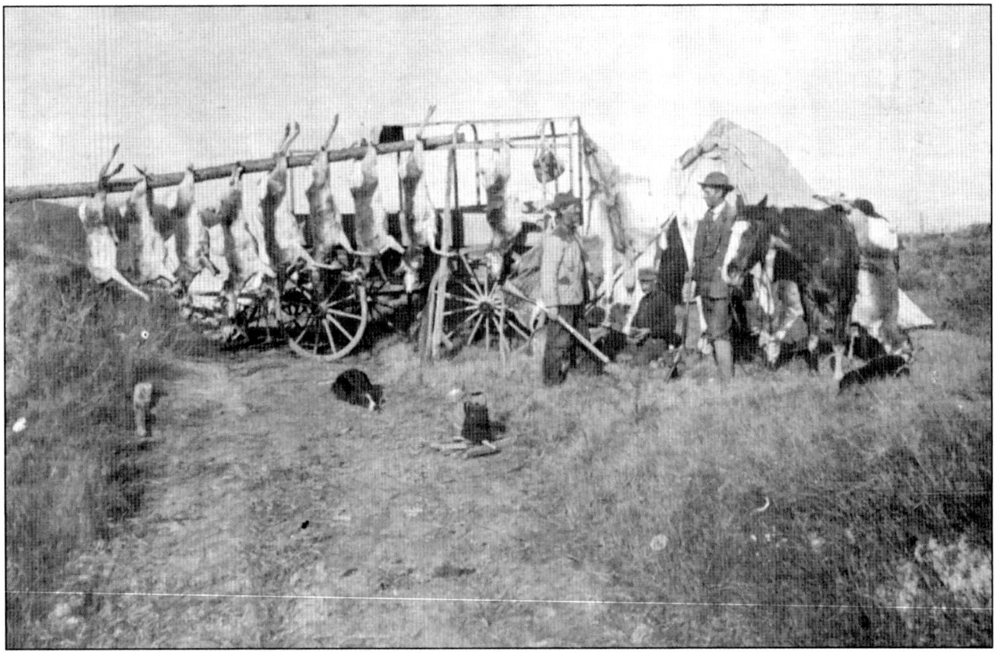

Game was plentiful on the plains for food for the miners. There are 11 antelope in this photograph, as well as the hide of a plains wolf. Many of the antelope and buffalo were killed for sport. If the pioneers did use the animals for meat, only parts were taken, with the rest left to spoil, unlike the Native tribes, who used everything. (GHM.)

Arapaho chiefs Little Raven, shown in this photograph, and Left Hand (Niwot) welcomed, in English, the white newcomers. They called the white settlers "spider people" but learned too late the significance of the web of roads and fences the pale-faced people had made. They accepted the gold seekers, who trespassed on what the federal government had recognized as Arapaho land, with generosity that they later regretted. (DPL.)

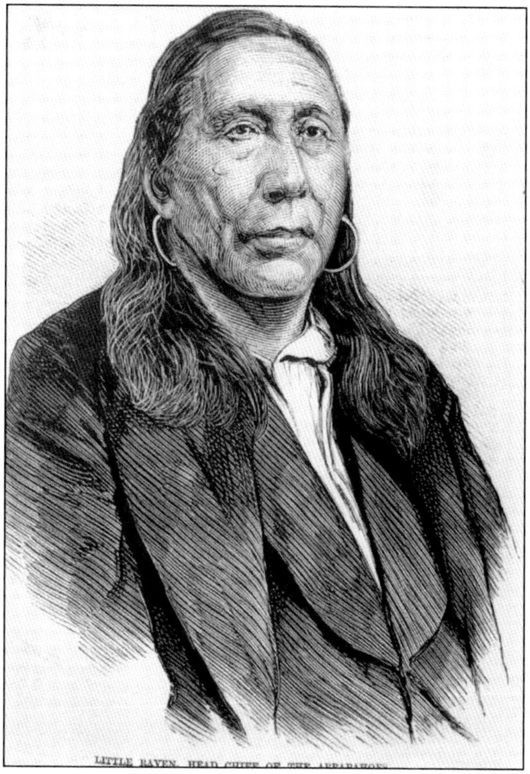

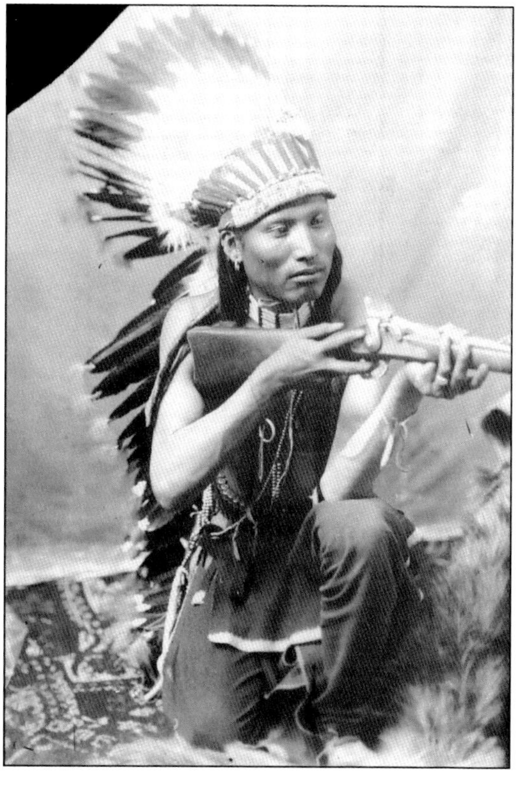

As many as 5,000 members of various tribes, mostly Arapaho and Cheyenne, lived along the South Platte River. That changed when the gold seekers found gold and began to settle in the 1850s. The Indians were doomed. As thousands of white settlers set up homesteads along rivers and creeks that had been Arapaho campsites, hostilities arose. (DPL.)

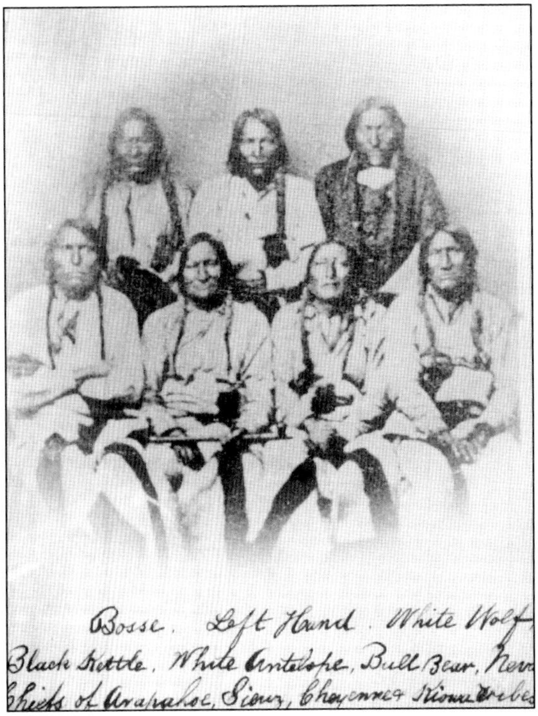

In 1864, the council on war and peace was initiated by Black Kettle, a Cheyenne chief, on the left of the first row of this photograph. He was trying to make peace between the whites and the Indians. People snickered when Black Kettle arrived, his American flag proudly flying on his wagon, but that flag meant a great deal to the Cheyenne leader. (DPL.)

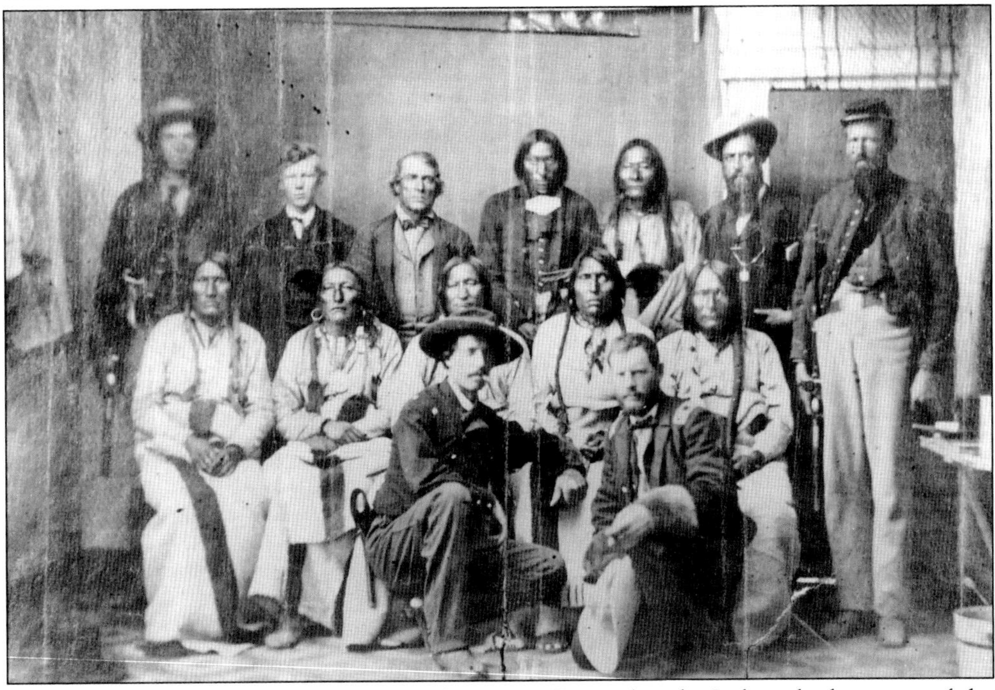

Although Black Kettle reminded territorial governor Evans that the Indians had not started the hostilities, he maintained that he and the other Indians wanted peace. The Arapaho leaders Left Hand and Little Raven did not attend the conference. They remained in their villages in order to keep the young warriors from further acts of aggression that could destroy the peace-keeping efforts. (DPL.)

When word came that there would perhaps be a peace agreement, the settlers were furious. They demanded an end to the attacks by the Indians. The 3rd Colorado Regiment was raised, mustering in troops for an enlistment period of 100 days. Governor Evans ordered the peaceful Arapaho and Cheyenne to camp near Fort Lyons on Sand Creek in a remote part of eastern Colorado on the plains. (DPL.)

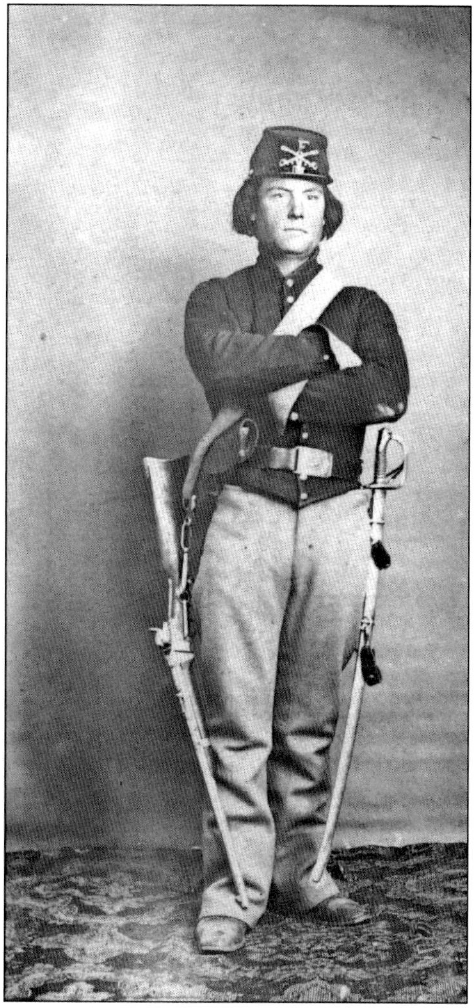

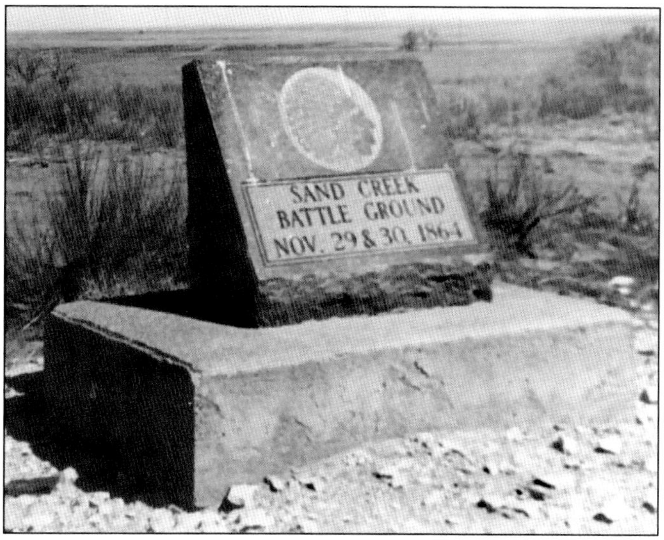

After months of patrolling, the 3rd Colorado, led by Col. John Chivington, attacked at dawn on November 29, 1864, completely surprising the sleeping native families. Black Kettle hastily raised his U.S. flag and a white flag of surrender. Left Hand, who felt such anguish at having led his people to Sand Creek, made no effort to protect himself and died that morning, along with 180 others. (DPL.)

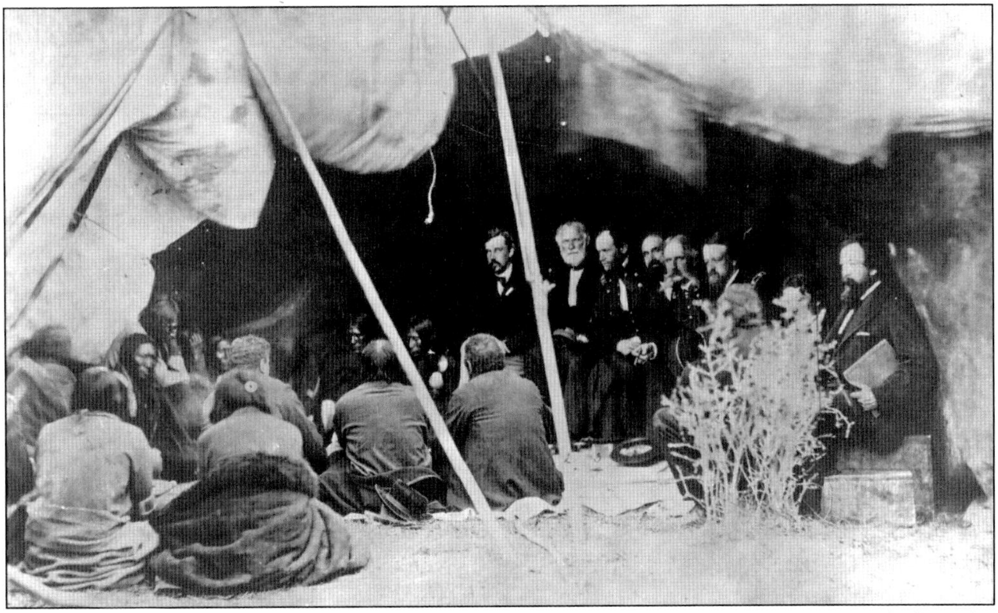

Sand Creek united the tribes as they had never been before, and it was not long before the frontiersmen on the Platte felt their wrath. The Civil War ended in 1865, freeing thousands of troops for action in the Indian wars. Gen. William T. Sherman, shown in this photograph, became the commander in the West. (DPL.)

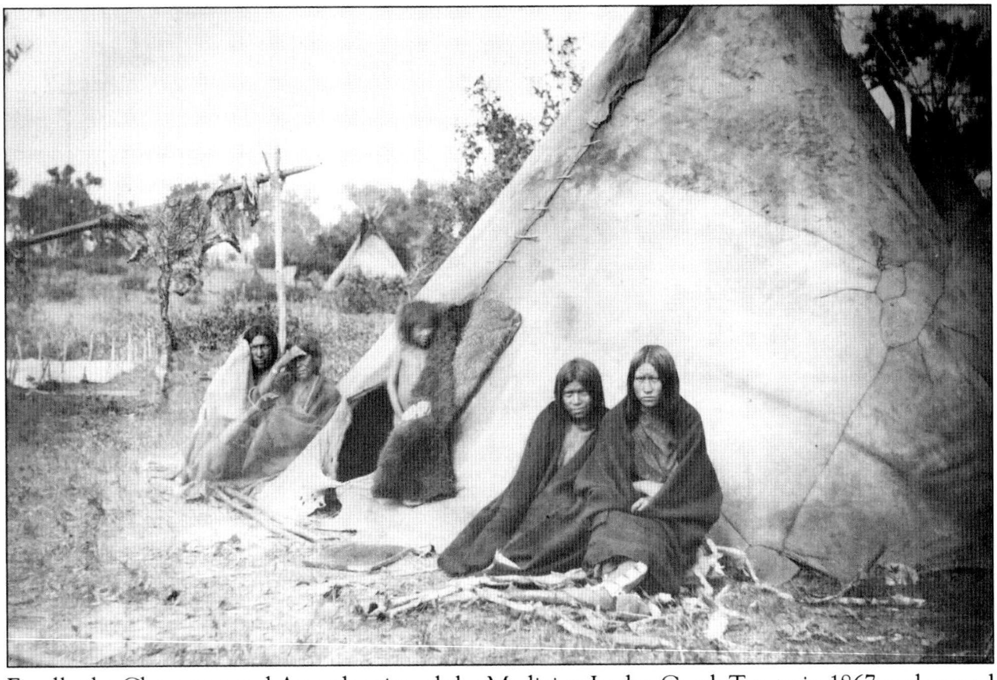

Finally the Cheyenne and Arapaho signed the Medicine Lodge Creek Treaty in 1867 and agreed to relocate to Oklahoma. Little Raven, who survived the Sand Creek Massacre, led the Arapaho people to Fort Sill, seen in this photograph. The last Plains Indian battle in Colorado was at Summit Springs in 1869, which was a rerun of Sand Creek. The Plains tribes were driven out of Colorado forever. (DPL.)

Two

Life on the Plains

Many came to the Rockies seeking gold but very few discovered much value from the mines. Some of these unsuccessful miners were "go backs" who went back to where they originated. Others stayed. Some who stayed went to the Johnstown area on the plains to meet the demand for supplies for the gold mining camps. This meant farming for some and ranching for others. Sometimes it meant stopping one unsuccessful enterprise and trying something else. These men were determined to make a life for themselves and their families, despite all the hardships of living on the plains. The cattlemen were the first permanent settlers. They were in the prime of their lives with their large herds, extensive ranges, and ready markets for their meat in the mining camps of Colorado. The miners who became farmers caused the development of the county to become the rich agricultural empire it is today.

Soon after gold was discovered in Colorado, the Homestead Act came into effect. A homesteader could claim 160 acres of land and keep that land, if they made improvements and lived there for five years. The early settlers brought their wives and families to the area to homestead. These wives were special. They all needed a certain iron determination, or they would not have survived. These women were like the cowgirls who Dale Evans wrote about in *The Queen of the Cowgirls* in 1992: "Cowgirl is an attitude, really. A pioneer spirit, a special American brand of courage. The cowgirl faces life head on, lives by her own lights, and makes no excuses. Cowgirls take stands. They speak up. They defend the things they hold dear."

Women established the moral and social values for their communities. The time of gold mining was a time of lawlessness. There was a need for law and order. When Colorado became a territory in 1861, it soon established rules that made it a place where all people, women and children included, could endure.

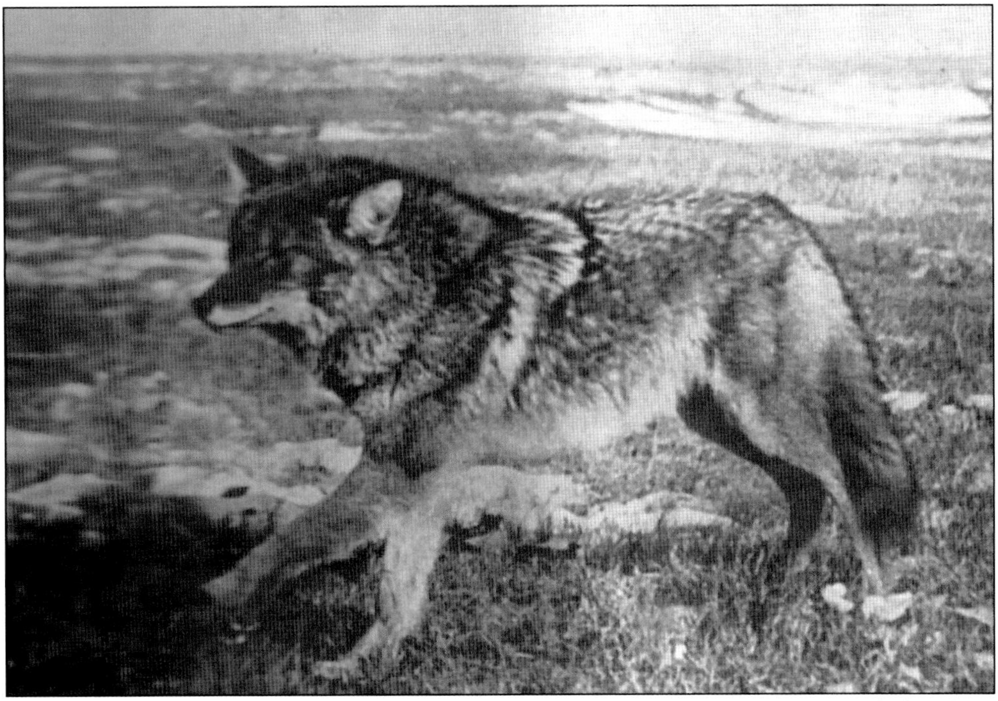

Many of the early settlers experienced disappointment. There was not enough water, and what there was did not go far. The crops that remained had been eaten by range cattle. Even garden vegetables disappeared before harvest to the hungry animals. Cattle did fare better on the open range, even though some ranchers were plagued by coyotes, like this one caught in a trap. (GHM.)

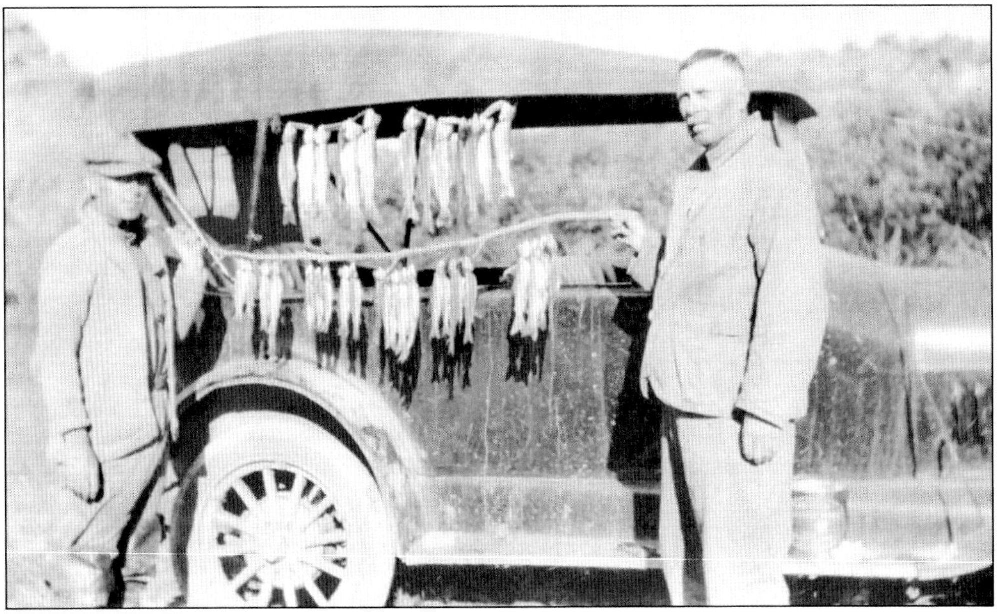

Many settlers had sunk all their available cash into seed and trees, which had not produced. They survived on the plentiful wild meat, such as fish, antelope, and buffalo. The Greeley newspaper described a herd of antelope that wandered into town. Many were shot by the settlers from their front doors. Buffalo meat was easily taken and the non-hunters could buy it for about 1¢ per pound.

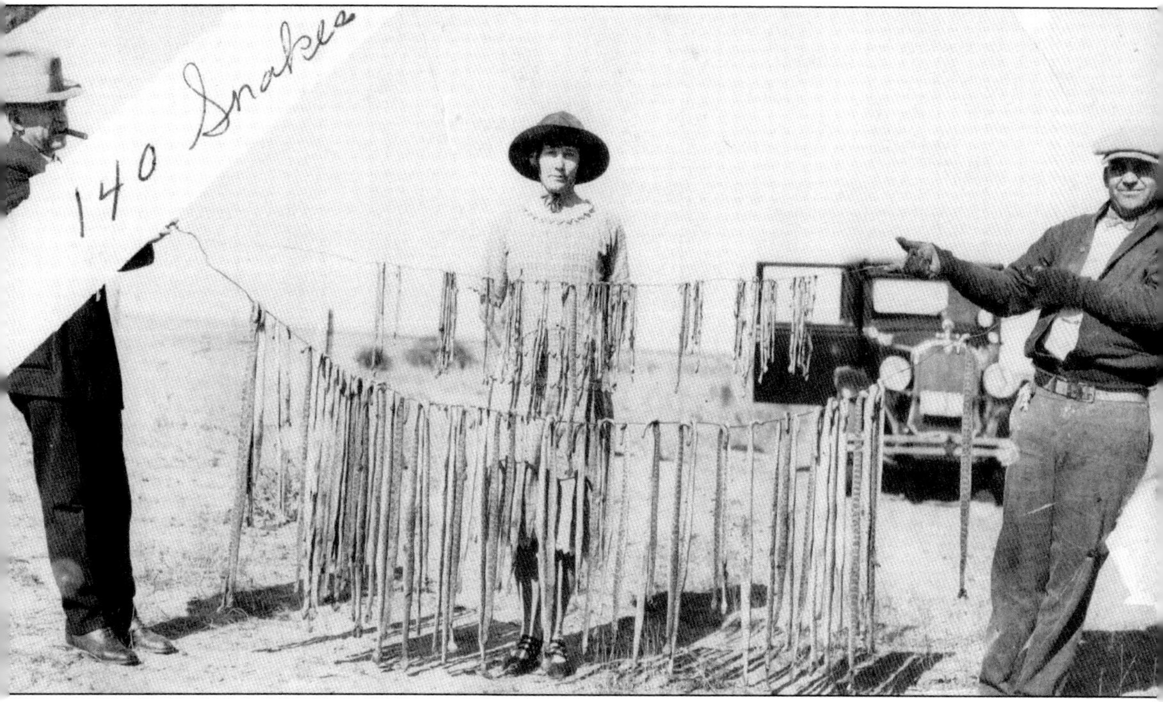

Dangers, like rattlesnakes, needed to be faced. Katherine McHale Slaughterback became known as Rattlesnake Kate. She was born in a log cabin in 1894, and she lived most of her life on the prairie. Kate rode out on her horse one day in 1925 with her three-year-old son and her .22 Remington rifle. When she got off her horse to open a gate, she saw a rattlesnake. She went back to her horse, got her rifle, and shot the snake. It was then that she noticed all the other rattlesnakes that soon surrounded her. When her bullets ran out, she took one of the fence posts and started beating the rattlesnakes. After two hours, 140 rattlesnakes lay dead at her feet, everyone safe. She later tanned the snake skins and sewed them into a dress, with matching shoes and headband. She made a necklace from the rattles. All are on display at a museum in Greeley. (GHM.)

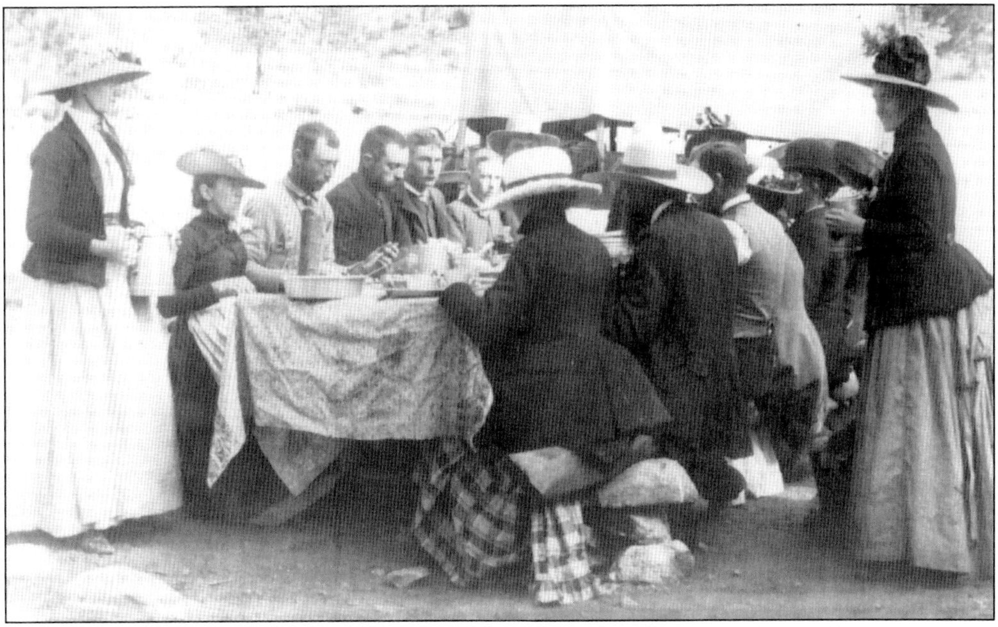

Women added a semblance of social graces and entertaining. An unusual way of entertaining is shown in this early photograph of a picnic in the Rocky Mountains by the Big Thompson River. In the days of traveling by horse and covered wagon, the picnic involved a one-day trip each way. Because the trip was so long, the travelers needed to spend the night. (GHM.)

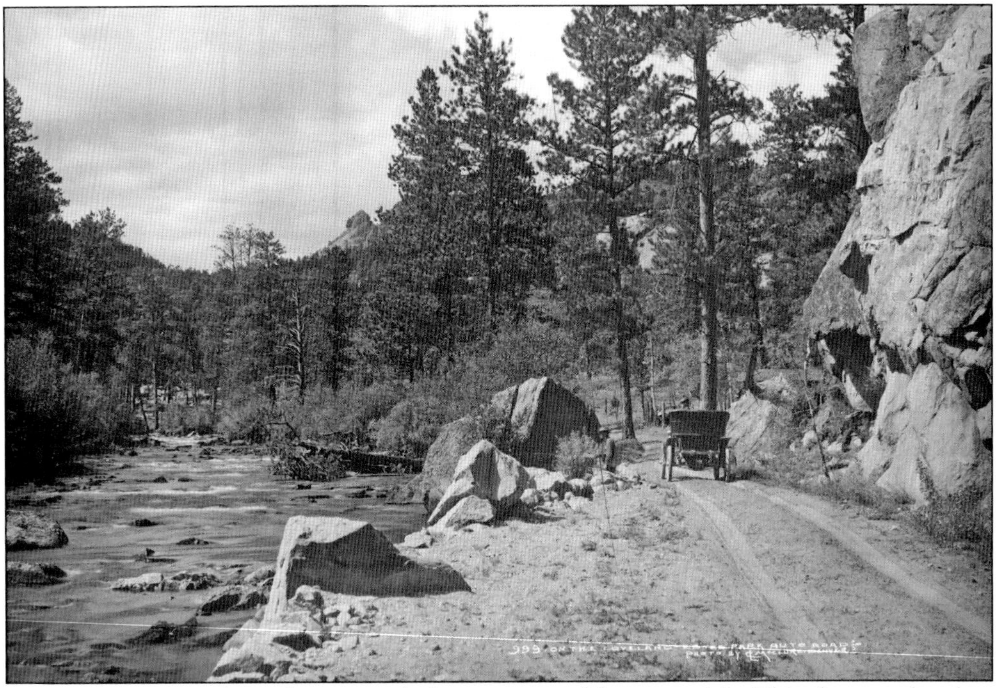

Later a picnic was made much easier with the invention of the automobile. This photograph, taken in the narrows of Big Thompson Canyon by the river, shows a car that was perhaps headed to Estes Park. Although easier, the trip still cannot be compared with the ease of today's 20-minute drive up the canyon on a paved two-lane highway. (DPL.)

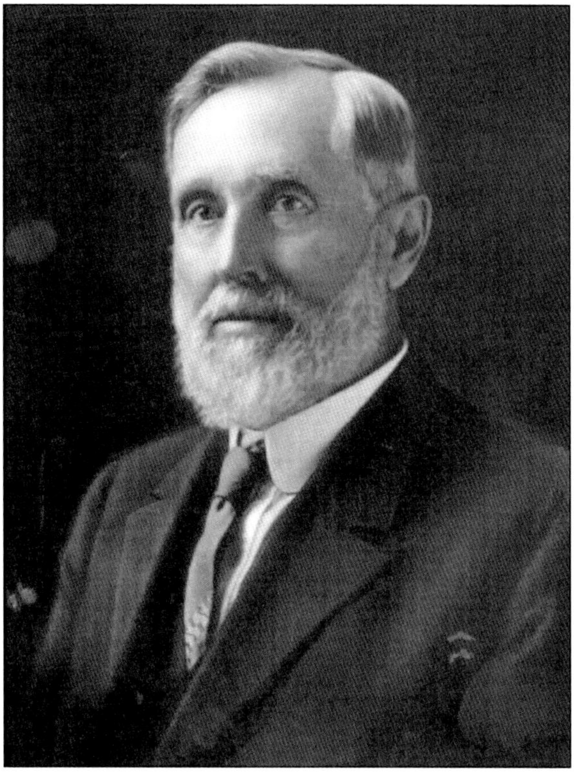

Jared L. Brush left Ohio in 1859 to seek a fortune in the gold mines with a team of oxen and $1.35 in his pocket. He reached Boulder City in the early part of July. Jared's brothers, John M. and William, joined him at Central City and later that same year, the three bought a gold mine. The first day they worked the mine, they took out $60 worth of gold, but that proved to be all they would get out of it. They sold the mine in spring 1860 and settled on the banks of the Big Thompson River, near where Johnstown is today. Jared's first wife of 11 years died in 1877. His second marriage in 1879 was to Mary Doolittle (pictured below), a widow with two children and a native of Ohio. (GHM.)

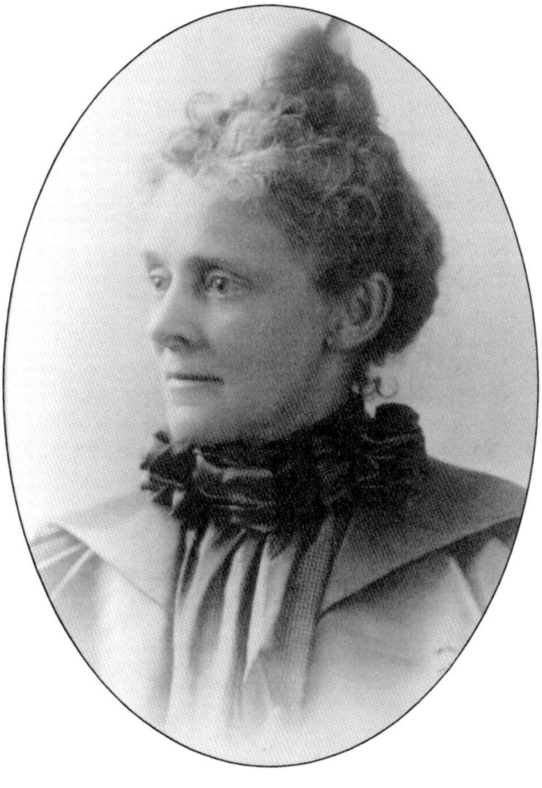

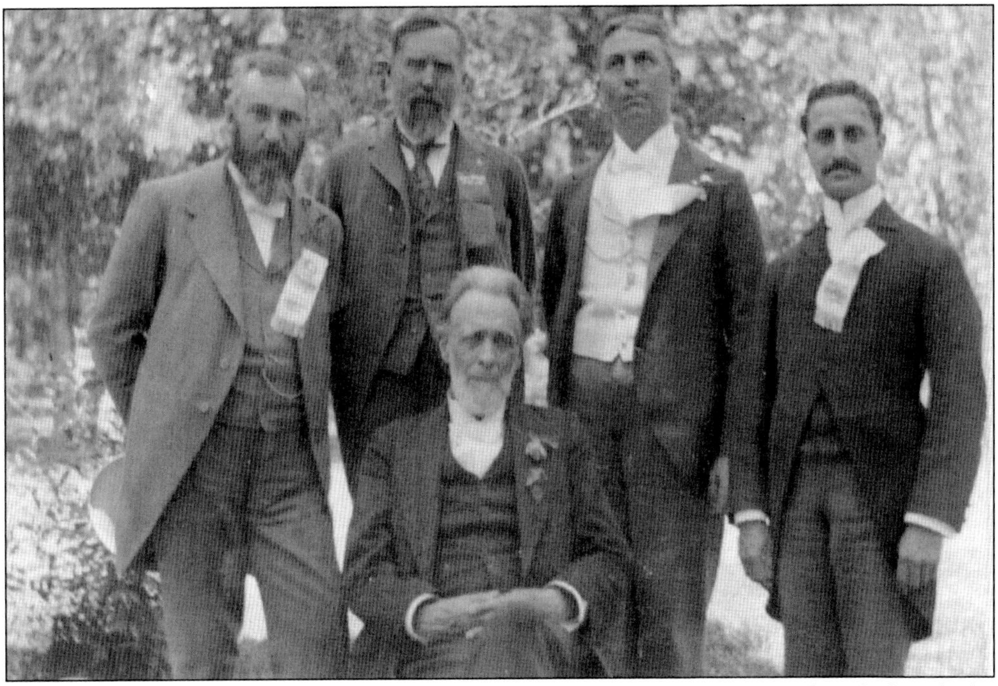

Jared L. Brush became known throughout Colorado. In 1871, he became identified with the colonists who founded Greeley. He served in several elected county positions, including county commissioner, before he was elected to the state legislature. He served as lieutenant governor (shown here with Governor Teller) twice in later years. The town of Brush in Morgan County is named for him. (GHM.)

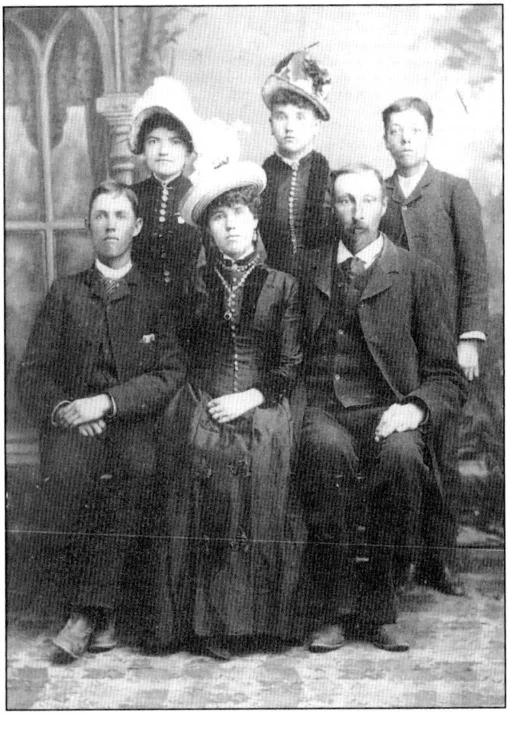

John Brush, shown with his family, came with William to the gold mines with a train of mules and joined their brother. After that business went bust, the three of them found the valleys were rich with natural native hay. During the summer of 1860, they cut native hay in Johnstown and sold it in Central City for $175 a ton, a huge amount for that time.

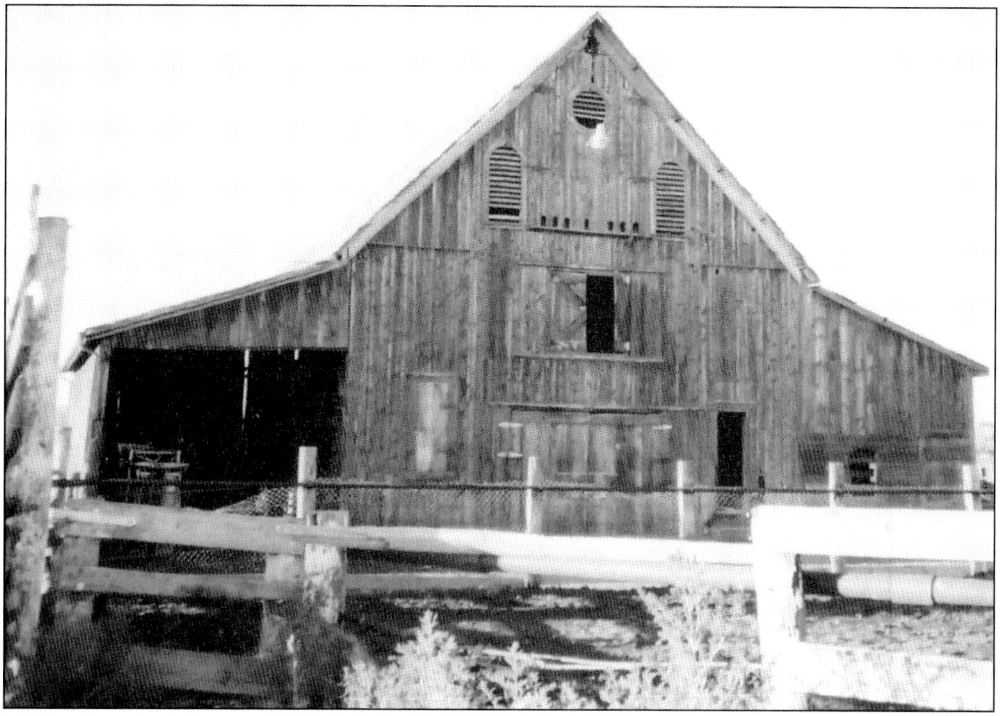

When the Brush brothers settled in Johnstown, they were the largest taxpayers in Weld County, excluding the telegraph company, for several years. The Brush brothers built this barn, with a huge hayloft, in the mid-1860s with heavy timbers that were tied together with round wooden pegs. The house they built, along with the barn, still stands.

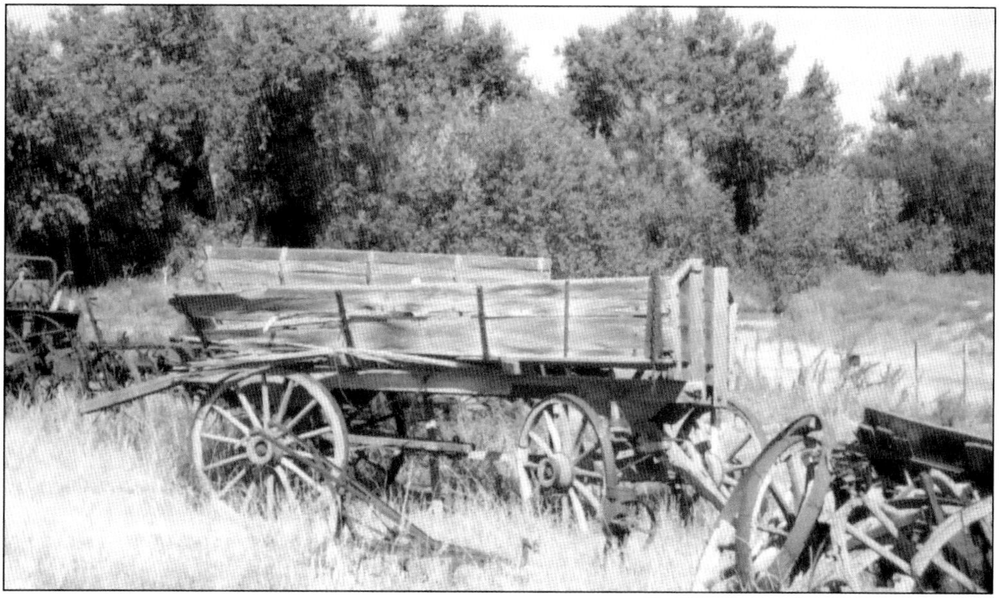

For the first 10 years on the ranch, Jared Brush was also a freighter and cattleman. Although he started freighting goods to the mining camps with wagons such as the one pictured, in the late 1860s he devoted most of his time to the cattle business. He engaged extensively in the raising, buying, and selling of stock near the present town of Brush, which was named after him.

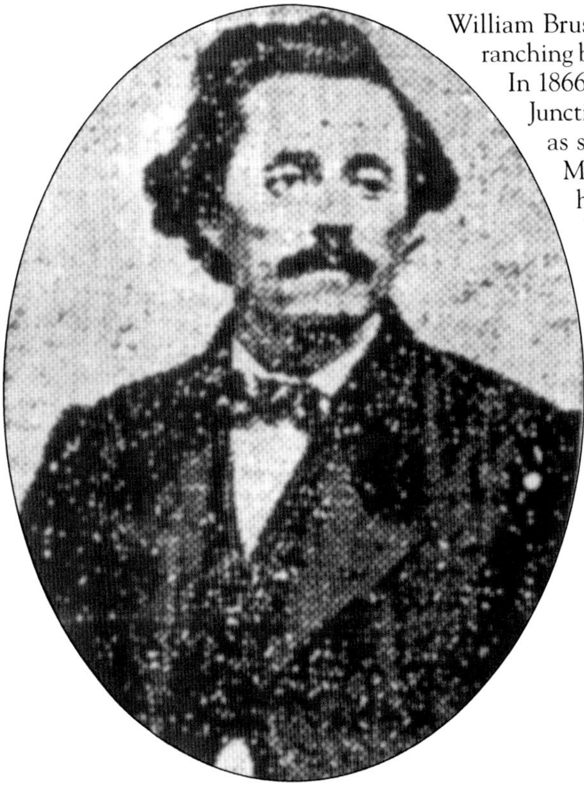

William Brush was a partner in the freighting and ranching business with his brothers Jared and John. In 1866, they also established a stage station at Junction, near old Fort Morgan, and were listed as station keepers. In 1867, Will married Martha Margaret Way, who was sister to his brother John's wife Mary, and they had a daughter, Minnie Belle, who was born in March 1868.

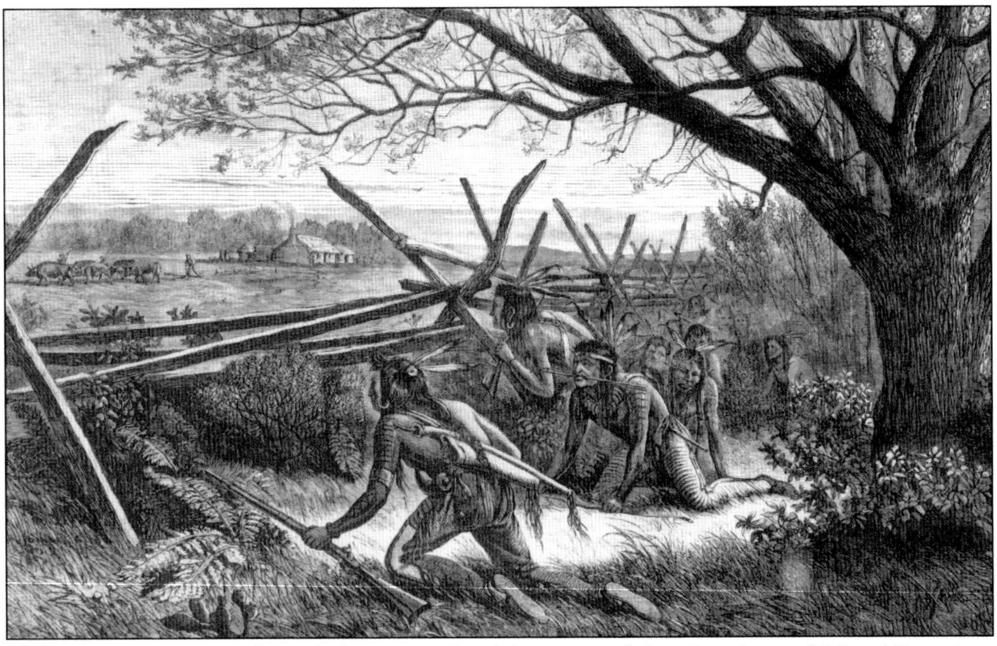

In late summer 1868, Will Brush, his cousin Jared Conroy, and their hired man, Halstad Dunning, went to the early trapper Eldbridge Gerry's ranch to cut the natural hay growing there. Oglala Sioux Indians, led by Chief Swift Bird, came to the ranch, asking to be fed. Brush obliged, then the Indians turned on the men and killed all three. (DPL.)

The bodies of the slain men were not found until the next day. Eldbridge Gerry learned of the deaths from his wife, whose brother was Chief Swift Bird. Gerry and the chief had been feuding for a long time, and Swift Bird had stolen Gerry's horses several times. Gerry informed William's brothers, and they laid him to rest on the north side of William's farm in Johnstown. (GHM.)

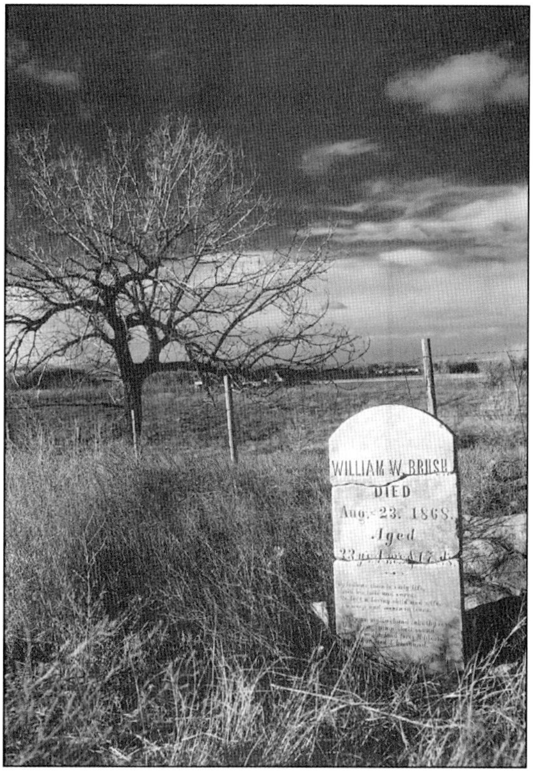

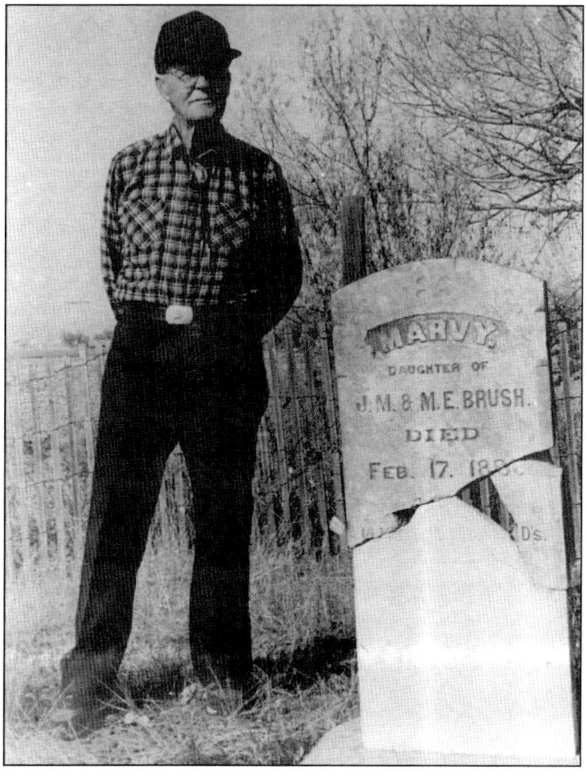

Zenas Brush, John Brush's grandson, stood next to Marvy Brush's grave at the Brush-Daniels cemetery. Until the Elwell Cemetery opened in 1902, the Brush cemetery was the only cemetery in the area. Although some of the graves from the Brush cemetery were moved, William Brush, Marvy Brush, the 14-year-old daughter of John Brush, and three children of the Daniels family are still buried there.

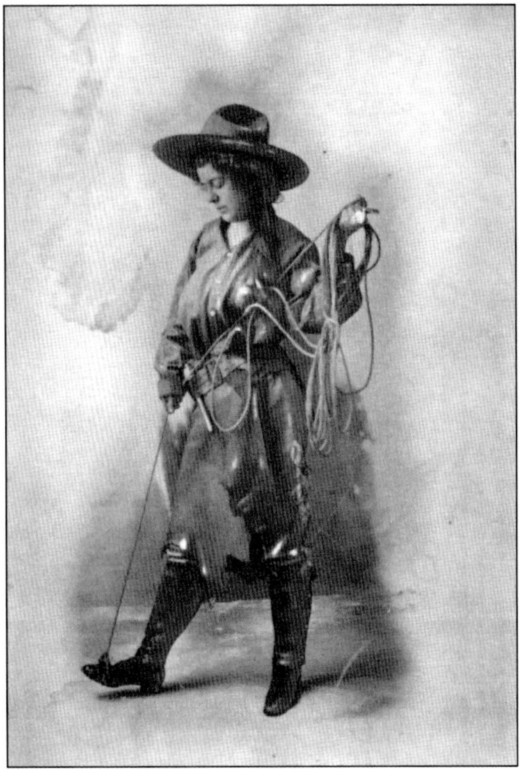

Women of that time needed to be rugged, independent cowgirls by nature. Often left alone for days at a time while their husbands looked for wild game to provide for the family, women were expected to take care of everything at home and keep everyone safe. Work never ended. (GHM.)

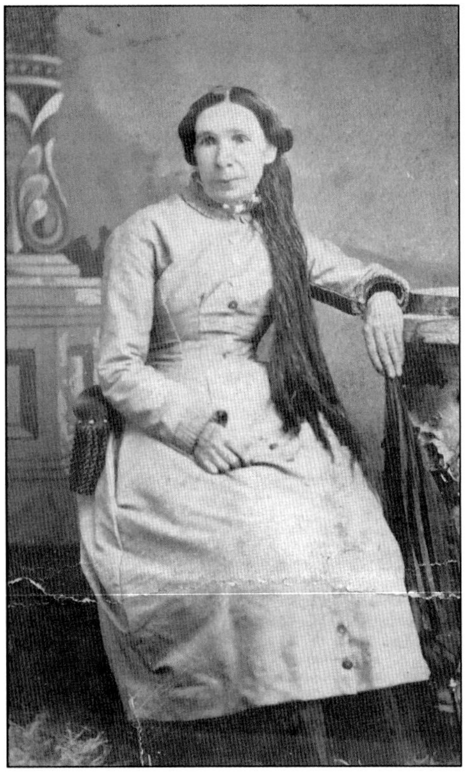

Elizabeth Parish was one of these independent women. She and her husband, Lewis, purchased 40 acres of land for $1.25 an acre in the Territory of Michigan in 1834. Lewis went hunting one day and never came back. Elizabeth bundled up her baby son John and walked 20 miles to the nearest people. She was the grandmother of Johnstown founder Harvey Jay Parish.

That pioneer spirit of Elizabeth Parish must have instilled a sense of adventure in her son John. In 1865, he left his family in Iowa and he and a partner came to Colorado, looking for gold. They paddled up the South Platte River in a canoe, traveling only at night and sometimes going without food so the Indians would not hear gunshots.

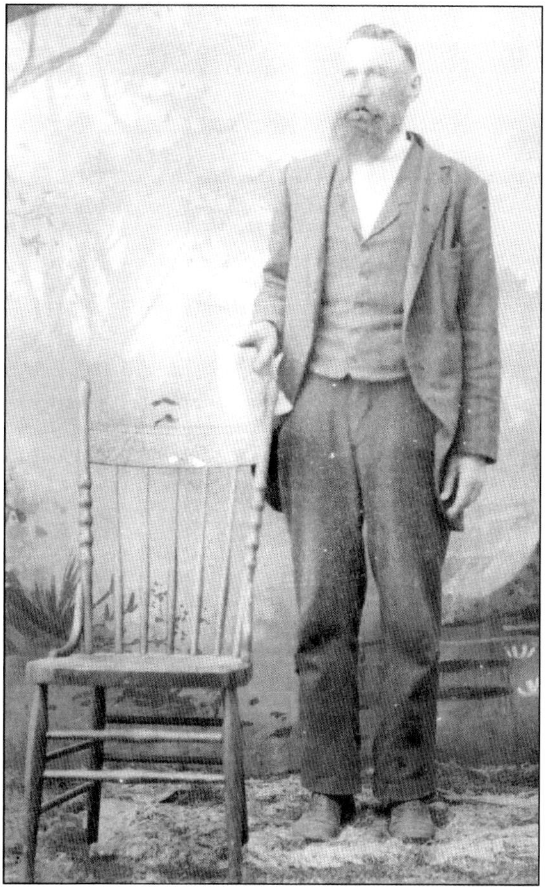

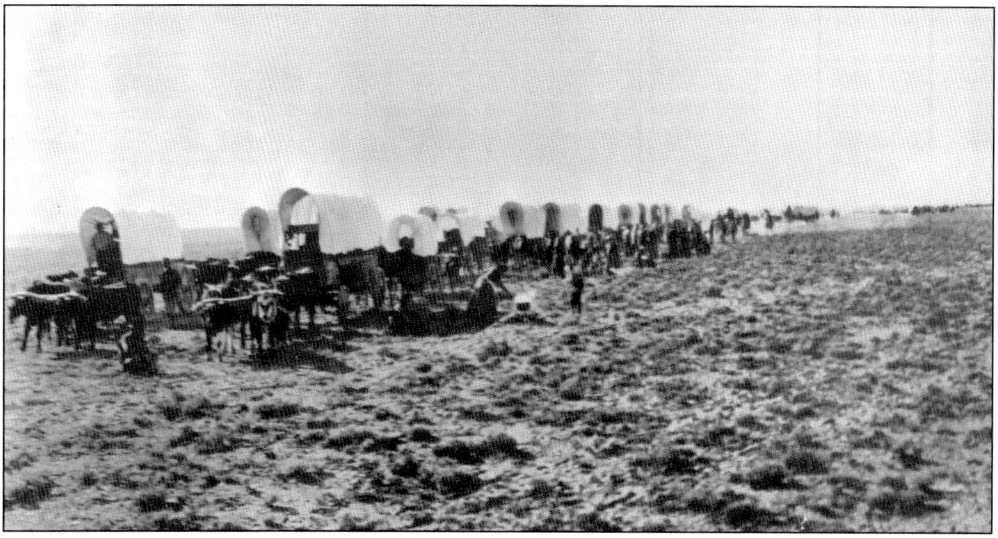

Finding no gold at the mouth of the Big Thompson River, John went back a year later to Iowa to get his family. John, his wife Mary, and his four-year-old son, Harvey Jay, joined a wagon train. The wagons were called prairie schooners because they looked like sailing ships on the prairie. They traveled to what is now Loveland, Colorado, a few miles west of Johnstown. (DPL.)

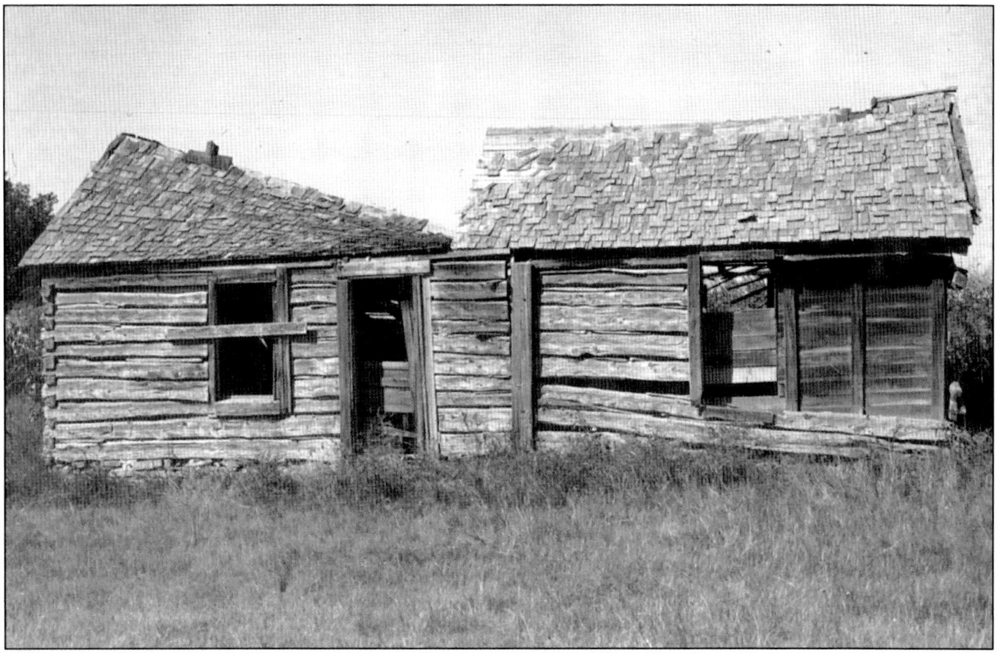

The John Parish family lived in a log cabin, probably like this Daniels family cabin. In 1868, there came word of a roving band of Indians in the area. This was the same group that had attacked and killed William Brush. John was away working as a blacksmith, so Mary took Harvey in blankets down by the river and hid until morning. (GHM.)

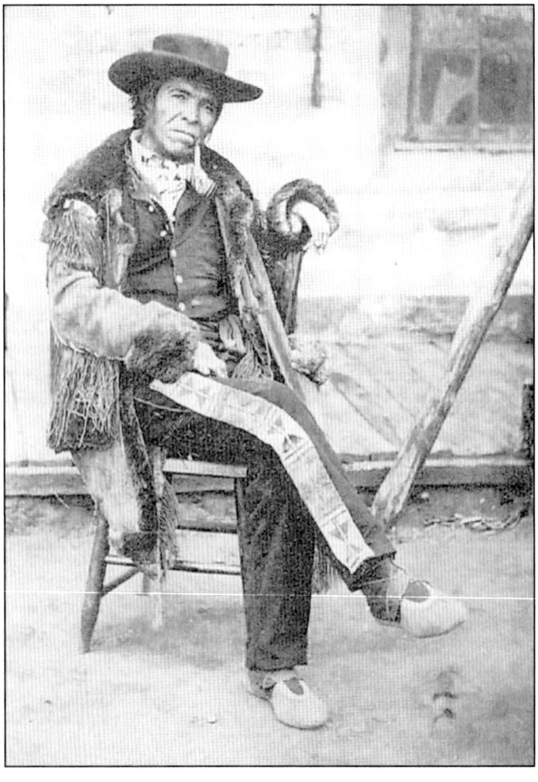

Mariano Medina was the first permanent settler in the Big Thompson Valley, west of Loveland. The John Parish family lived next to Namaqua Butte, at Medina's settlement. Namaqua had a home station on the stage line running north and south from Denver to Cheyenne. Mary Parish was well educated for the time, and she taught school in their cabin. Some of her pupils were Medina's children. (DPL.)

John Parish secured a contract to supply a large number of ties for the railroad. Many men were employed cutting and dragging timber to the banks of the Big Thompson River. When the water became so high that the ties could be floated, men with spiked poles followed along the river, poking the logs out of places where they would lodge. (DPL.)

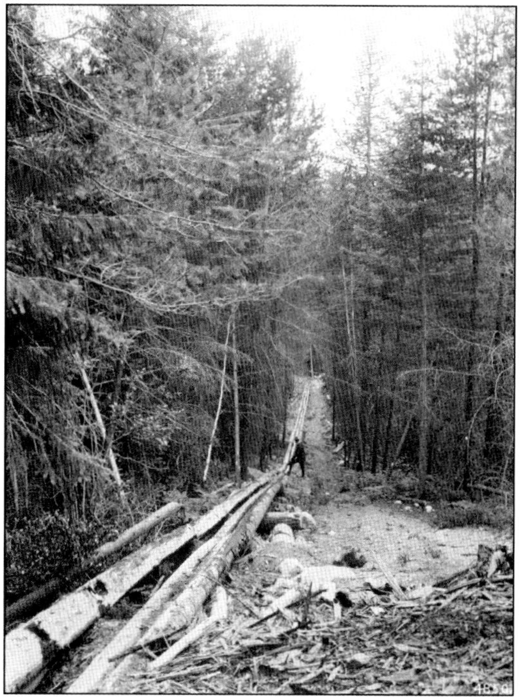

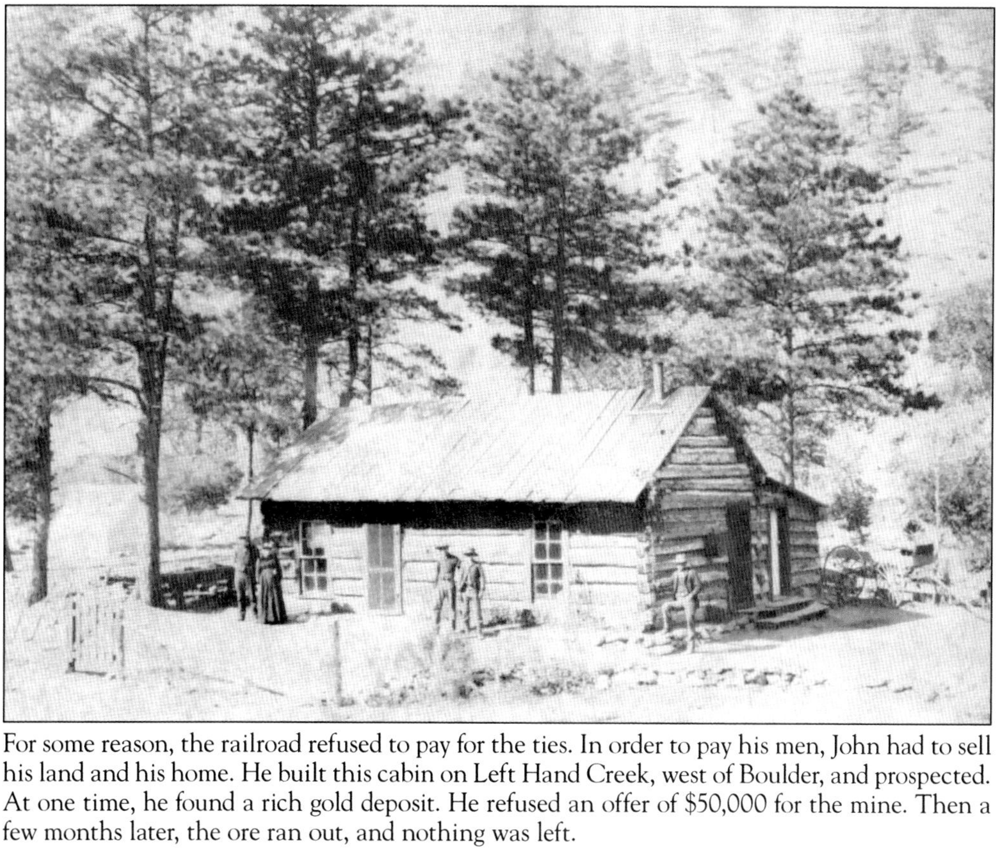

For some reason, the railroad refused to pay for the ties. In order to pay his men, John had to sell his land and his home. He built this cabin on Left Hand Creek, west of Boulder, and prospected. At one time, he found a rich gold deposit. He refused an offer of $50,000 for the mine. Then a few months later, the ore ran out, and nothing was left.

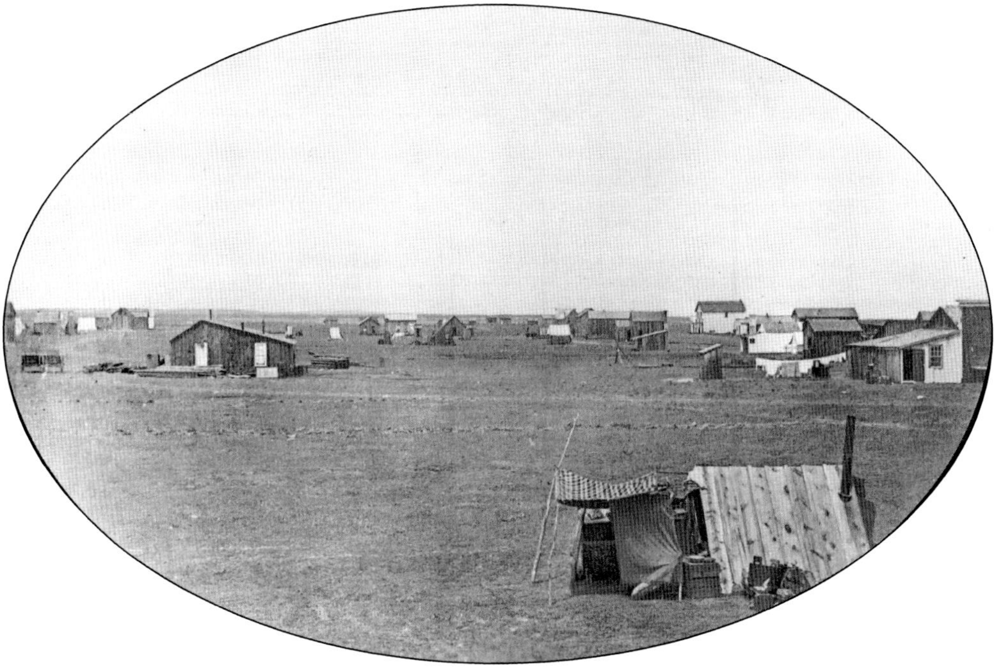

Harvey Jay Parish did not move with his parents to Boulder. At age 21 in 1883, he homesteaded an 80-acre farm that adjoined Johnstown. At first he lived in a tent, like this one. He was able to develop this tract of land and acquire other farms, until at the time of his death he owned 720 acres of choice irrigated farmland. (DPL.)

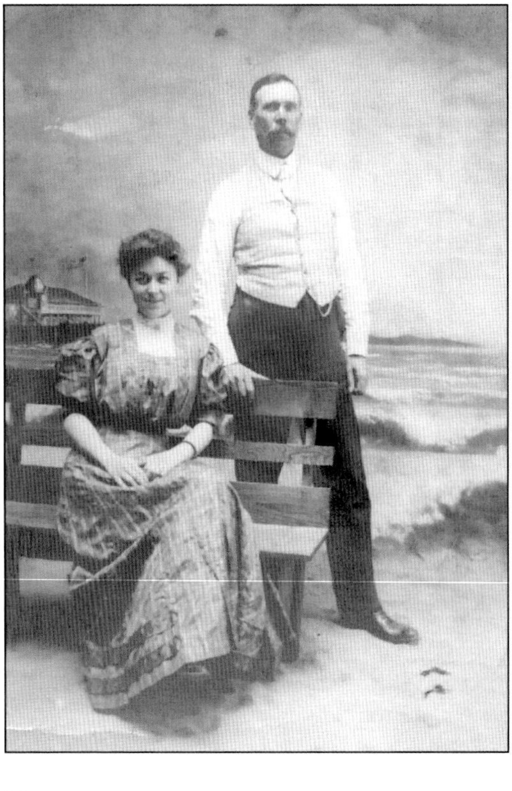

Harvey Parish and Mary Wygal were married in 1884. Mary's father, Rufus Wygal, came to Colorado in 1859, looking for gold. Not finding anything, Wygal dropped back into the Poudre Valley. He returned to Missouri after his wife and son James William. They crossed the plains to Windsor with an ox team. Mary was one of the first children born at the old sod fort.

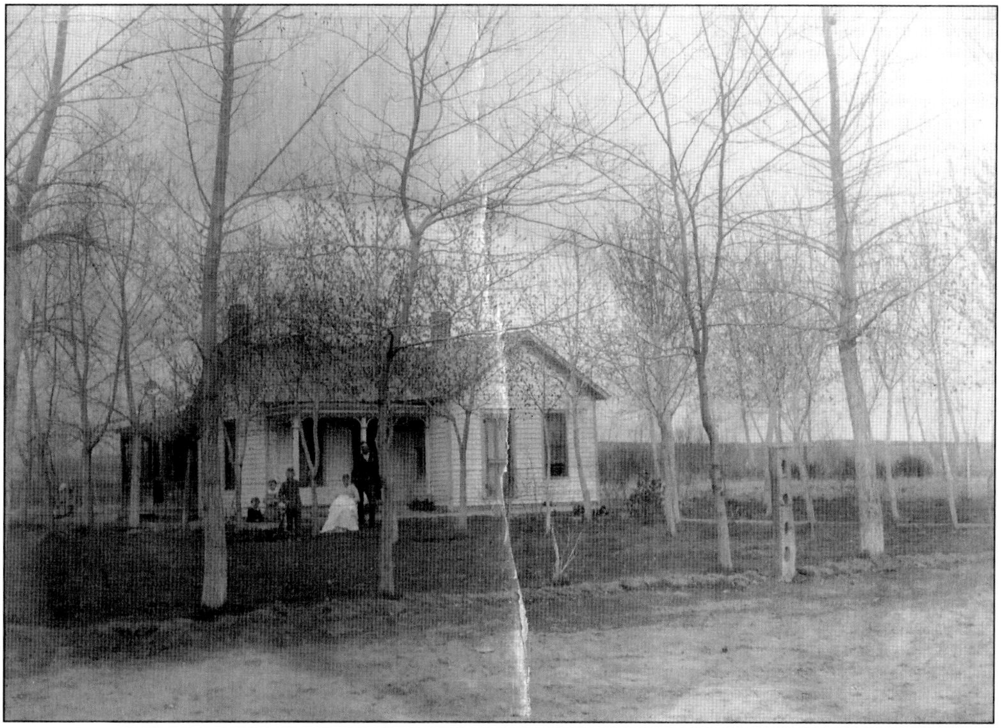

At the time that Harvey and Mary Parish homesteaded, there was not a tree or fence in sight on the prairie. Here they struggled together to build a home. Enduring the many hardships that came to them in those pioneer days, they succeeded in establishing a comfortable home for themselves and their family.

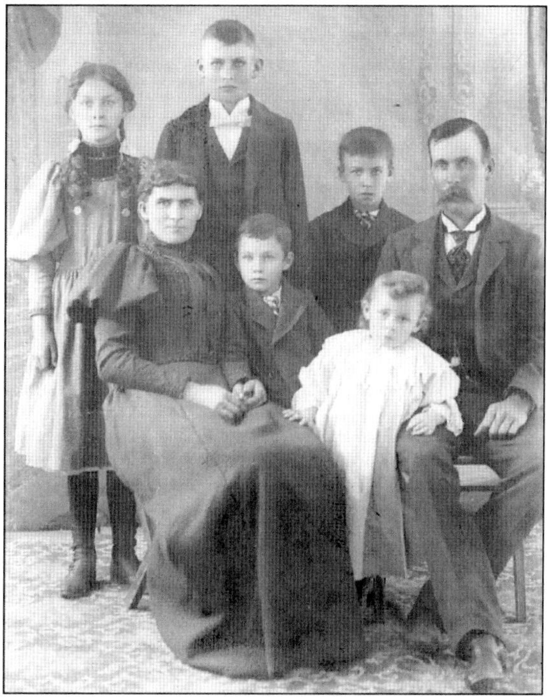

The Harvey Parish family is shown here in the late 1800s. Harvey had learned about irrigation from his father when they lived west of Loveland, and he was one of the first successful farmers in the area because of his use of irrigation. His sons learned to work farm machinery, like threshing and hay-cutting machines, all pulled by horses. They also became farmers.

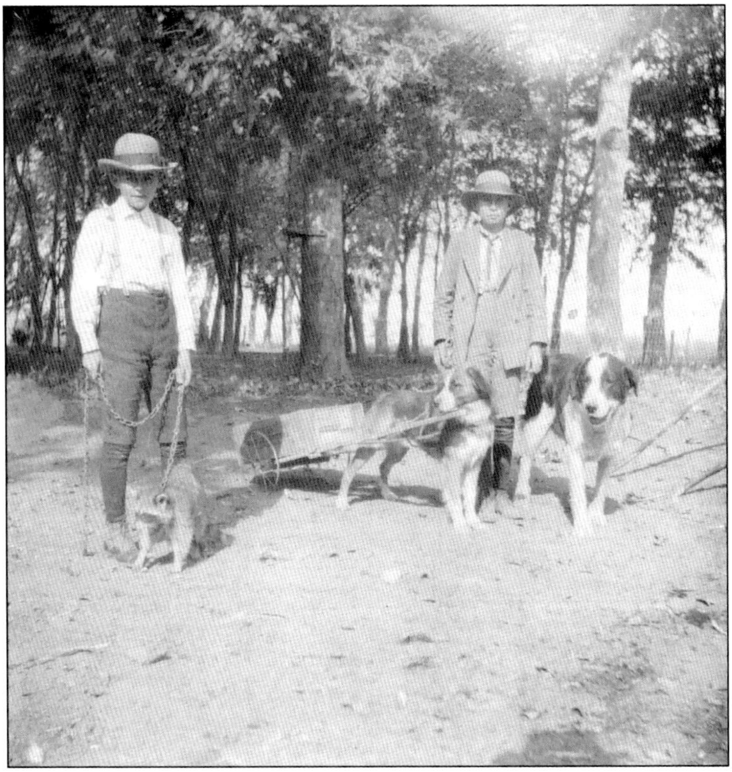

Growing up on the plains of Colorado was not all work and drudgery. These two Parish boys, Raymond and Ruthford, are playing down by the river with their dogs and pet raccoon. When other children from neighboring farms got together, they may have played games like dog-and-deer, but everyone on the plains played baseball.

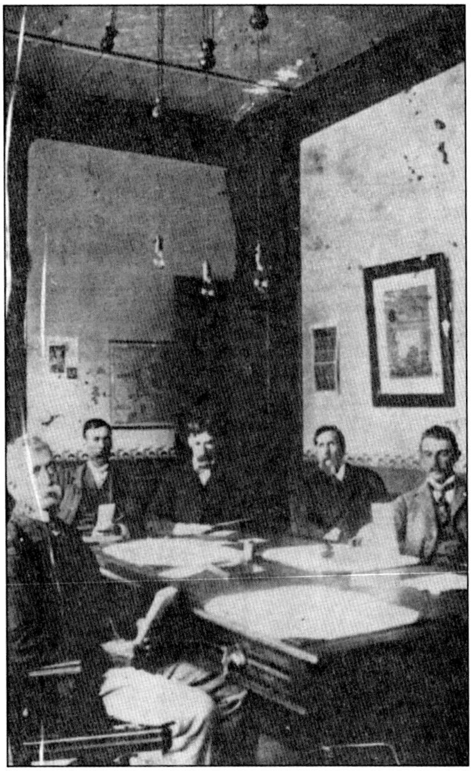

In the late 1800s, Harvey Parish, second from the left, served as a county commissioner. Soon after, Parish would found the town of Johnstown. Another early Johnstown pioneer, Jared Brush, is shown second from the right. This photograph was taken in the old courthouse in Greeley, which was built in 1882 on the site of the present courthouse and razed in 1915.

Although not as numerous as the English or the Irish, the Scots had a Colorado population of around 2,000 by 1890. Like the English, the Scots assimilated into the dominant Anglo culture and made less of their ethnicity than most other groups. A Scottish family that settled in Johnstown was the Thomas Wailes family, shown here. Three Wailes brothers and one sister came from Scotland in the early 1880s.

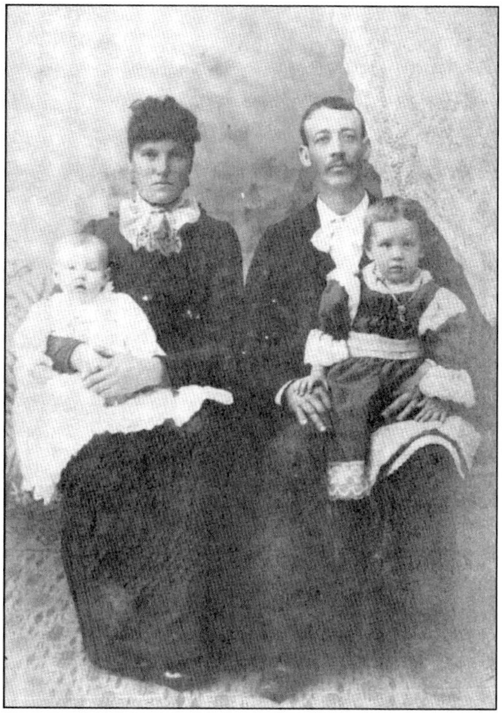

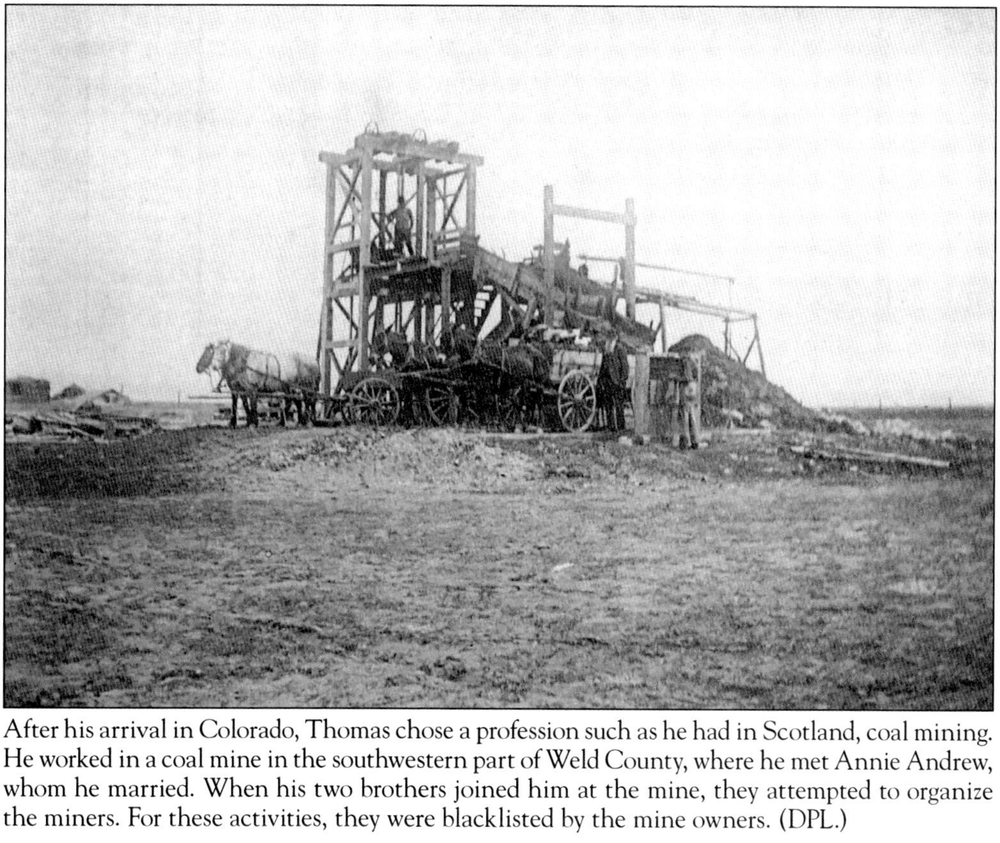

After his arrival in Colorado, Thomas chose a profession such as he had in Scotland, coal mining. He worked in a coal mine in the southwestern part of Weld County, where he met Annie Andrew, whom he married. When his two brothers joined him at the mine, they attempted to organize the miners. For these activities, they were blacklisted by the mine owners. (DPL.)

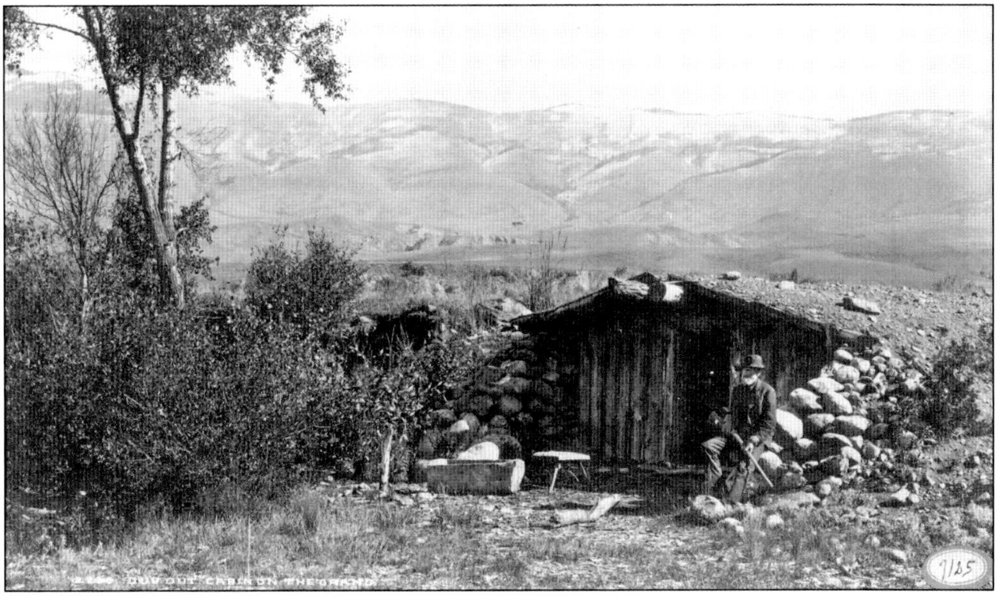

The Wailes families soon homesteaded land near Johnstown and became farmers. At first, Thomas and Annie lived in a dugout. The dugout was quite elaborate, and Thomas had no desire to move to the new place they had bought. Annie took matters into her own hands. She moved the stove to the new place and refused to cook until the rest of the belongings were moved. (DPL.)

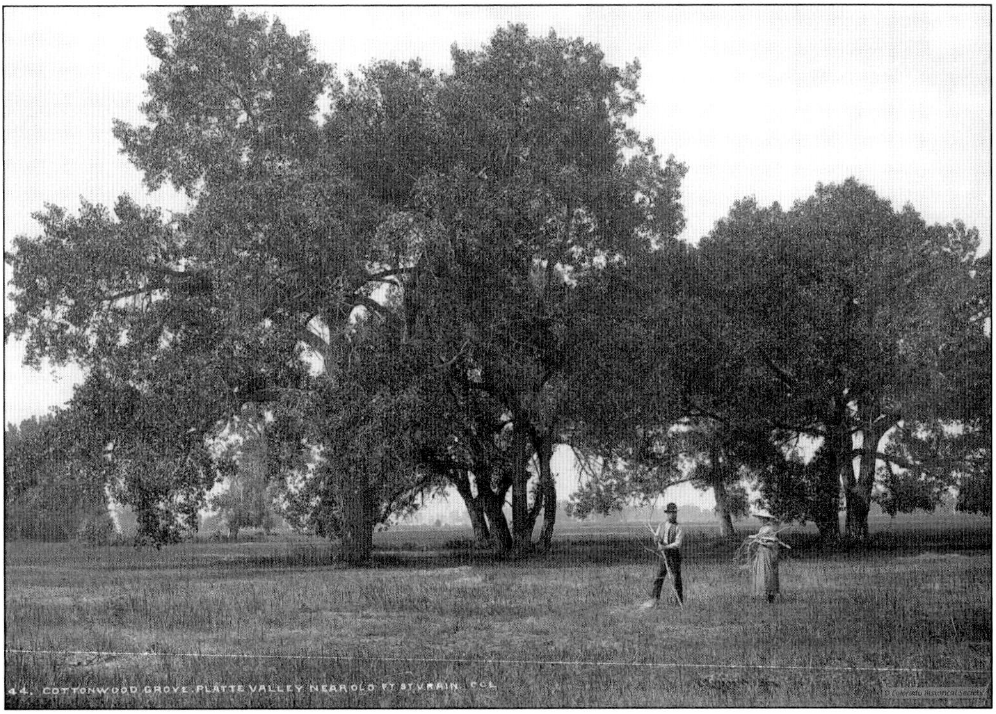

Sometimes winter fuel could be found by the rivers, as illustrated by this couple gathering wood. Most often though, the younger children were sent on the prairie north of the dugout to pick up cow chips to burn in the stoves. Some of the younger children also went with their father to the coal mines to lay in the winter supply of coal. (CHS.)

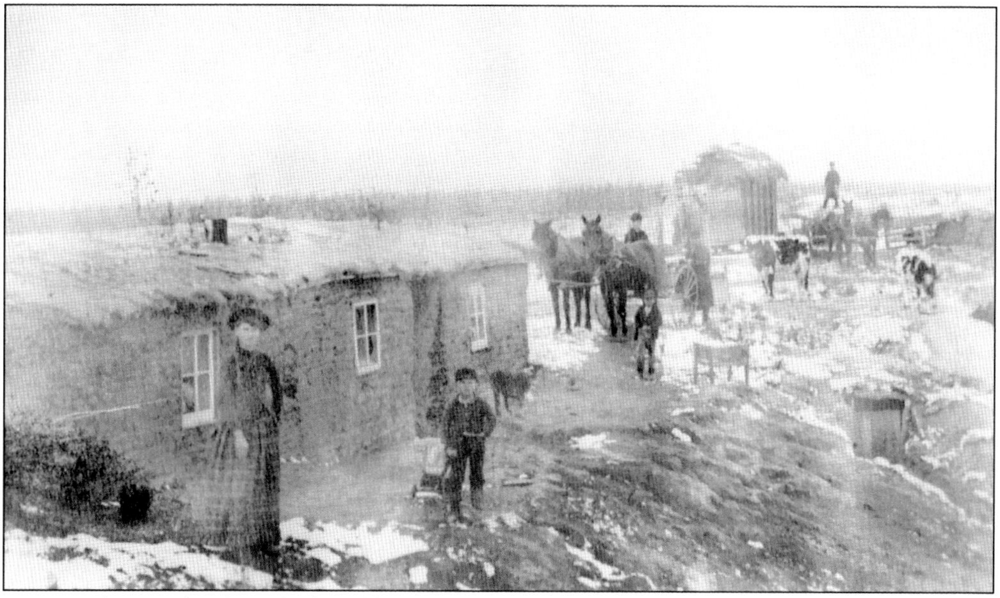

Some settlers on the plains built sod houses. Roots of the prairie grass held the soil tightly together, and the sod was cut up to make bricks. Other settlers who built sod houses had to plow almost an acre of land to get enough grass to build a house. There was not enough grassland in Johnstown to build many sod houses. (GHM.)

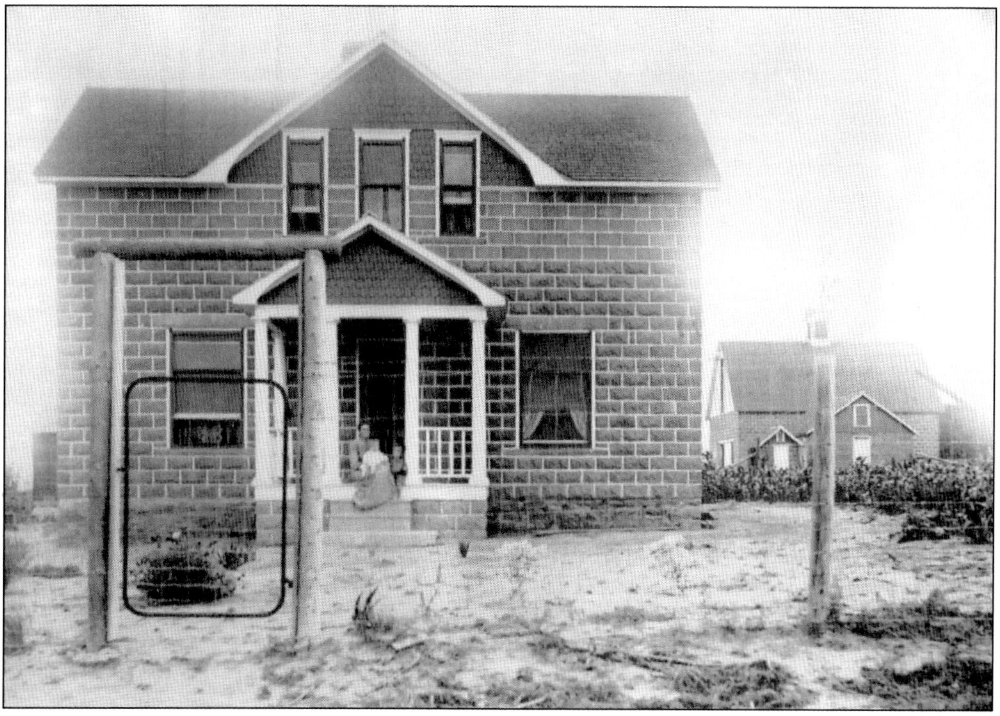

Thomas and John Wailes purchased a half-section of ground north of Johnstown, and they farmed it together for a few years. Then they divided the farm, with John taking the west half and Thomas taking the east half. Thomas's east half is still in the Wailes/Mellon family. Their brick house is shown in this photograph.

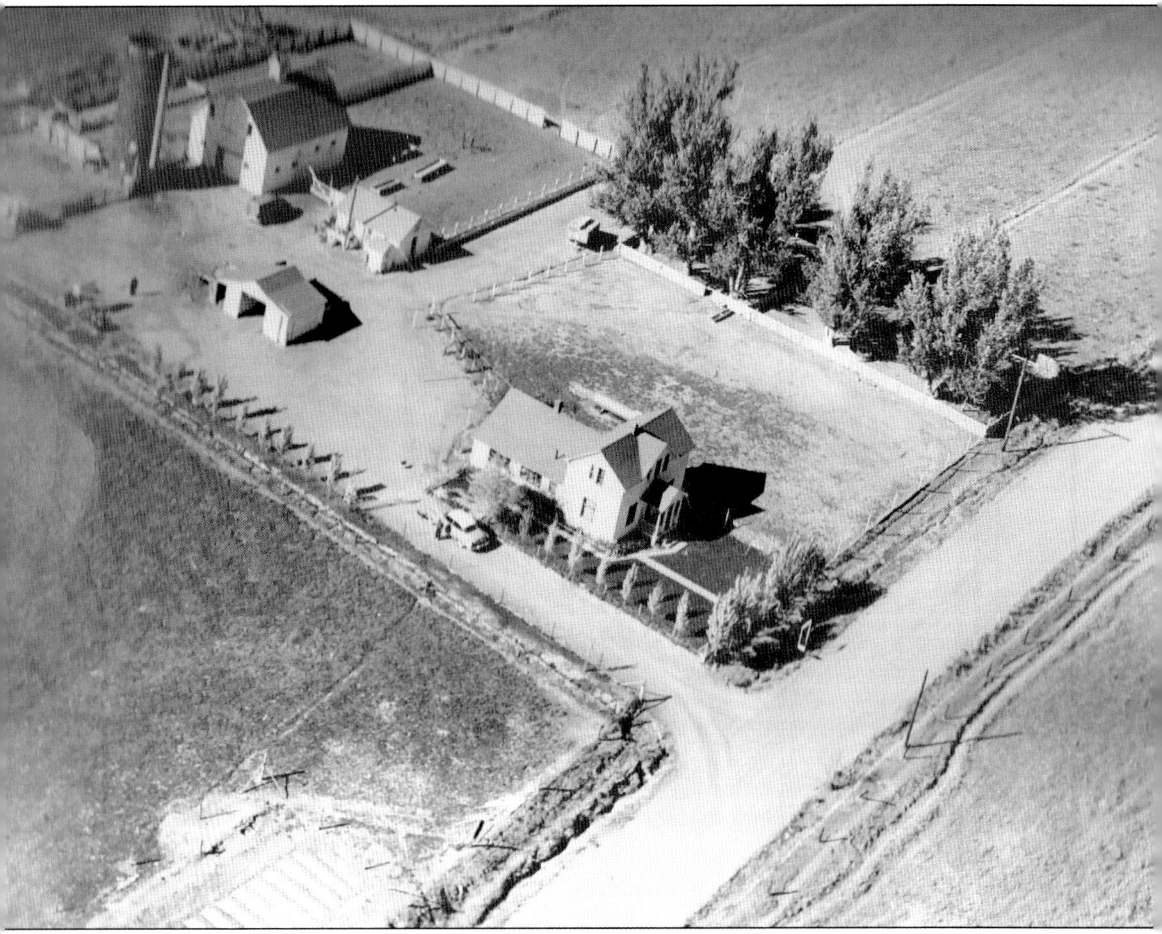

When Thomas started farming, he did not know how to hook up a team, but he would not admit this to anyone. To learn how to do it, he got up at 3:00 in the morning and walked a couple of miles to the home of a nearby neighbor on the pretense of a visit. He talked to the neighbor and watched while the neighbor was getting ready for the day's work. He then went back to his farm and did the same thing. When he was ready for the next step, he paid the neighbor another visit. The descendants of Thomas Wailes must have appreciated his efforts. Monte and Marvin Mellon currently own their great grandfather's farm. It was honored by being named as a Colorado Centennial Farm by the Colorado Historical Society.

Three

Water, Water, and Water

Most of the pioneers who settled in Colorado came seeking gold, but only a few succeeded in making a living out of the mines. In the Johnstown area, the early settlers turned to agriculture (ranching and farming).

The first settlers along the Big Thompson River, including the Brush family, were ranchers. The cattle industry thrived during an era of open grazing. The drought that occurred in the 1890s, however, caused the ranchers to extend their herds beyond what the land could sustain. The land became overgrazed. In the early 1900s, ranchers had to adapt to new practices rather than depend on free grazing. They now had to invest in land, fences, farm machinery, and crops such as alfalfa to feed their livestock. The cowboys of the past century gave way to businessmen, investing in real estate. The cowboys became ranchers and farmers.

The Homestead Act allocated 160 acres for a family farm. The first wave of farmers came to Johnstown in the 1880s, hoping to build a new life. Many new towns in the area such as Berthoud, Loveland, Longmont, and Greeley were established and grew during this time, and farmers were realizing their dreams. The drought of the 1890s that had affected the ranchers also affected the farmers. Many abandoned their farms because they were not skilled at dry-land farming. They soon learned the truth of the saying, "The three most important things about living in the West are: water, water, and water." Conventional farming techniques used in the East did not work in the West. A new wave of homesteaders came at the turn of the 20th century, with the hope of practicing new techniques for irrigation and improved technology for dry-land farming.

Even though living off the land has been a constant struggle, the agricultural people of Johnstown adapted to natural elements and other difficulties confronting them and have thrived.

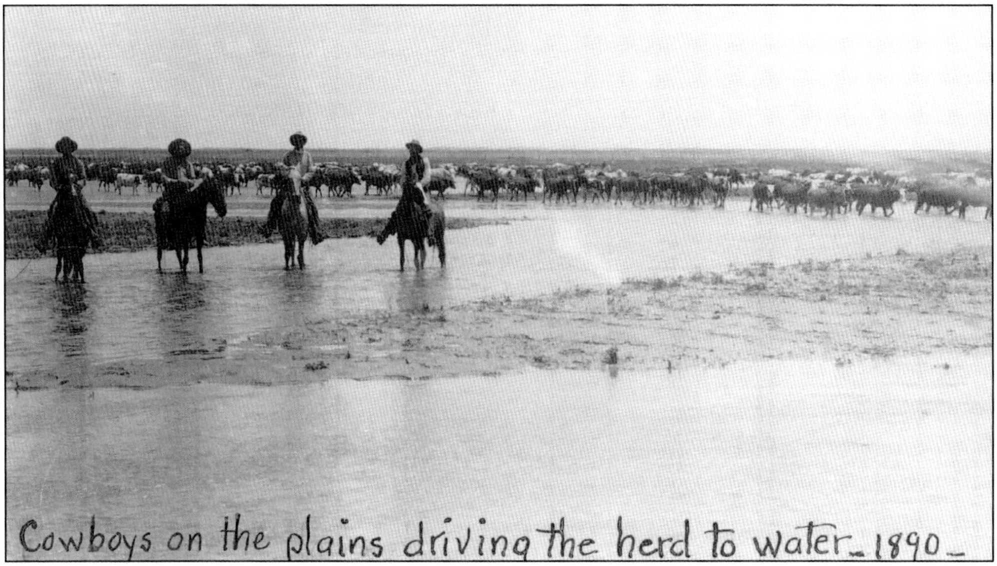

In the early days of cattle ranching, cowboys depended on finding natural streams and springs that were scattered throughout the prairie. The native grasses were also prized by the range cattle, as they had been by the buffalo before them. They did not wilt in the autumn but cured themselves, thus providing forage for the cattle in the winter. (GHM.)

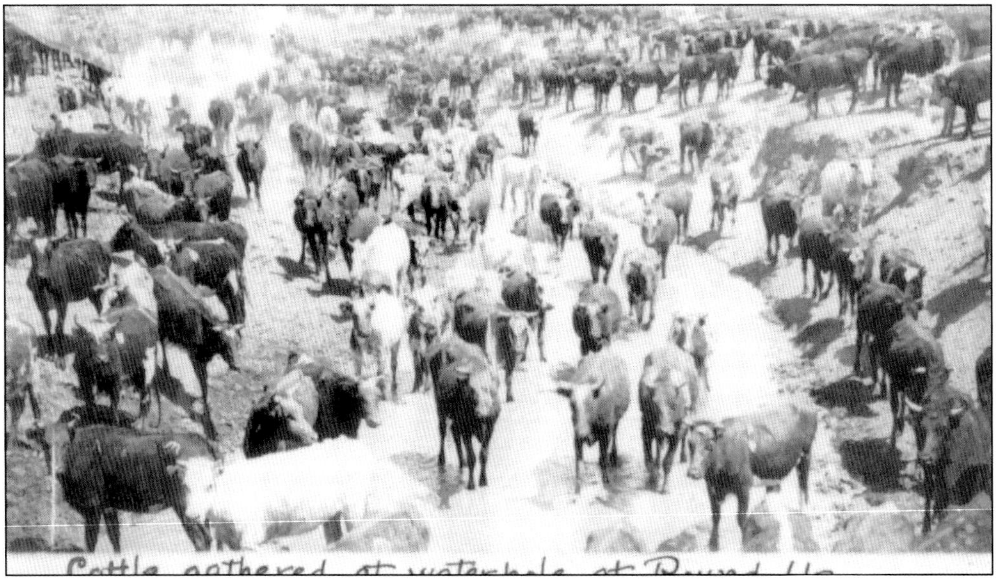

Two roundups were held each year when cattle were kept on the open range. The spring roundup was for branding calves, and the one in the fall was to round up the animals that were to be shipped to market. The roundup in this photograph was probably on its way to market and shows the mixed variety of range cattle in the early days, including longhorns. (GHM.)

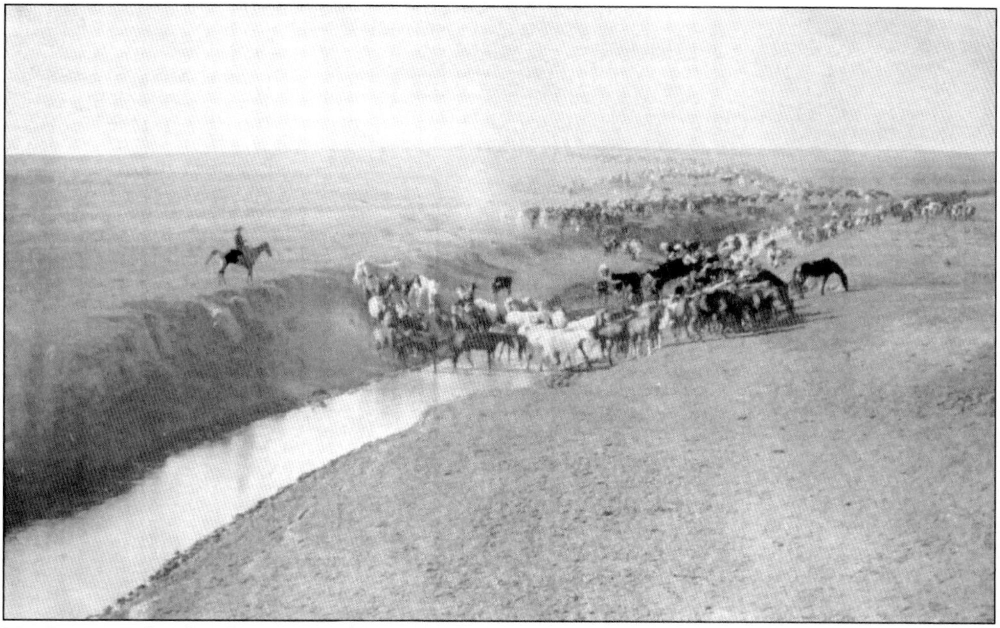

Tending vast herds of range cattle required hundreds of head of horses. In preparation for the roundup, usually seven horses were furnished each cowhand and this string was his for the duration. Each cowboy would usually change horses three times each day. In this photograph, about 40 horses can be counted, a good indication of the size of the outfit. (GHM.)

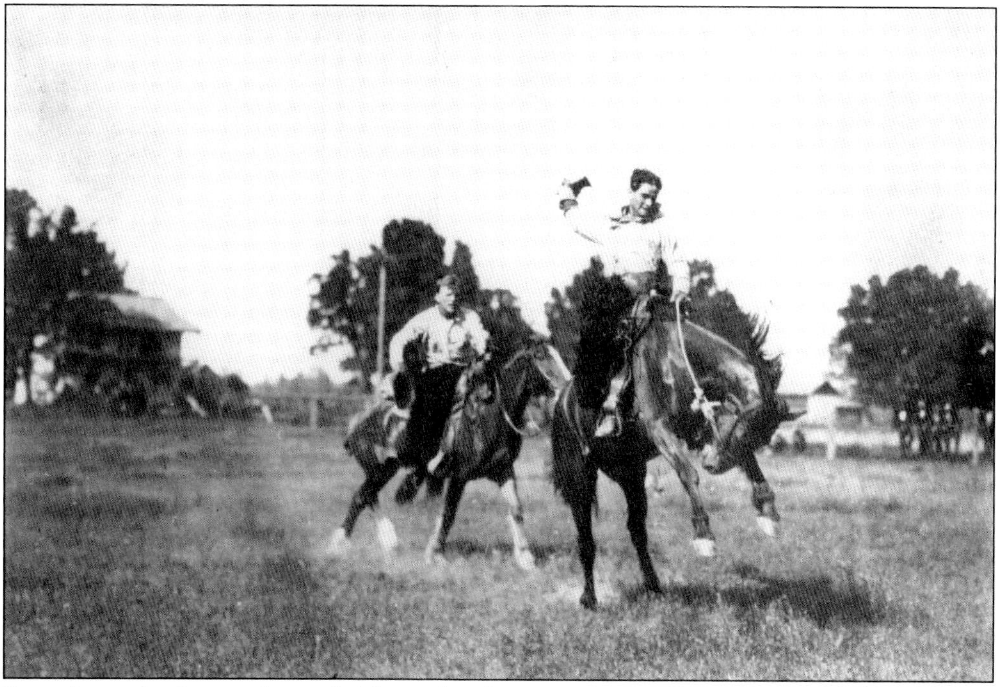

Part of a cowboy's everyday work life was breaking new horses. A story was told about Mike, a cowhand who attempted to tame Poncho, a horse that was thought to be unbreakable. After weeks of patience, the cowhand was able to put a saddle on Poncho, and he seemed tame. However, Poncho later took advantage of a weak moment and trampled Mike to death. (GHM.)

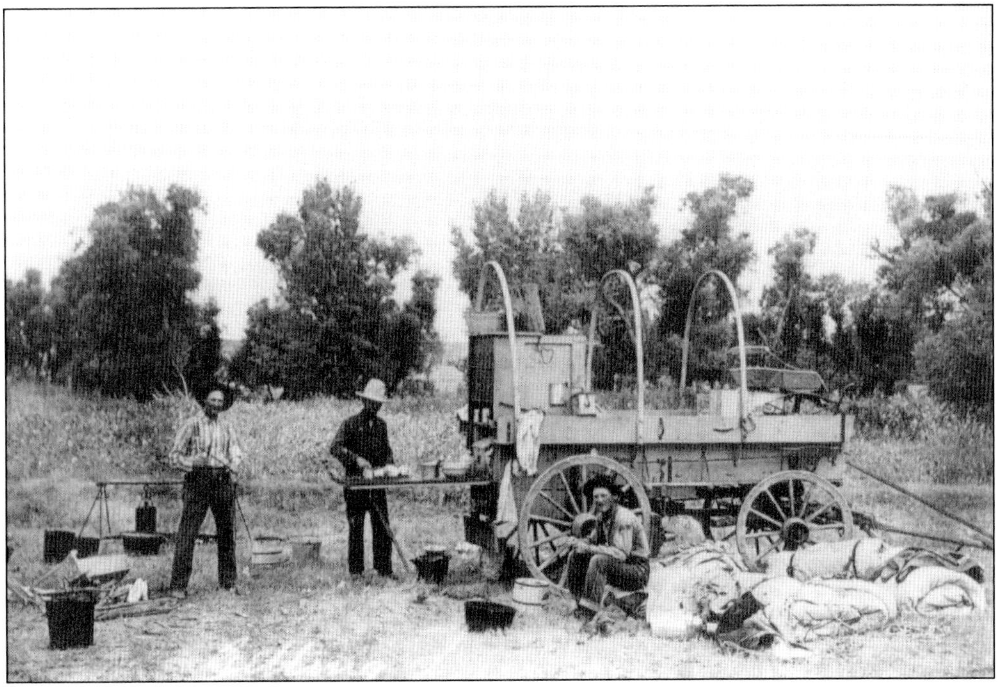

Provisions were very important in the middle of nowhere, so precautions were taken to keep the chuck wagon safe in case of a stampede. Cowboys set up the chuck wagon a full mile away from the cattle, in the direction the herd was headed. Cattle on the trail only stampeded in one direction, back along the trail they had just passed. (GHM.)

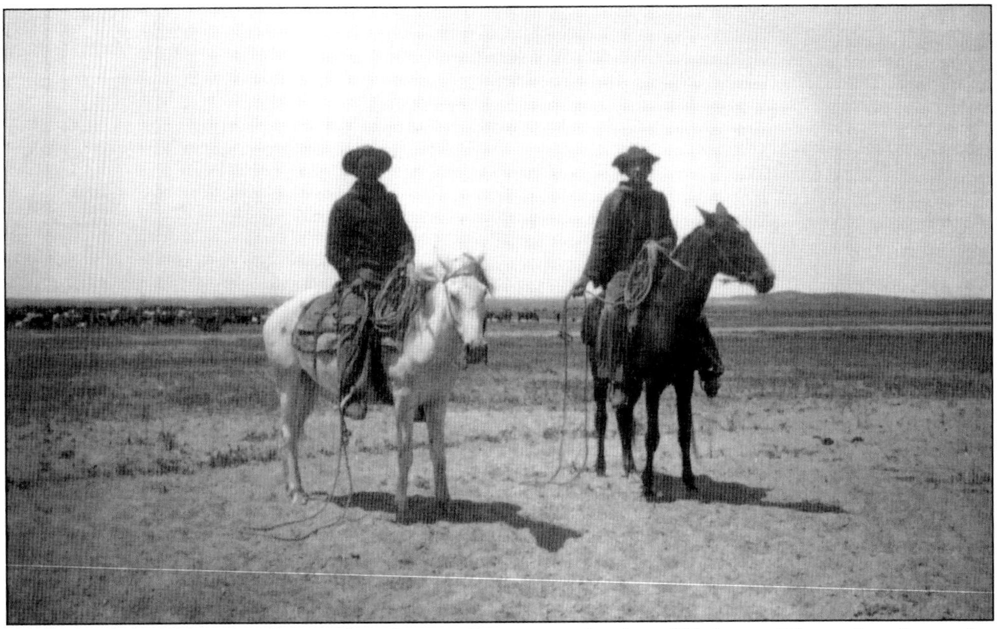

One stampede started with a strike of a match on a cowboy's saddle horn. Three days later, the cowboys finally got the cattle back to where they had started. Two hundred of them were dead or had to be shot, and hundreds had their horns broken off and hanging by slivers. It cost at least $10,000 in damages. (GHM.)

The three most important things about living in the West are water, water, and water. The early settlers quickly learned this lesson. Water engineers are fond of saying that 80 percent of the water in Colorado falls on the west side of the Continental Divide, but 80 percent of the people live on the east side. (GHM.)

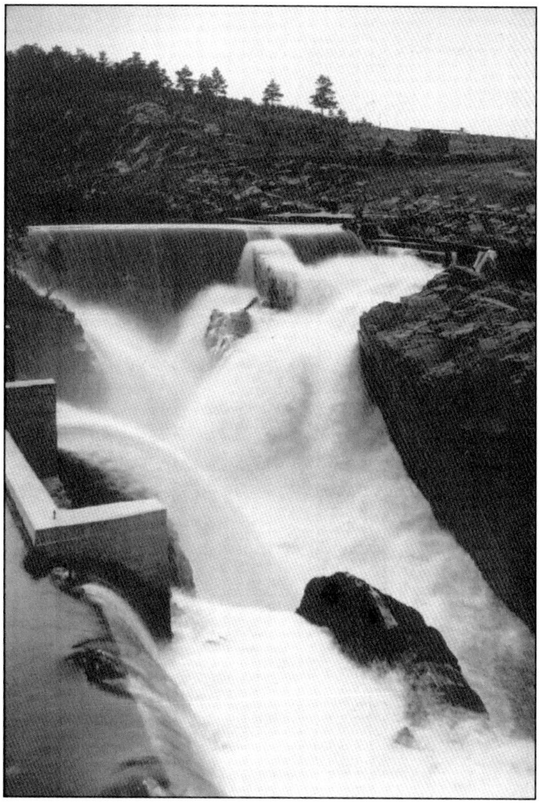

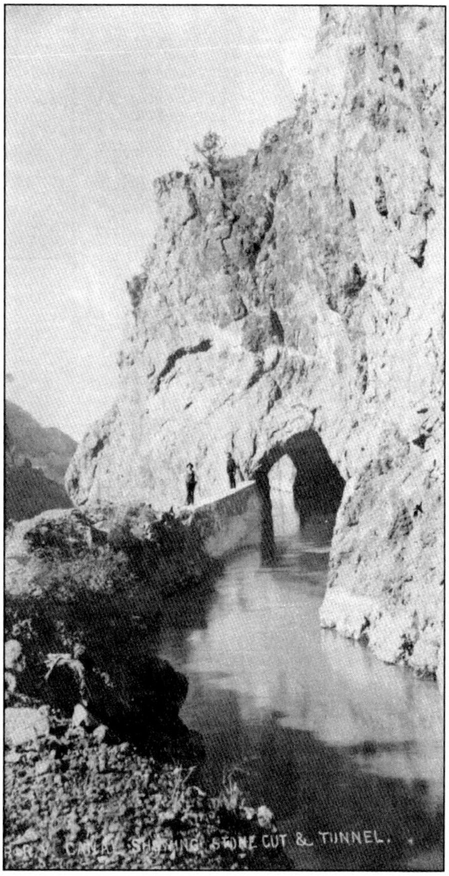

Since water was not naturally provided on the eastern slope, it was diverted from the Colorado River on the western slope, through a series of dams, ditches, and a tunnel, to the eastern slope. Water projects needed to be developed in the early days also, as shown in this photograph of a canal with a tunnel cut through a mountain. (GHM.)

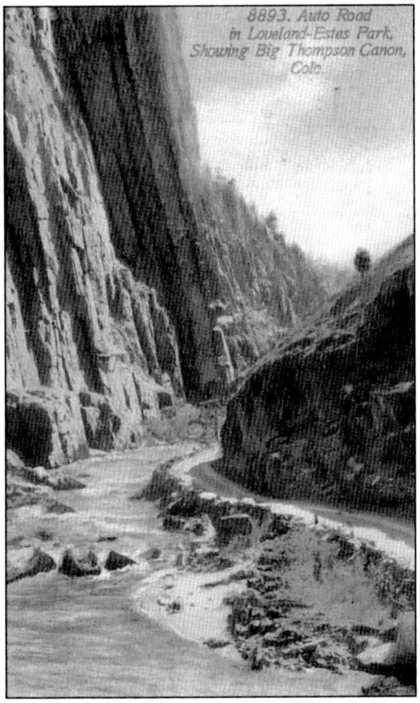

Johnstown is between two streams, the Little Thompson River and the Big Thompson River, shown here. In the first few years of settlement, almost every acre along the banks of these rivers was brought under an irrigation system of some sort.

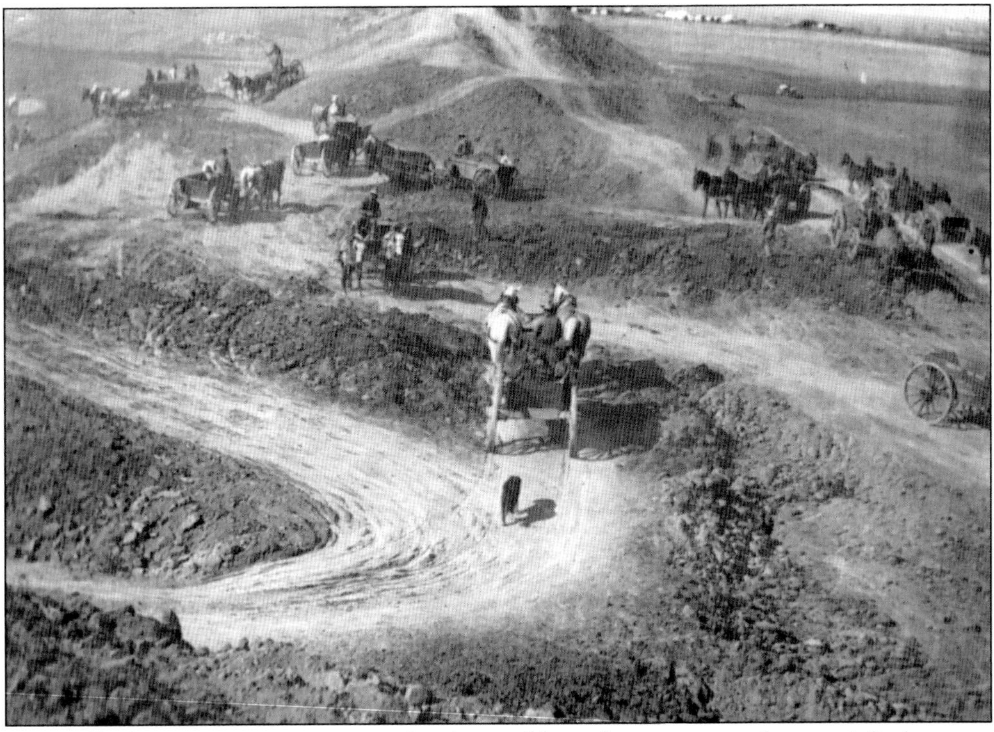

Eventually there was no more water to be obtained from the streams, so dams and ditches were constructed to catch runoff from the smaller streams and from irrigation systems themselves. Harvey Parish, Johnstown's founder, possessed more practical knowledge of ditch building than any other man in this part of the state. This photograph shows how a nearby dam for Fossil Creek Reservoir near Greeley was built. (GHM.)

This photograph shows the last length of pipe of the Greeley water system. Early settlers gave preference to people who needed water for domestic or agricultural use. They also adopted a principle of "first in time, first in right." Whoever had been the first to use the water obtained the water rights to that stream. (GHM.)

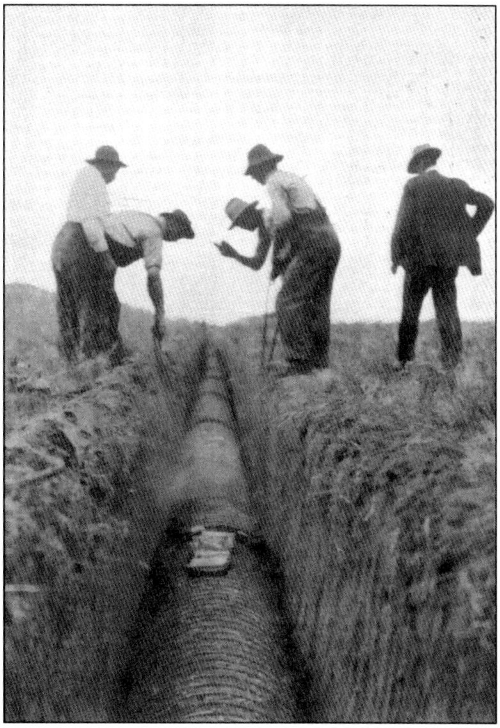

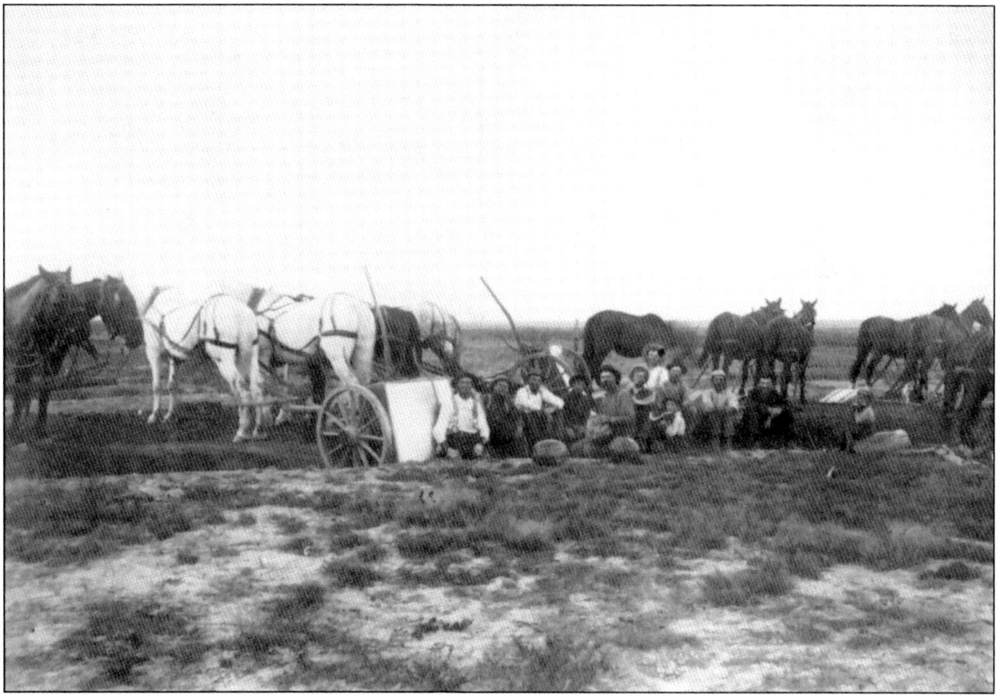

The ditches that the original settlers built soon proved to be too small. The flow of the water in the irrigation ditches was not enough to meet farming needs. The ditches had to be widened and deepened, as this photograph shows. This allowed them to come closer to carrying the amount of water needed for their crops. (GHM.)

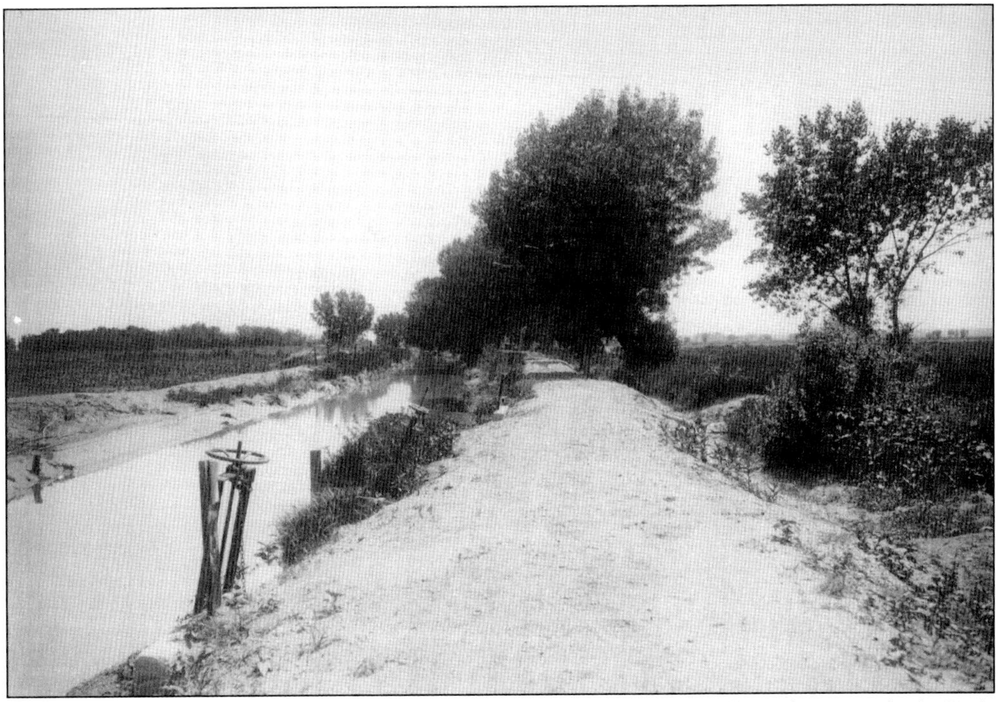

The purpose of the lifting valve, or head gate, was to control the water from the main ditch. Each farmer was allotted a certain number of shares of water. When farmers used the same ditch, they sometimes fought over whether or not they were getting their share. To help solve this problem, a lifting valve could be adjusted to send more water or turn it off. (GHM.)

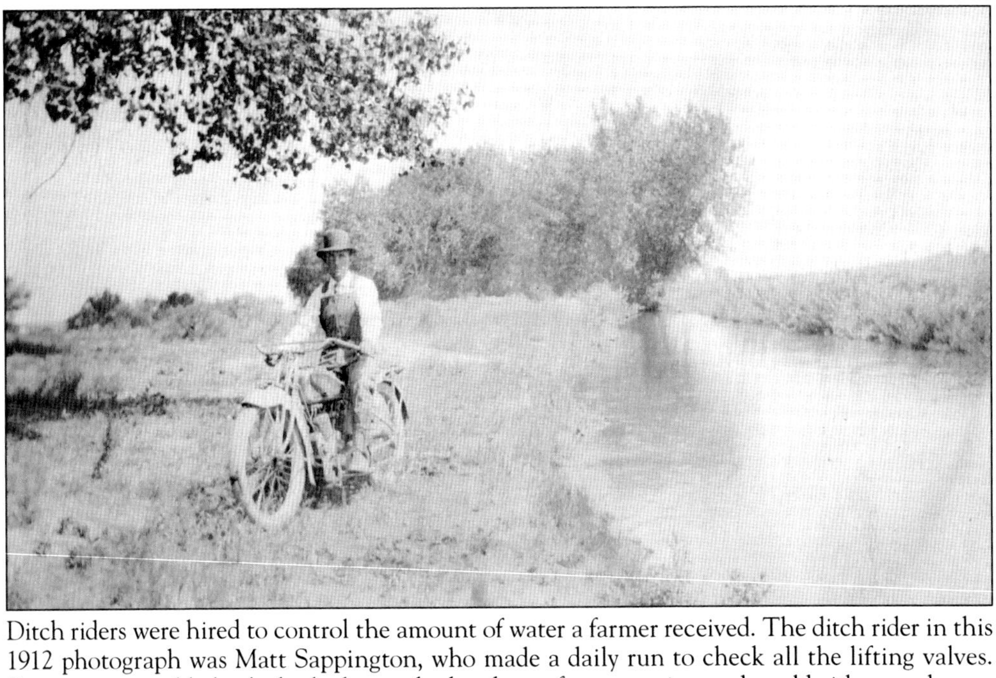

Ditch riders were hired to control the amount of water a farmer received. The ditch rider in this 1912 photograph was Matt Sappington, who made a daily run to check all the lifting valves. Sappington would check the locks on the head gate for tampering and could either send more water to the farmer or turn it off.

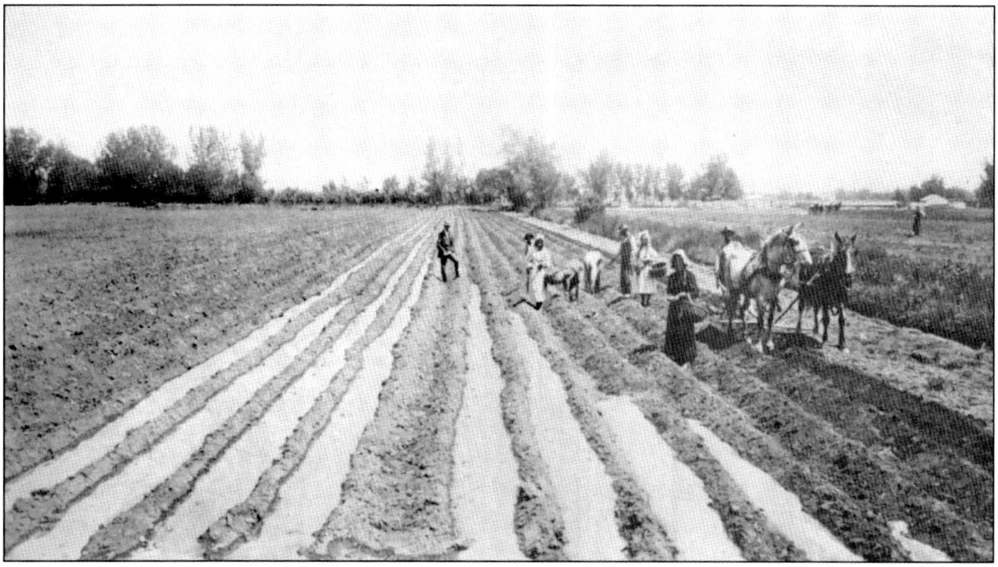

Water rights still are an important commodity on the Front Range of Colorado, and one share can be worth a great amount of money. Irrigation water was so necessary because it made a virtual paradise of the vast semi-arid plains in the county. This photograph shows cabbage plants being set and irrigated in the 1890s. (GHM.)

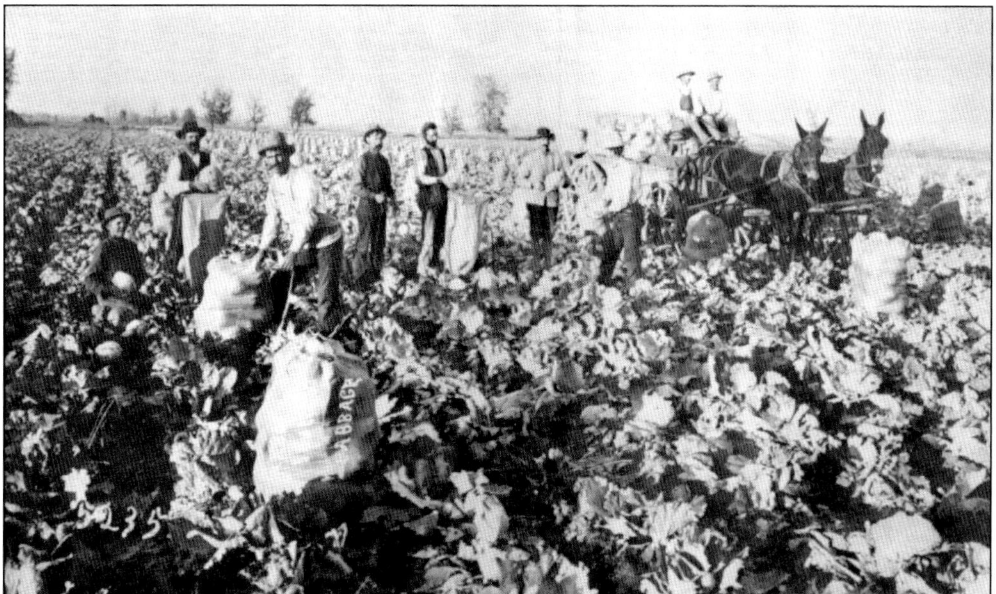

The same crop of cabbage that was planted in the previous photograph may be the crop that is being harvested in this scene. Workers sacked and loaded cabbages grown under irrigation, then the produce was shipped to markets in Denver and eastern cities. (GHM.)

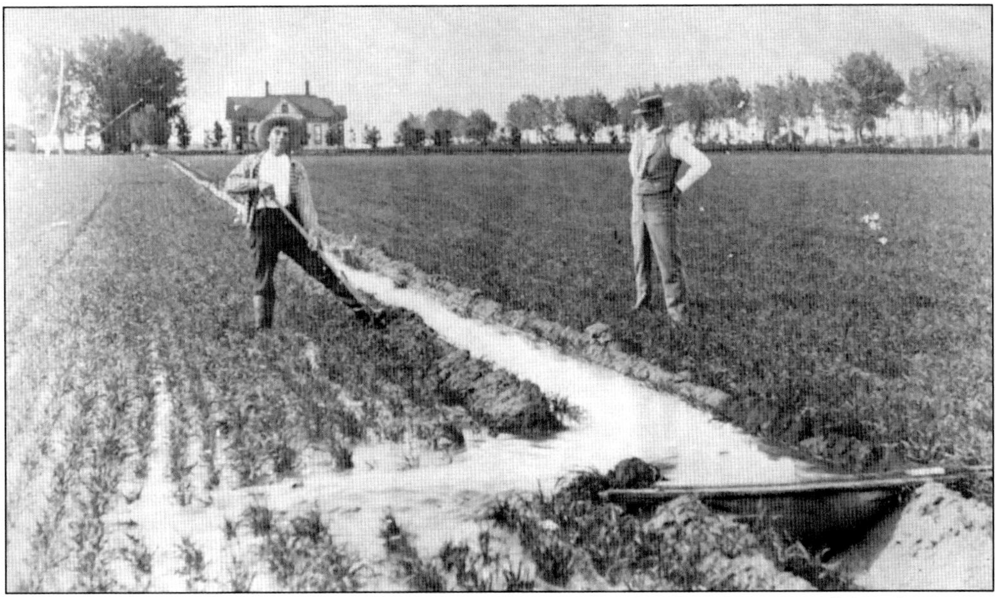

This photograph of the Ben Reinke farm west of Johnstown showing irrigation of the wheat crop was a typical scene in the 1890s. Bringing water from the rivers to provide moisture for crops, through irrigation, has paid off for Weld County for more than a century. Weld County has consistently ranked among the top agricultural counties in the nation. (GHM.)

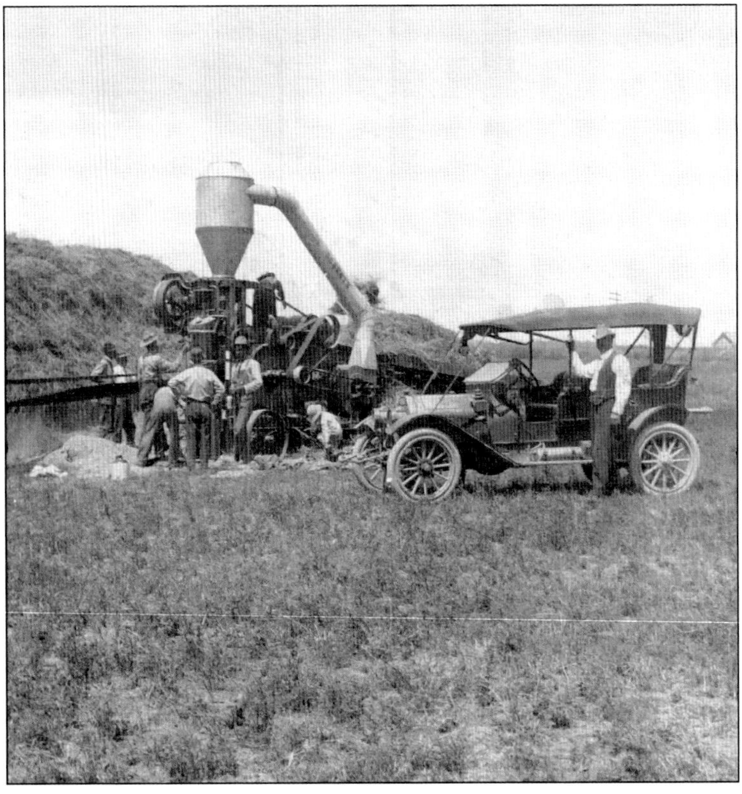

Enterprising farmers such as Ruthford Parish did not use irrigation to produce wheat but depended on precipitation to meet crop requirements. He is shown in this photograph on his farm in Las Animas in Bent County. Today most wheat is grown with this dry-land farming technique in eastern Colorado, while irrigated land in this area produces sugar beets, corn, potatoes, and similar crops.

In the early days of Johnstown, farmers like Herman Lammers, shown in this photograph, gathered and tied their crop into bundles. Bundles then were placed together in a shock. The grain was separated from the straw with a threshing machine. The grain was shipped to flour mills, and the straw was used as bedding for animals in the winter.

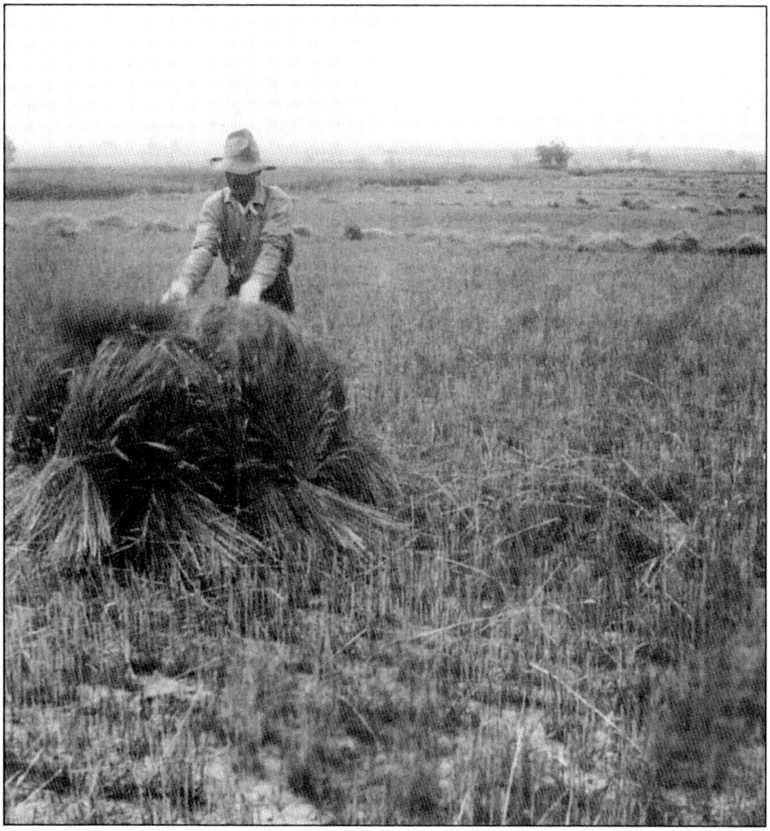

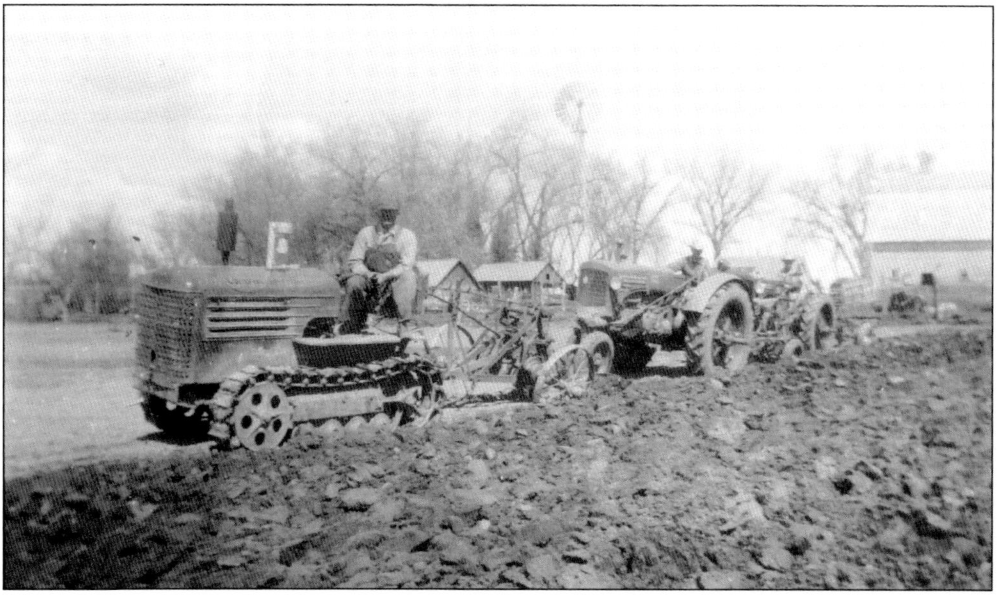

Clarence Schwalm used a Cletrack crawler tractor in the 1930s to plow his fields. This tractor had wire-rimmed wheels, with roller-chain tracks. Although the work was slow, Schwalm was able to easily plow land that was muddy or lacked traction.

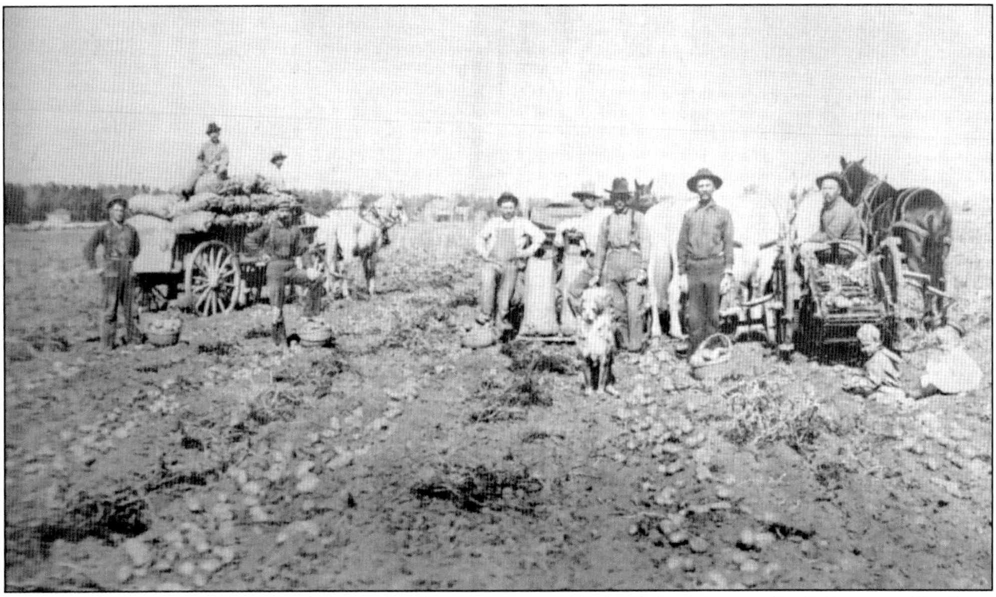

Hundreds of men were needed to grade the potatoes in this field as they picked them up. Baskets were used instead of potato sacks, and the potatoes were stored in an underground cellar or taken to a potato dock for shipment. At the time this photograph was taken, Weld County produced the most potatoes of the region, but blight caused the downfall of this crop. (GHM.)

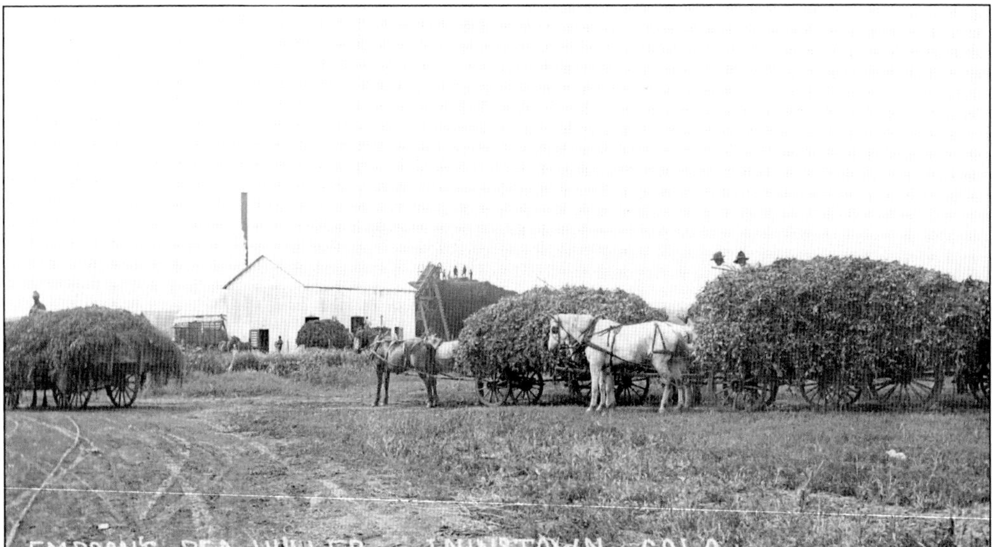

Peas were another early crop in Johnstown. Farmers brought peas from about 600 acres of farmland each year to the pea huller, operated by the J. H. Empson Canning Company. Then the peas, along with other vegetables of the area, were shipped to the factory in Greeley to be canned.

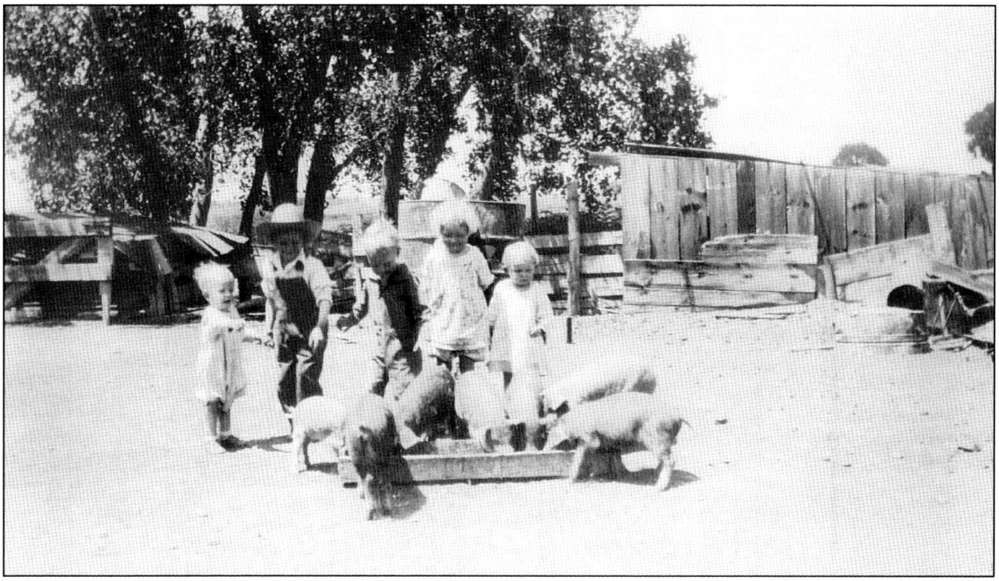

Farming in Johnstown involved hard work. Farms generally consisted of a small house and a barn for livestock. Sometimes a cistern for water would need to be used if a well could not be dug. A water truck would come periodically and fill the cistern with "liquid gold." The families led lonely lives, as the nearest neighbors were usually several miles away.

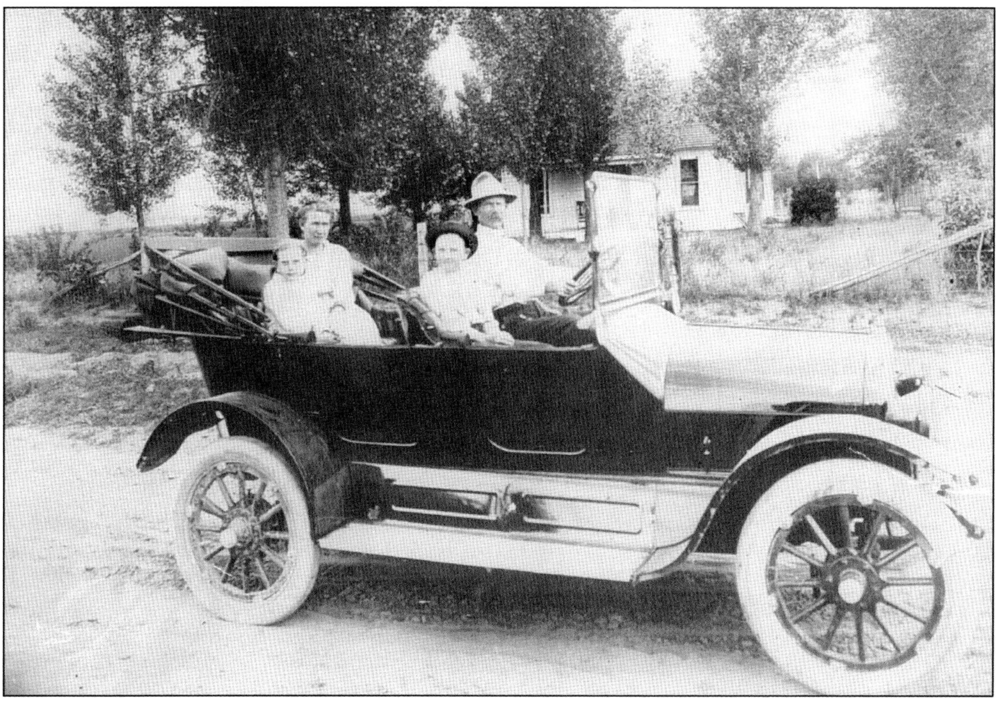

Not every day was a work day. On Saturday, the family would "load up" in the new car and go into town to shop and socialize. Shown in this photograph are Herman, Bertha, Anna, and Joseph Lammers. Anna (Miner) spent almost her entire life in Johnstown. When she moved to Greeley in 1999, she had lived in Johnstown for 92 years, making her the longest living resident of the town.

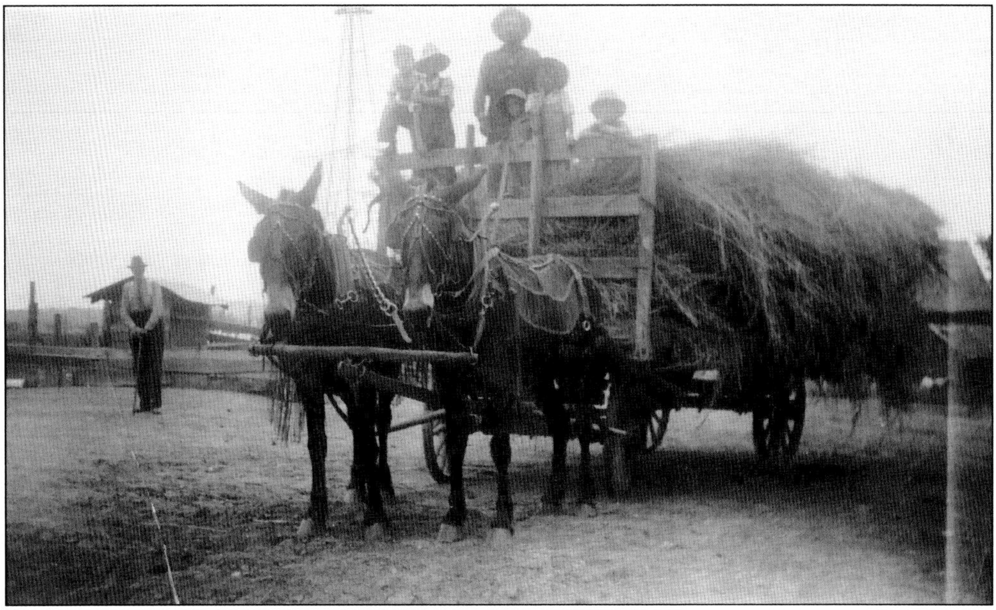

Some families, like the Schwalm family, may have waited for the Richie Wagon to pay one of its regular visits. This "moving store" carried almost everything the early settlers needed in a series of drawers and compartments on the wagon. On top of the vehicle, the driver carried chickens, crates of eggs, produce, and occasionally livestock that had been taken from farmers in exchange for goods.

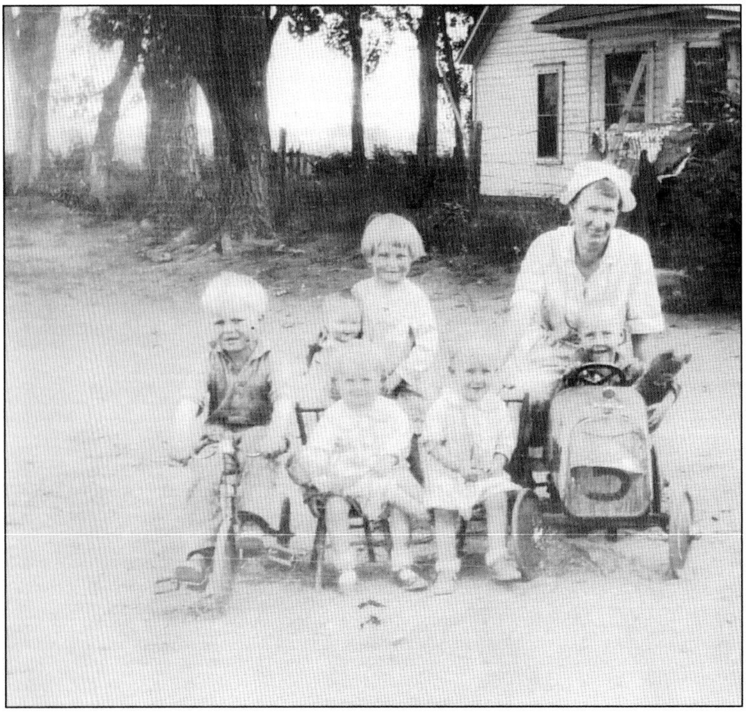

Although the farmers of long ago did not have the conveniences of today, they had something that many lack now—close family ties. Three or four generations of family members often lived in the same house. The children and grandchildren grew up together, as shown in this photograph of Bertha Lammers and her grandchildren.

Four

Building a Town

By the time Johnstown was founded in 1902, almost all of Colorado's population was already settled nearby along the Front Range, in larger cities. The only buildings within the present city limits were two farmhouses. The residents of this area were fairly self-sufficient, so trips to an established town were seldom. However, when someone did need goods or services, he had to go to Berthoud, Windsor, or Greeley—at least a 10-mile trip one way. Because this trip was made using a horse-and-buggy, it was long and tiring.

Three main factors came together in 1902, which caused Harvey Jay Parish to start building Johnstown: sugar beets, irrigation, and the railroad. In the late 1800s, researchers at what is now known as Colorado State University in Fort Collins discovered that due to the high altitude, cool weather, and controlled irrigation, sugar beets could be effectively grown in this region. In 1901, several investors got together and built the first sugar beet plant along the Front Range. They chose Loveland as their site. By this time, many farmers along the Platte and Big Thompson river valleys began planting sugar beets. The Great Western Sugar Company decided to connect the Loveland plant with many of the surrounding agricultural centers. The presence of the Great Western Railroad was the main reason for Johnstown's existence. With the involvement of the railroad, Johnstown was turned from barren fields into a thriving town in just a few months. Johnstown was platted around the railroad line before the tracks were even built. The main street, which became Parish Avenue, ran parallel to the railroad tracks.

Three years after its founding, the entire town of Johnstown was getting ready to move to a different site 2 miles to the east because of the railroad. A survey for the Denver, Laramie, and Northwestern Railroad would leave Johnstown out of its path, so a move was in order. But the Denver, Laramie, and Northwestern Railroad never materialized, and Johnstown did not move.

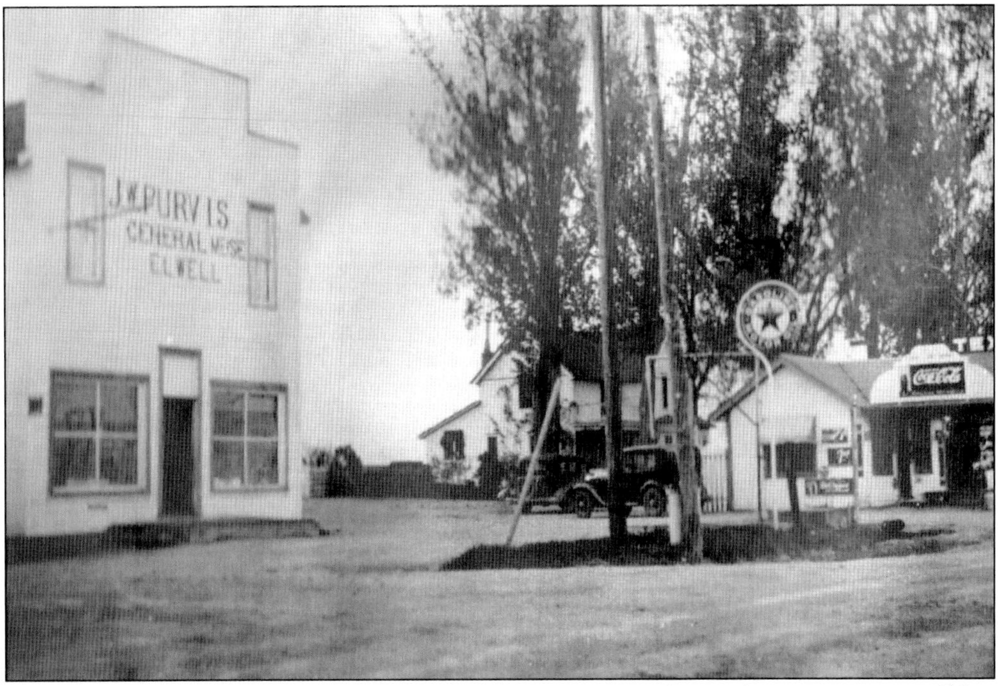

In 1900, the town of Johnstown did not exist. However, 2 miles to the west was a small but active settlement called Elwell. This settlement contained approximately six houses, a church, a cemetery, and several small one-room schools nearby. John and William Purvis came to the Elwell community in 1895 from Nebraska and worked on a farm there. In 1899, John built the J. W. Purvis General Merchandise Store.

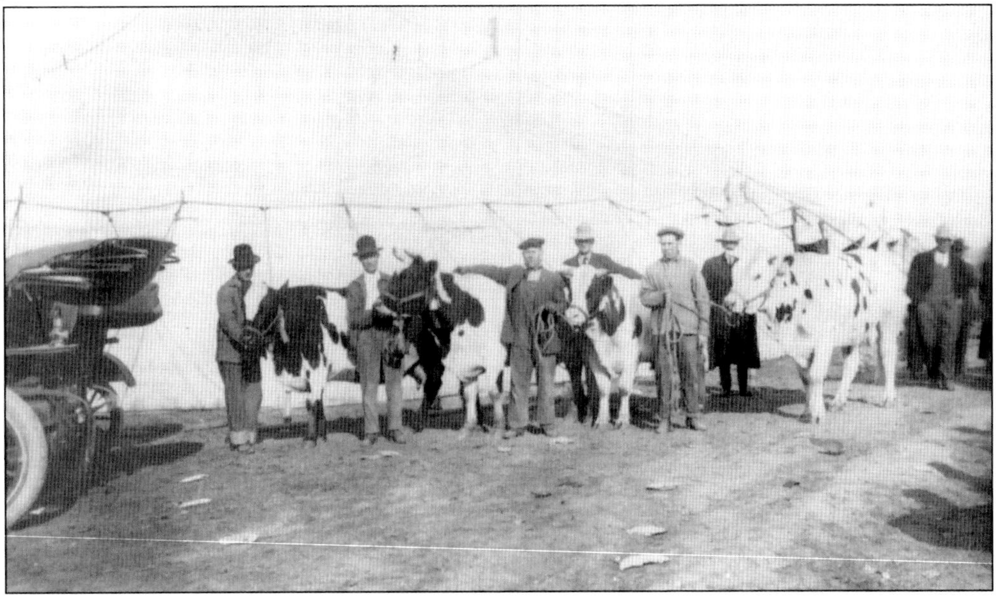

In 1929, Vernon Purvis bought a dairy business and continued with it for a number of years. Eventually Elwell melded into Johnstown, and few people today remember its existence. The church was moved to Johnstown and became the Catholic church, the Elwell Cemetery became Johnstown cemetery, and the schools became part of Johnstown's system. (GHM.)

The first branch of the new railroad line ran right next to the Parish farm. Realizing he was situated near a future railway hub, Parish bought the 160 acres north of his for $11 an acre. He then platted the land and founded the town of Johnstown in 1902.

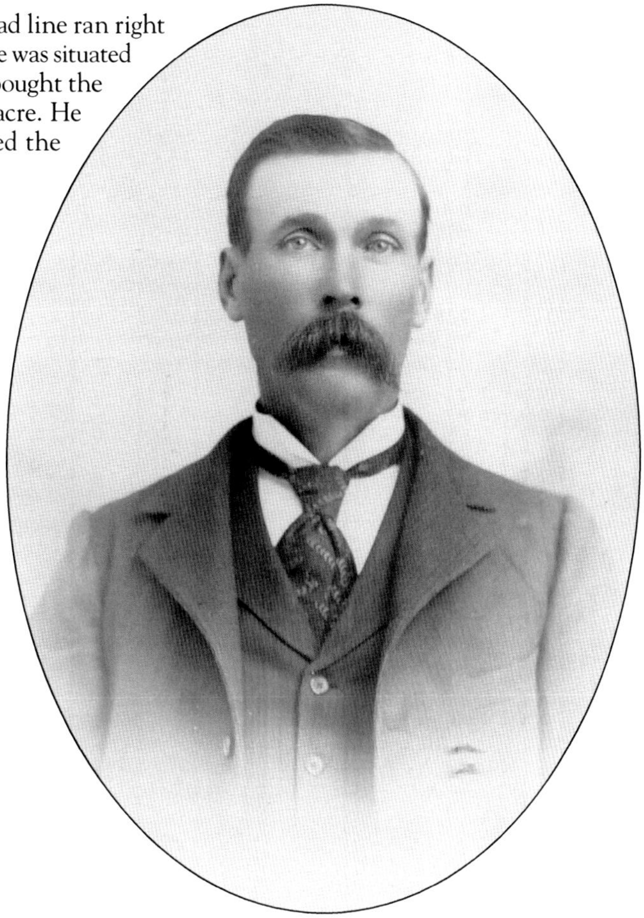

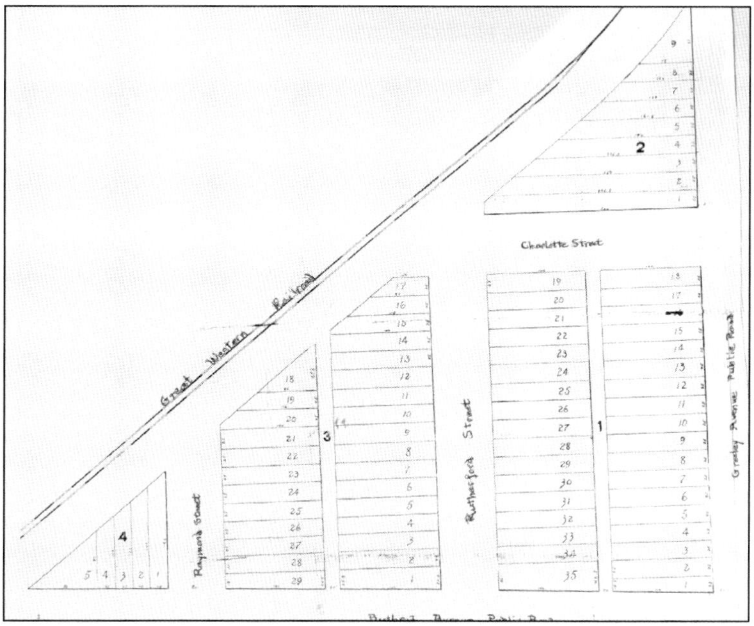

The original plot of Johnstown contained no more than 10 acres. It was platted in 25-by-140-foot lots to 20-foot alleys, with wide streets, for that time. The main street was called Greeley Avenue Public Road, later to be known as Parish Avenue. Lots were formed only on the land that Parish bought, on the west side of this main street.

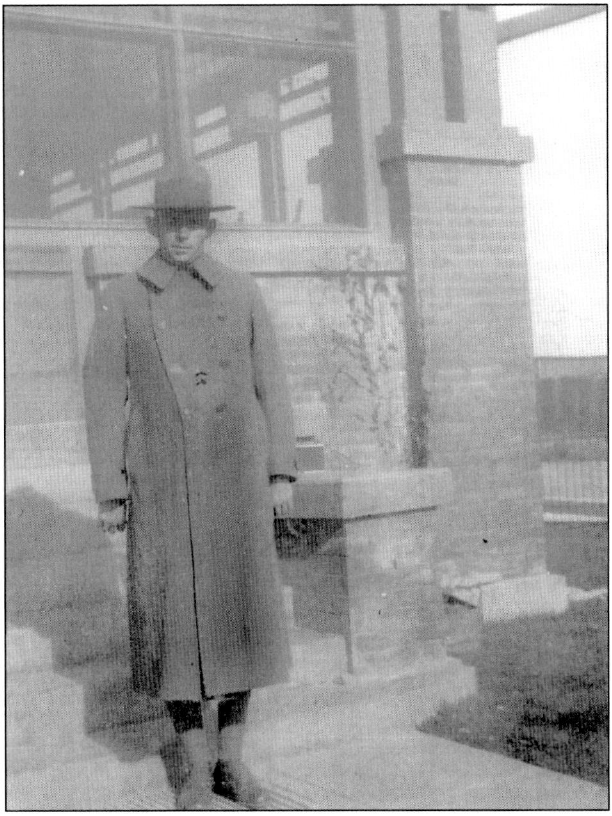

At the time H. J. Parish was planning the town, his youngest son, John, was hospitalized in Denver for a ruptured appendix. To speed the boy's recovery, Parish urged him to get well because he was naming the town in his honor. Young John returned home to the new town named John's Town and later served in World War I and as the town's mayor from 1929 to 1934.

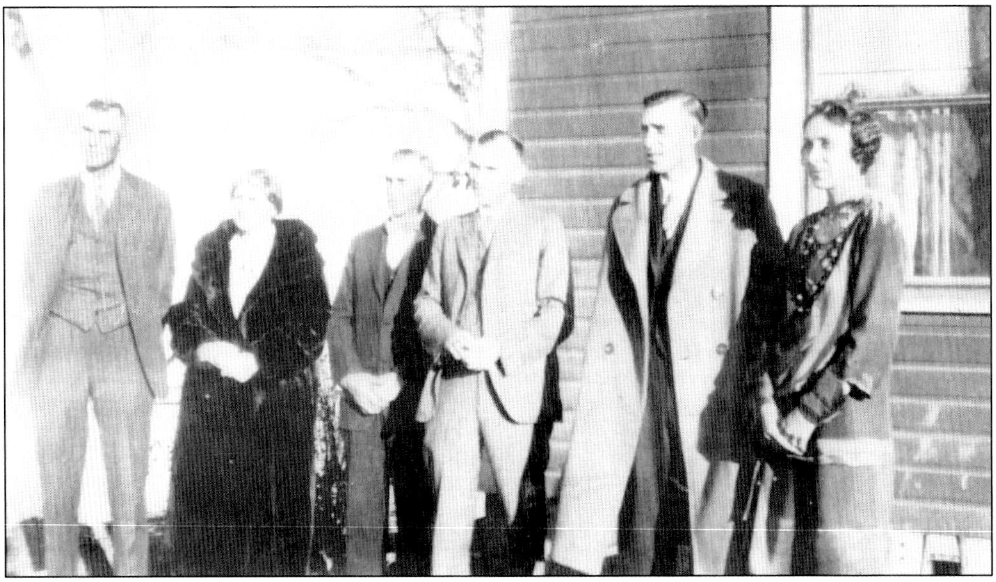

Three of the streets were named after Harvey Parish's children. From right to left are Charlotte, Rutherford, John, and Raymond. There is not a street named after his oldest child, William Albert, shown on the left. It is unknown why, nor is it known why he and his immediate family were buried in unmarked graves in a cemetery 20 miles away from the rest of the Parishes.

Five years before his death in 1923, Harvey Parish's health became affected to such an extent that he was forced to spend the greater part of his time in California. His legacy lives on today with the main street, a park, and many other streets named after his family.

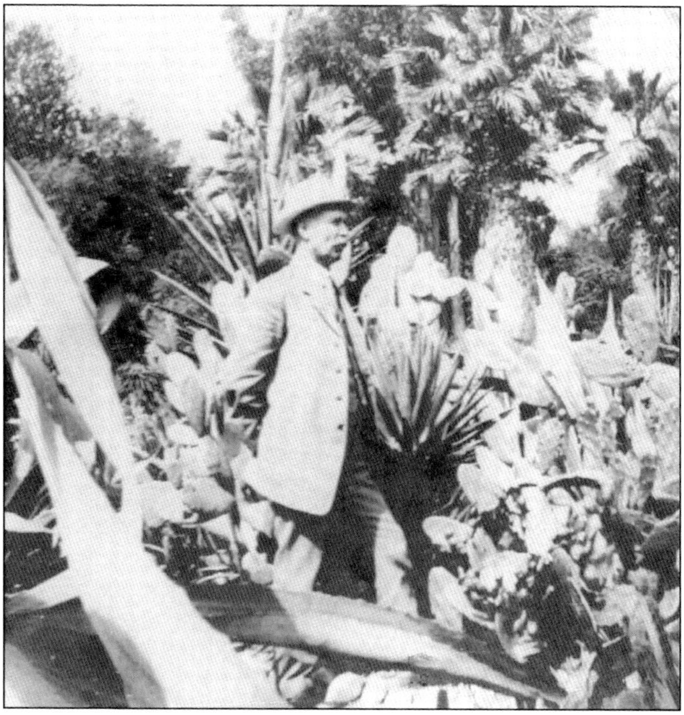

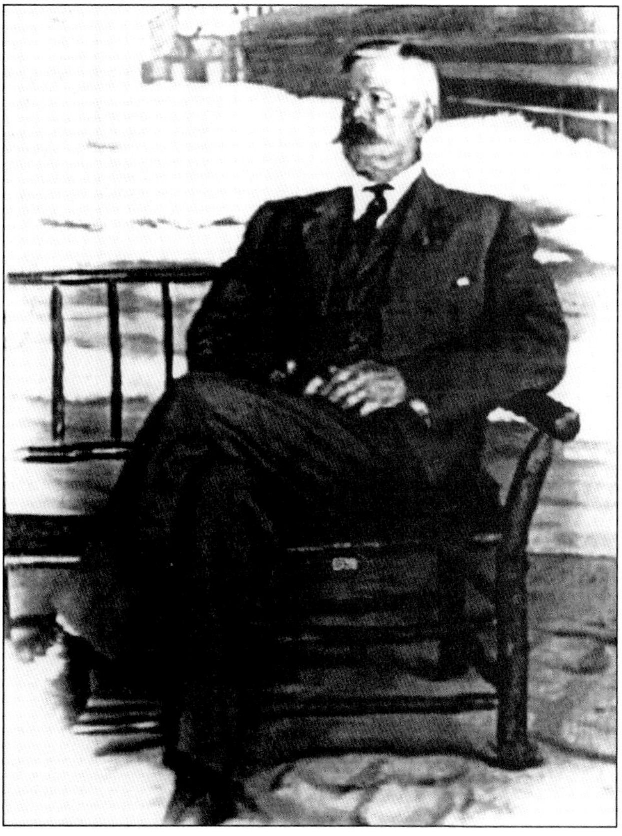

Joseph J. Becker and his wife Paulina were German immigrants who settled in what was to become Johnstown in 1894. Becker owned approximately 274 acres of land east of the new main street in Johnstown. He sold 40 of those acres to the Great Western Railroad, and it was immediately platted into lots and added to the town.

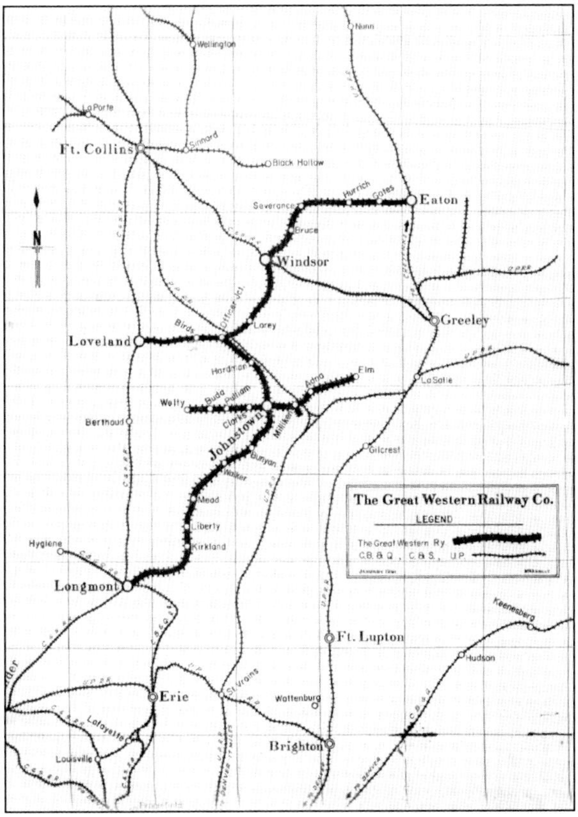

The Great Western Railway did make Johnstown a railway hub, as Parish predicted in 1902. As shown on this map of 1961, no other railroads came near the town. Great Western built a line from Johnstown to Berthoud and later extended it to connect with the railroad at Milliken. This railroad had been acquired by Great Western when the previous owners became bankrupt and sold the rails as scrap. (GHM.)

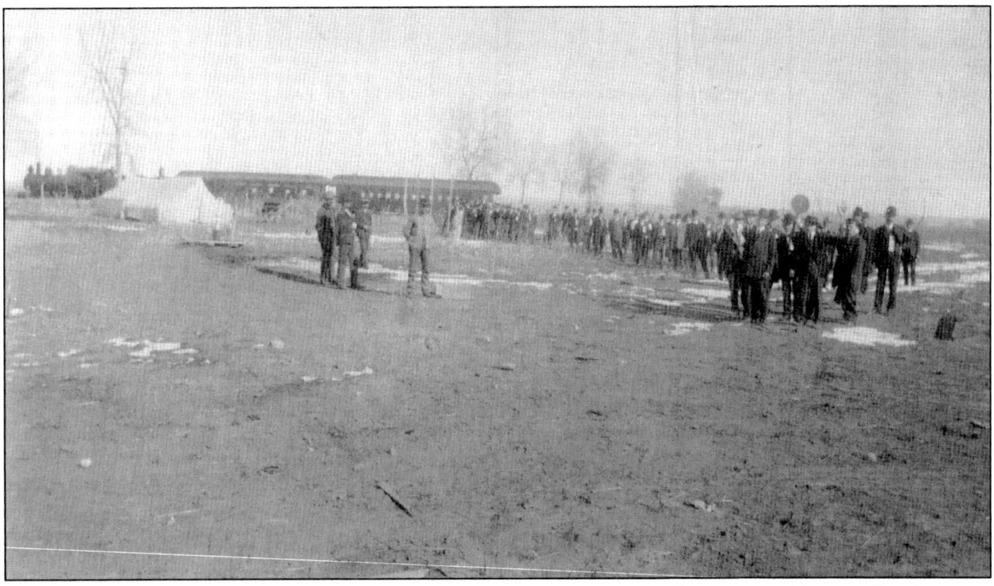

The Great Western Sugar Company started construction on the Great Western Railway in 1902. The purpose of the railway was to carry beets to the sugar factories located in Loveland, Windsor, Eaton, Johnstown, and Longmont. This photograph shows the first train to travel through Johnstown in 1902. Great Western Railway ran two trains weekly through Johnstown in 1902. (GHM.)

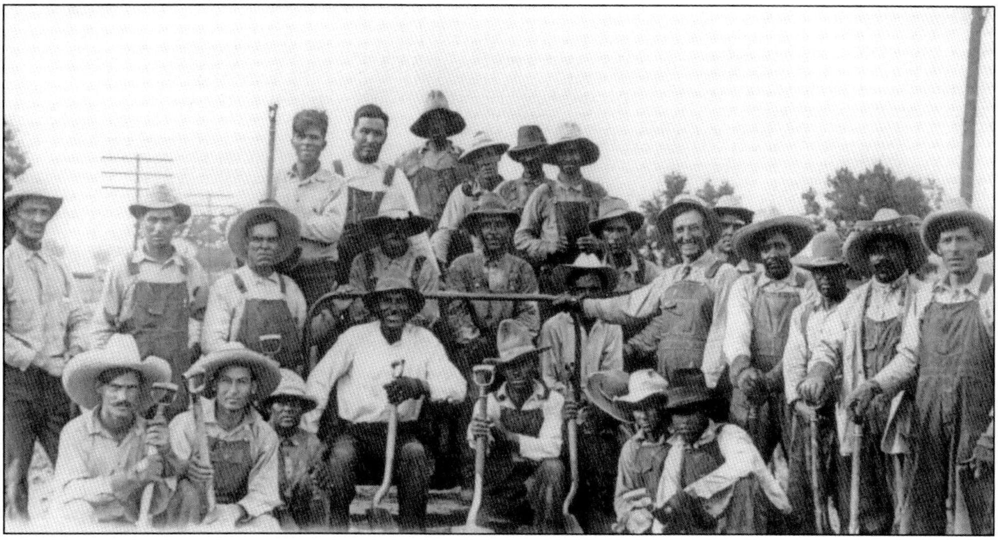

Mexican workers built the railroad from Johnstown to Loveland in 1912. In the second row, third from the right, is the father of Johnstown resident Paul Meza. The labor of workers from Mexico was vital to the development and success of the Johnstown area. There would not have been a town without the commitment of these workers to build the place that Johnstown is today.

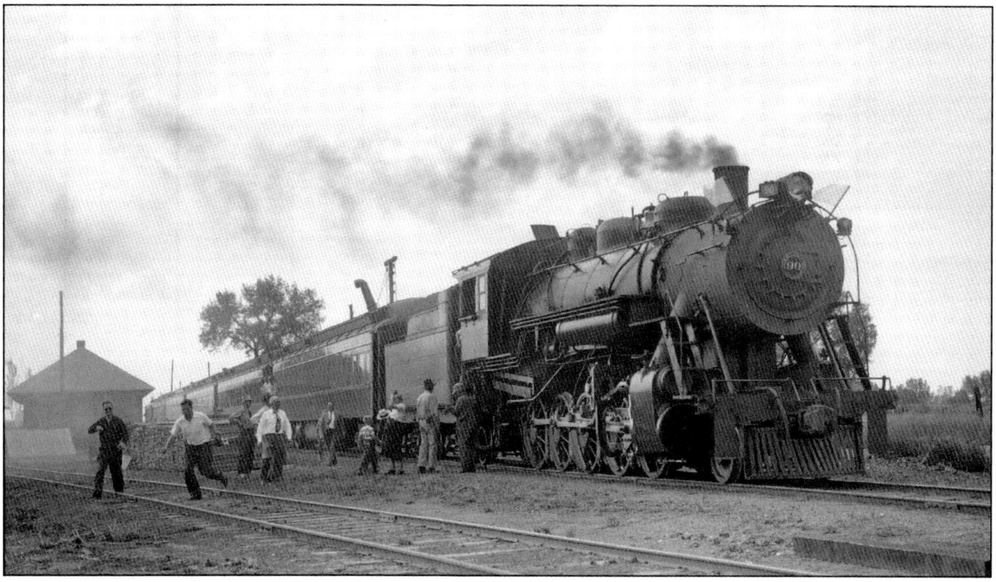

A town in the early 1900s without a railroad depot had difficulty surviving. The depot became a social area, with farmers and townspeople greeting the shipment of supplies and mail. The Johnstown train depot was erected by Fairbairn and Parish Company, the same company that built the first building in Johnstown. It burned down in November 1977. (GHM.)

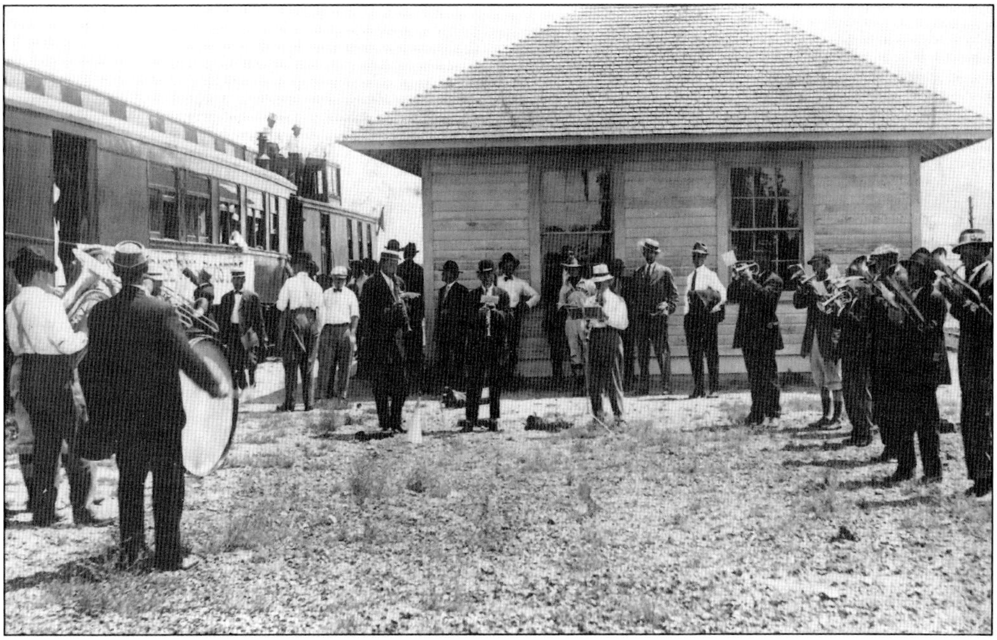

The sugar beet campaign was only during the fall and early winter, so eventually Great Western also began to offer passenger and freight service to earn money throughout the year. A wagon usually met the train to bring the mail and supplies into town. Railroad depots were frequently the center of town events, as shown in this photograph of the Johnstown band playing to welcome special passengers to town.

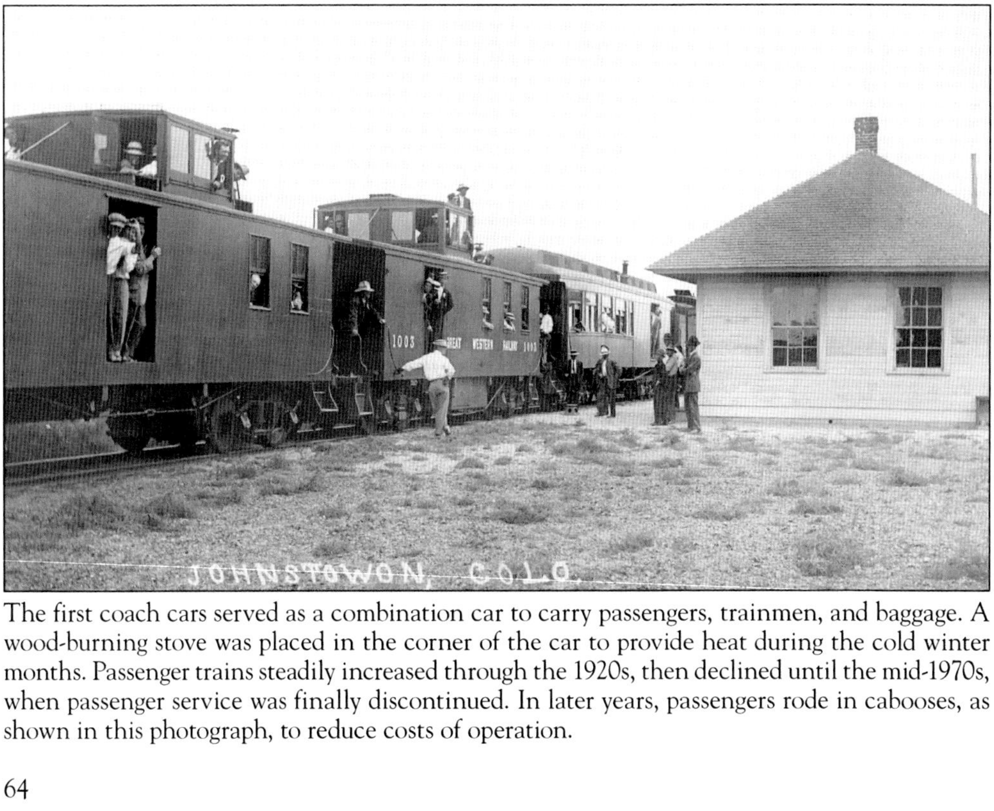

The first coach cars served as a combination car to carry passengers, trainmen, and baggage. A wood-burning stove was placed in the corner of the car to provide heat during the cold winter months. Passenger trains steadily increased through the 1920s, then declined until the mid-1970s, when passenger service was finally discontinued. In later years, passengers rode in cabooses, as shown in this photograph, to reduce costs of operation.

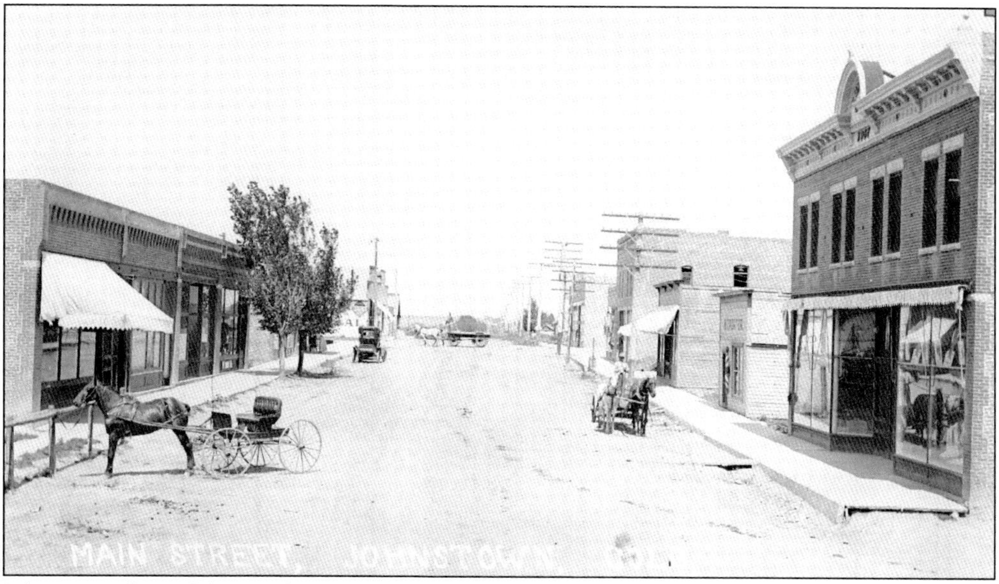

Johnstown thrived during the better economic times of the early 1900s. Local residents no longer needed to travel for miles to trade for goods and services. Downtown businesses were mostly built of wood. Fire was a common occurrence in the early days, and the buildings that burned were usually replaced with brick structures. As horses gave way to automobiles, the need arose for gasoline stations and garages.

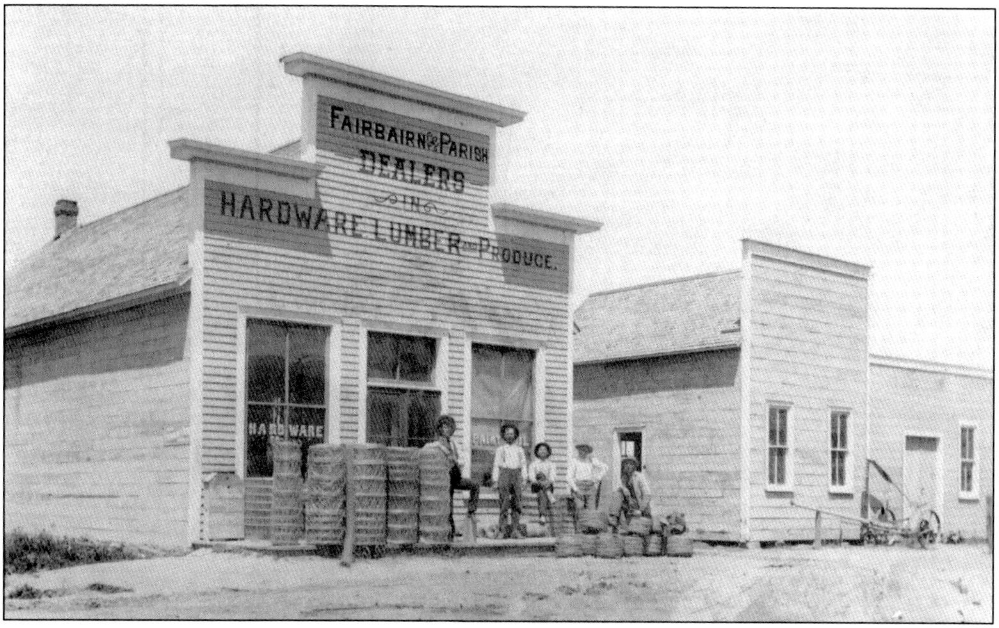

In August 1902, the site of Johnstown was an alfalfa field. Between September 1, when 13 wagonloads were delivered to the area, and January 1903, a town was built. The lumber company of Andy Fairbairn and Harvey Parish was the first building completed. Shortly after, A. R. Morrison built his blacksmith shop next door to the north. (GHM.)

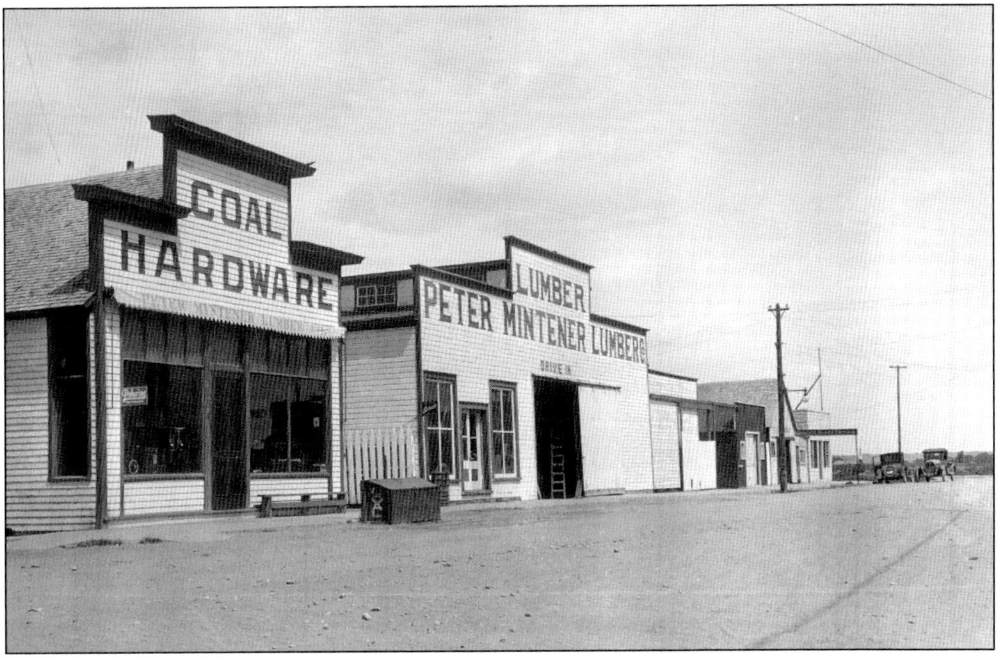

Fifteen years later, the Fairbairn Parish Company was owned by Peter Mintener. Eighty pounds of the finest kind of honey was removed from between the walls of the company. Bees, which had made a hive in the partitions of the building, were smoked out and the honey was secured with very little difficulty. Two cars are parked at the end of the street, in front of the blacksmith shop. (DPL.)

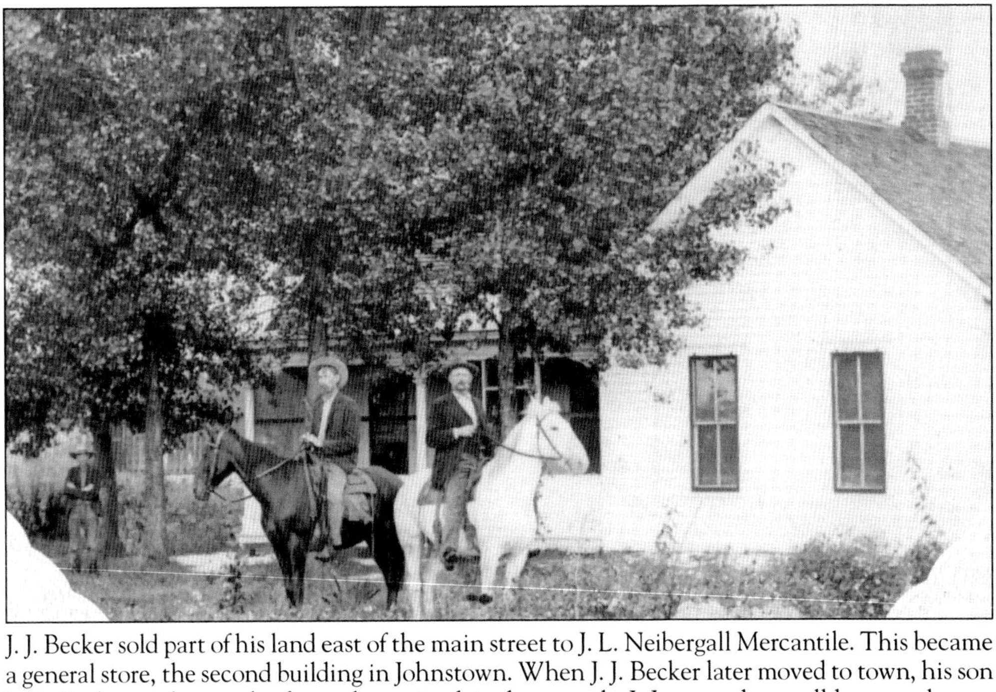

J. J. Becker sold part of his land east of the main street to J. L. Neibergall Mercantile. This became a general store, the second building in Johnstown. When J. J. Becker later moved to town, his son J. C. Becker took over the farm, shown in this photograph. J. J. opened a small harness, buggy, and implement repair shop next to the Neibergall building.

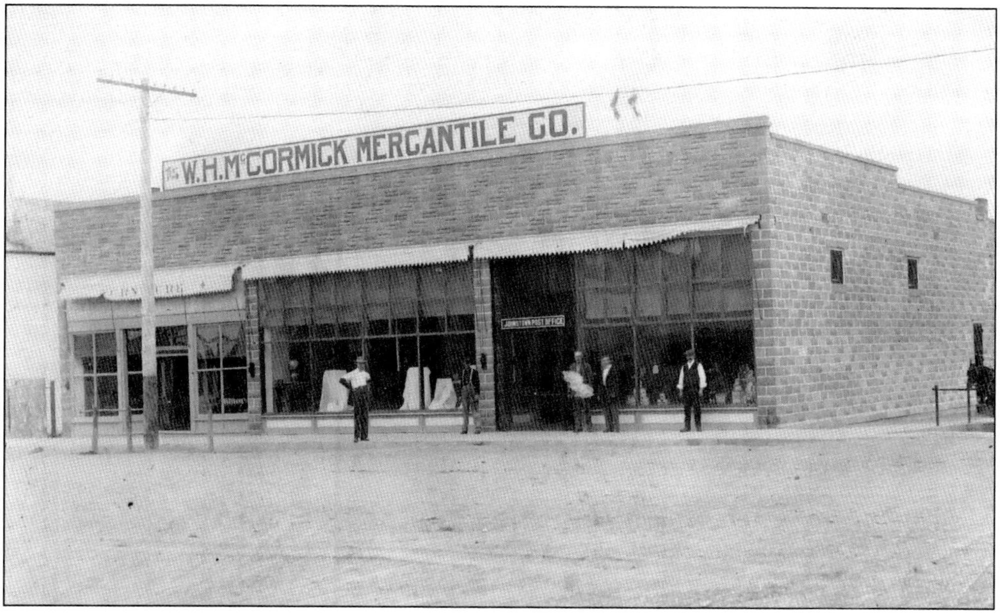

In 1909, W. H. McCormick of Berthoud opened a branch of his McCormick Sells Everything mercantile store at the same location as Neibergall's Mercantile. These stores sold a wide range of goods. In the truest sense of the word, they were general stores. For example, fruit, clothing, food, paper goods, and shovels were sold in the store shown in this photograph.

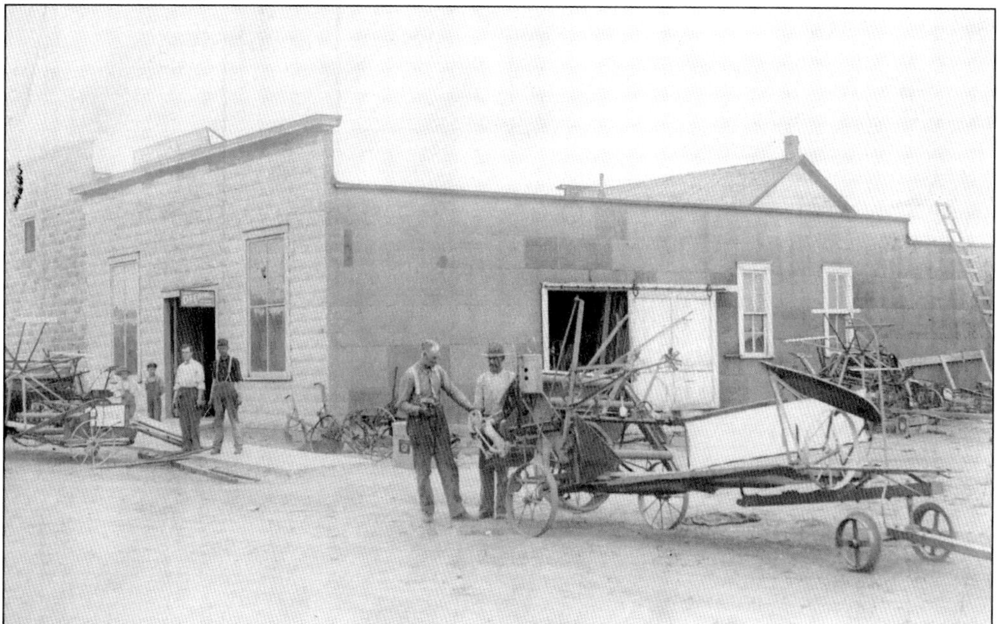

W. H. McCormick also opened McCormick Harvesting Machines, as shown in this photograph. McCormick came to Colorado in 1870 and settled in Berthoud. As well as being a merchant and farmer, he was a pioneer minister, organizing practically all of the United Brethren churches in Northern Colorado, including the one in Johnstown. McCormick was also elected as representative from the district to serve in the fifth general assembly of Colorado.

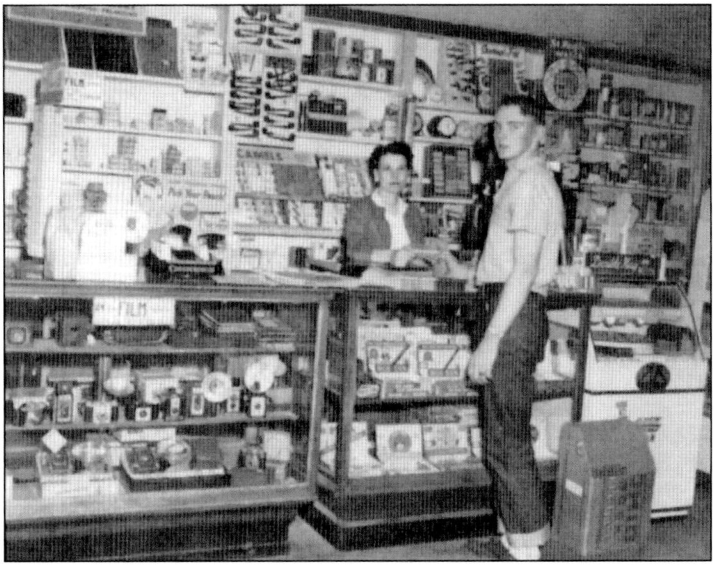

Throughout the years, the Neibergall/McCormick Mercantile building was used for different purposes. As horses and carriages gave way to automobiles, garages were needed. For over 30 years, this location held one garage after another. Finally the Johnstown Drug Company claimed this spot in the 1950s. It continued to be used as a drugstore until fairly recently.

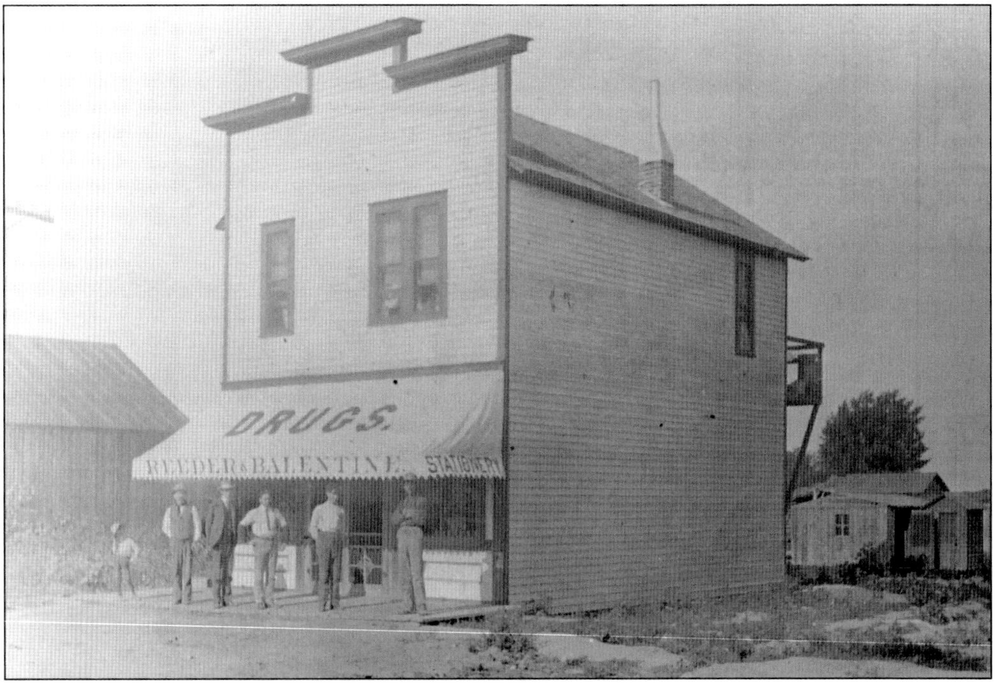

The first drugstore was not the Johnstown Drug Company nor was it in that location. The first drugstore was built in 1906 and was located on the corner of Charlotte Street and Parish Avenue. Like many of the early buildings, it was constructed with a false front to give the perception that it was larger than it actually was.

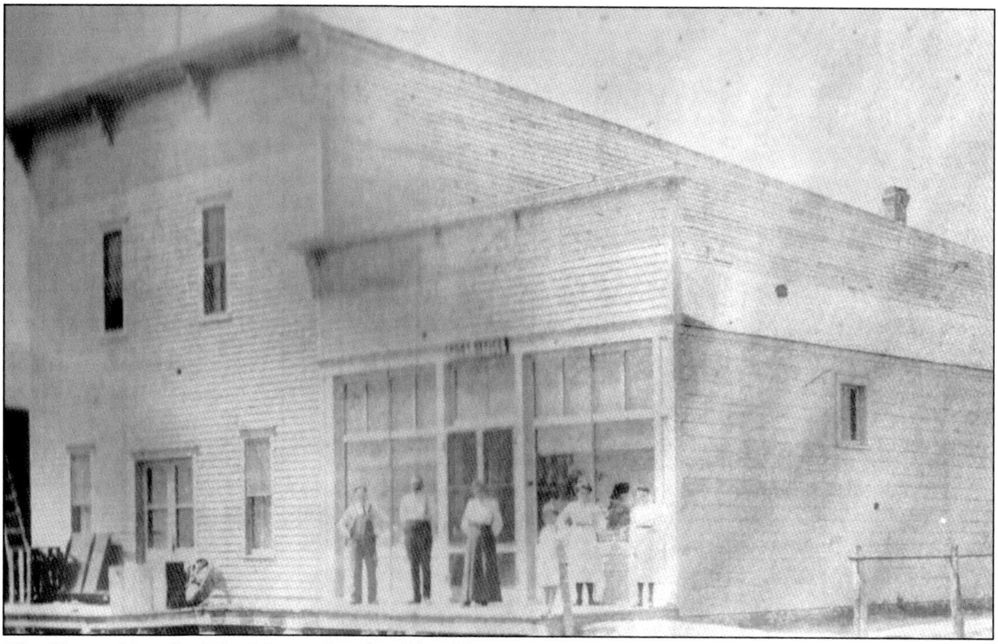

The Davis-Hartford Building, the third building in Johnstown, was also the site of the first post office in Johnstown. Mr. and Mrs. Rudolph Brunner managed the store, and Mrs. Orpha Brunner stamped the first letter in 1903. The mail came from Berthoud on a rural route. From early 1900 to 1976, there were only three postmasters in Johnstown: Mr. and Mrs. Brunner, Charles Dunn, and Charles Reider.

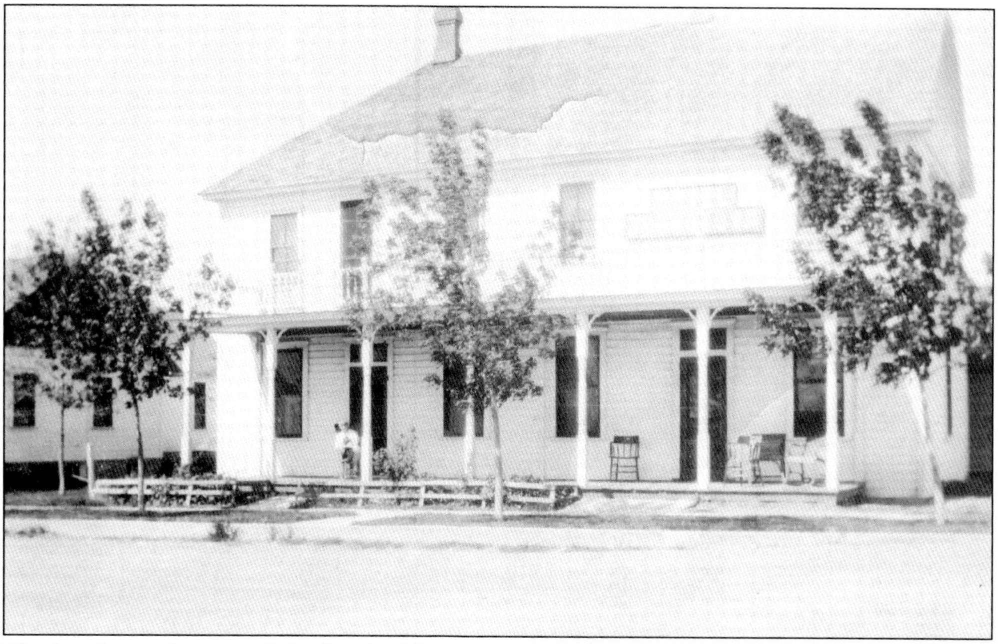

The hotel was also one of the first buildings constructed in the new town of Johnstown. It was needed to house construction workers, salesmen, and agricultural people. Mr. M. H. Tucker built the Horner Hotel with 14 rooms and offered room and board for $5 a week. It was later added to and called the Johnstown Hotel. It was destroyed by fire in the 1950s.

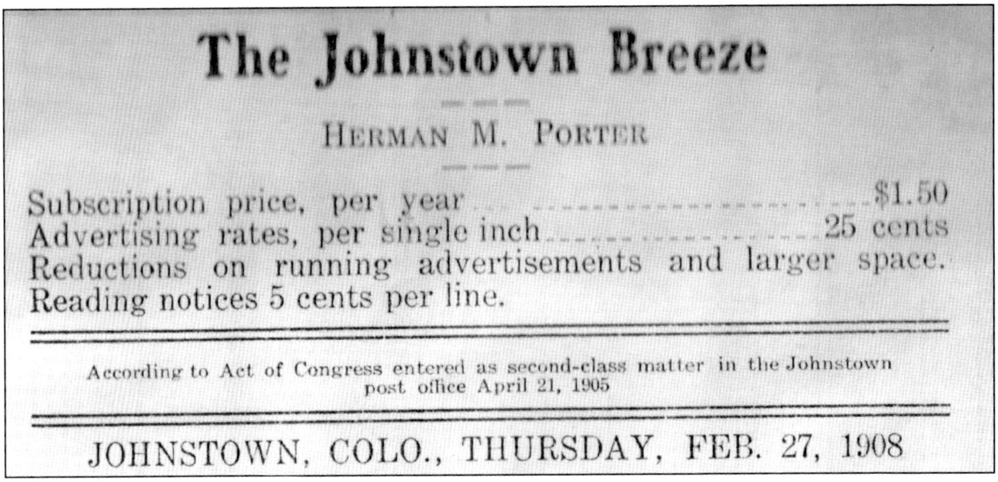

The Johnstown Breeze

HERMAN M. PORTER

Subscription price, per year $1.50
Advertising rates, per single inch .... 25 cents
Reductions on running advertisements and larger space.
Reading notices 5 cents per line.

According to Act of Congress entered as second-class matter in the Johnstown post office April 21, 1905

JOHNSTOWN, COLO., THURSDAY, FEB. 27, 1908

Johnstown's first newspaper was published by J. Gordon Smith in 1904. The *Johnstown Breeze* still maintains its downtown location, as it has for over 100 years. Its weekly publication includes local news and a weekly column of the history of the area. At one time, the caption under the name of the newspaper read, "Tis an ill breeze that blows nobody good."

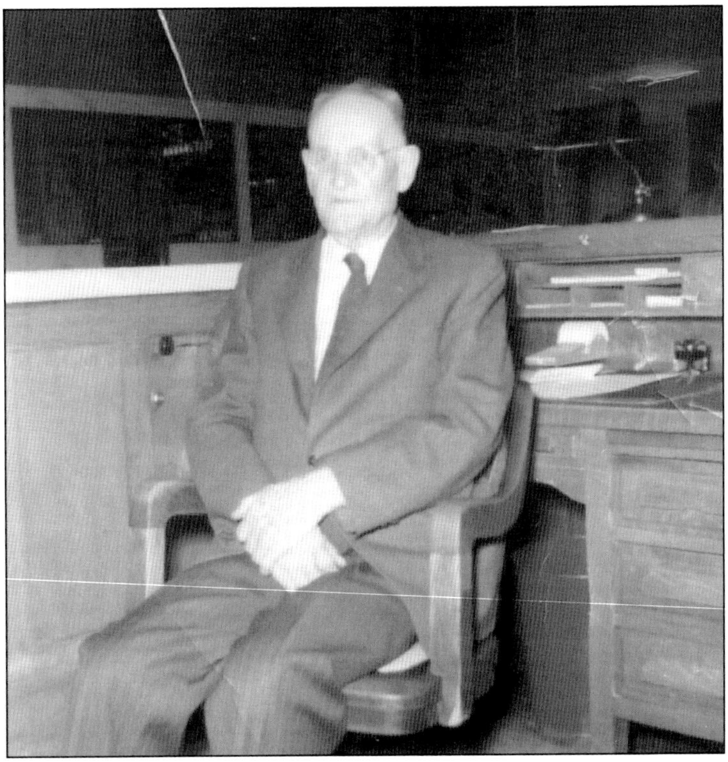

In 1904, Willard E. Letford, T. M. Callahan, and Harvey Parish started a private bank that would become the First National Bank of Johnstown. Mr. and Mrs. Letford lived in the back of the bank and operated it themselves using all handwritten ledgers. The total cash on hand at that time was $1,000. Luckily no one wanted to cash a check over that amount.

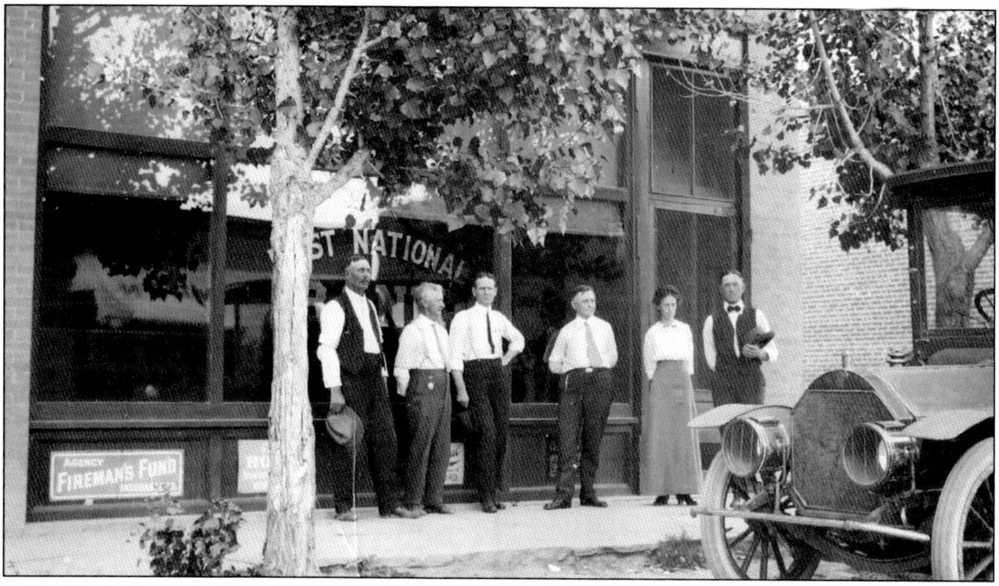

On April 6, 1907, the Johnstown Bank was awarded a national charter and became the First National Bank. Also around that same time, one of the first brick buildings was constructed a few doors down from the previous location. The new location of the bank is shown in this photograph, along with Harvey Jay Parish on the left and W. E. Letford in the middle.

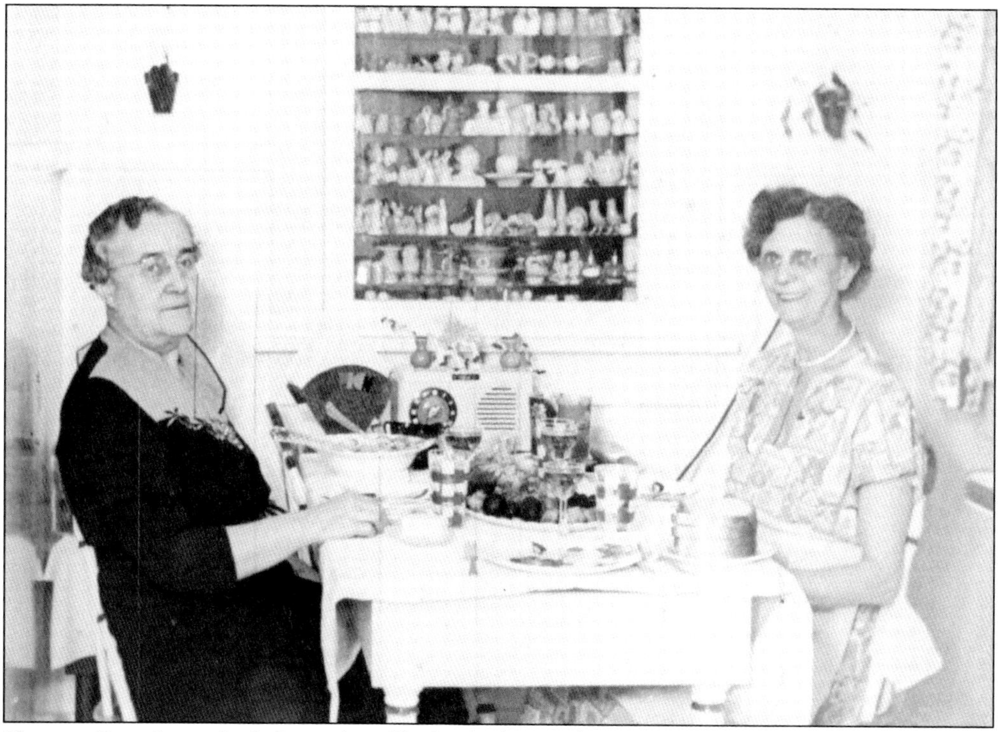
Florence Brandt, on the left, was hired by Letford to work at the First National Bank in 1920. She served for 43 years, retiring before her 80th birthday. Brandt and her children came to Johnstown in early 1919, during the time of the influenza epidemic. The woman on the right is Marie Brust, former co-owner of the *Johnstown Breeze*.

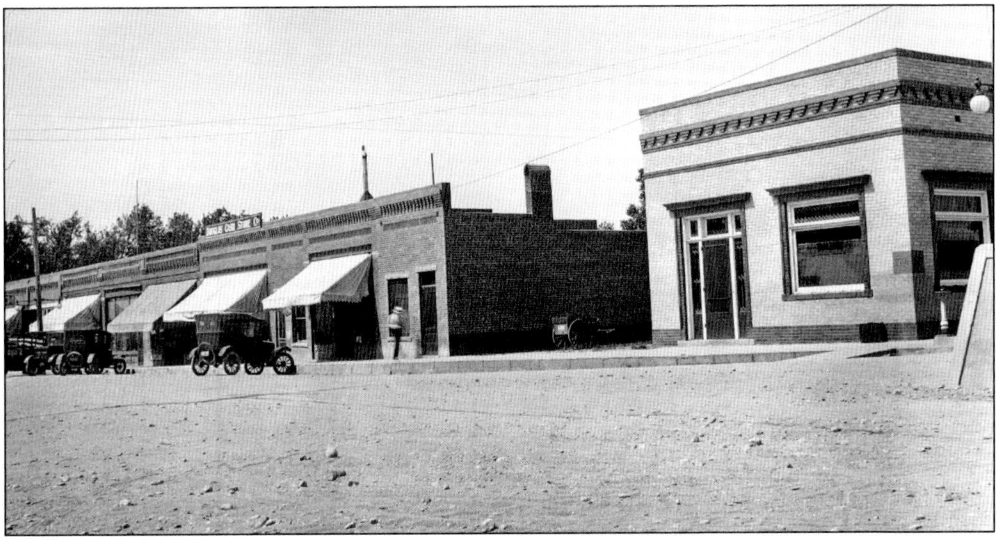

Although its business was short lived, the Johnstown State Bank provided the First National Bank its first competition in 1916. Two years after its opening, Johnstown State Bank sold out to the First National. The building on the right in this photograph became the First National's property, and the bank moved to that location. Shown to the left of the bank in this photograph is some early fire equipment. (DPL.)

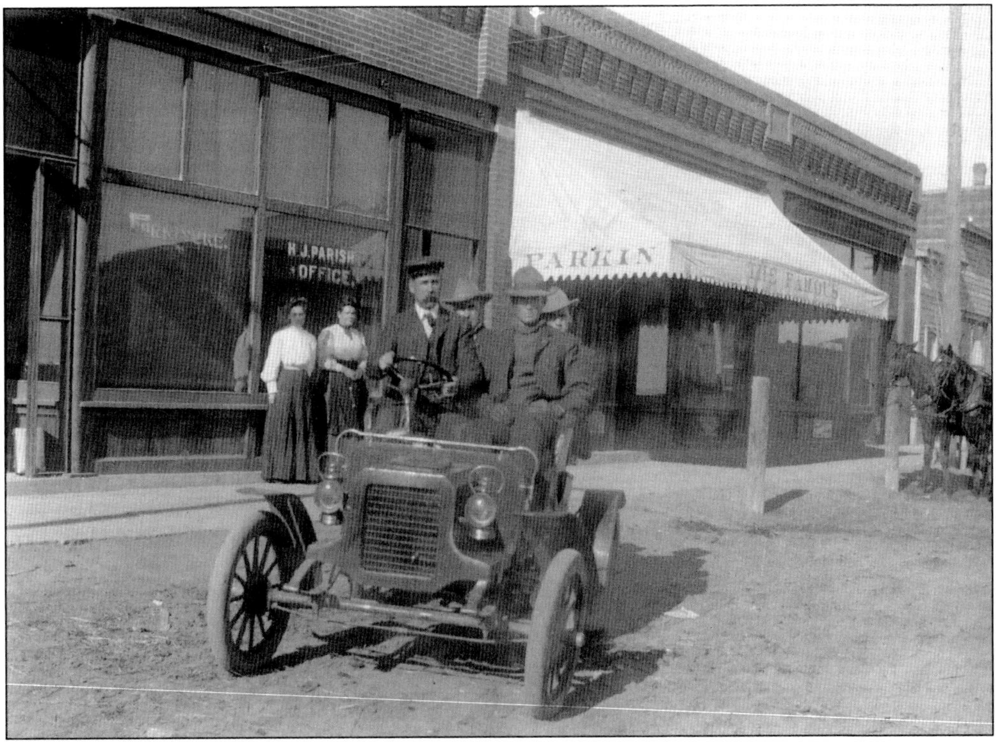

When the bank moved to its new location, Harvey Jay Parish opened his office in the previous place. Here he is in his new Reo automobile, in front of his office. Seated with him are Cody Powers, John Sandstrom, and Henry Clingenpeel. In front of Parish's office with his daughter Lottie "Parish" Parkin is Albina Clingenpeel. (GHM.)

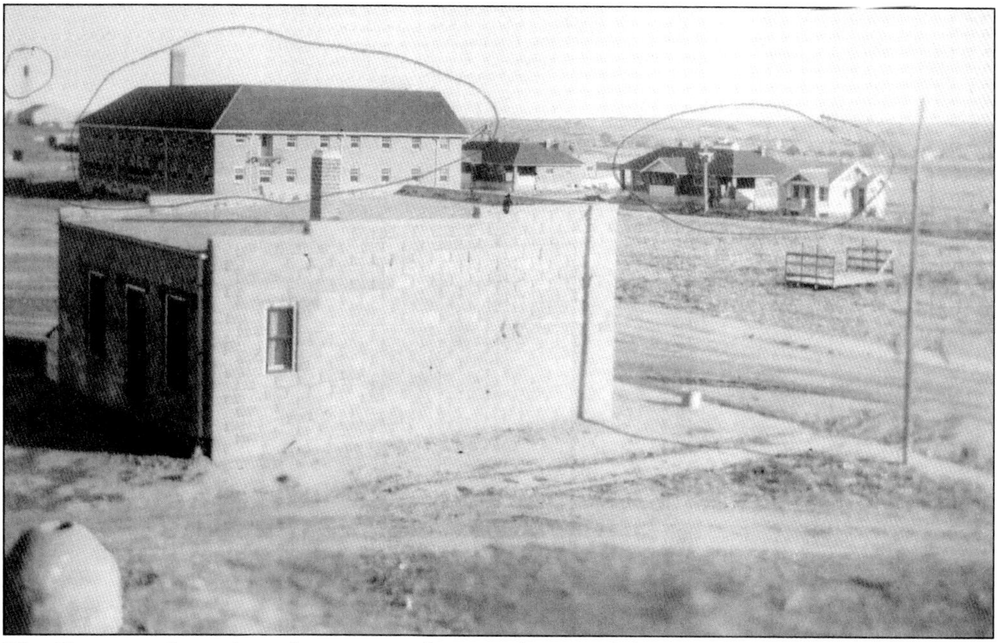

The Clingenpeel couple in the previous photograph opened the mortuary, shown in the forefront of this photograph. Albina Clingenpeel was born near Johnstown in 1870 to Marshall and Susan Cook. Her father was an Indian scout and pioneer of the area near Fort St. Vrain. After her first husband, L. E. Temple died, Albina moved back to Johnstown with her three children and married Henry Clingenpeel in 1905. (GHM.)

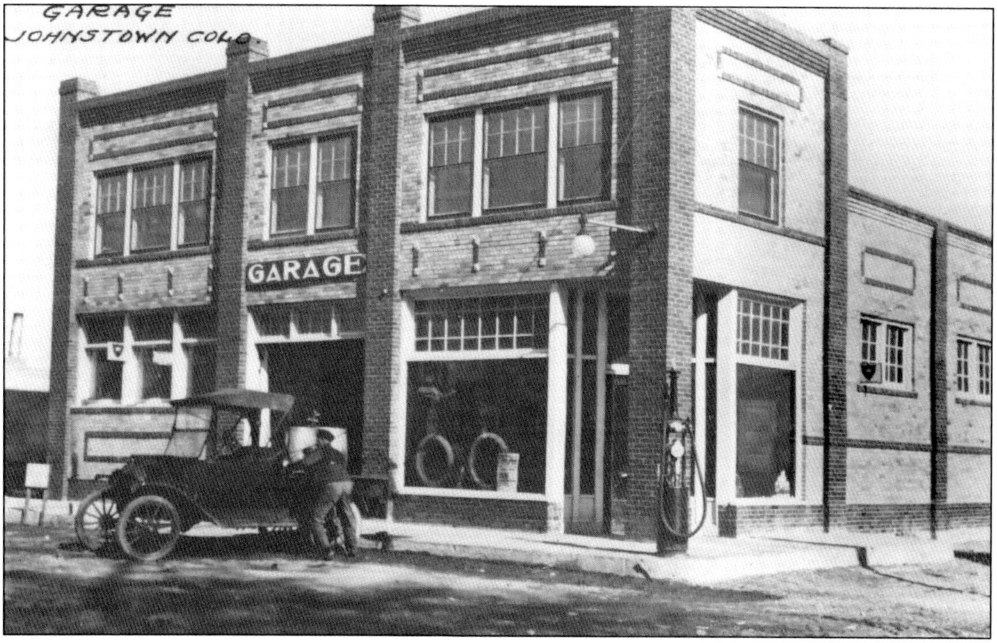

When horses were the only means of travel, a livery stable was necessary, but as automobiles were used more often, the need came for gasoline stations and garages. Charles Goodwin completed this garage in 1914. He later traded it off for a ranch. A man in this photograph loads an item onto a flatbed pickup truck. A gas pump is on the corner. (DPL.)

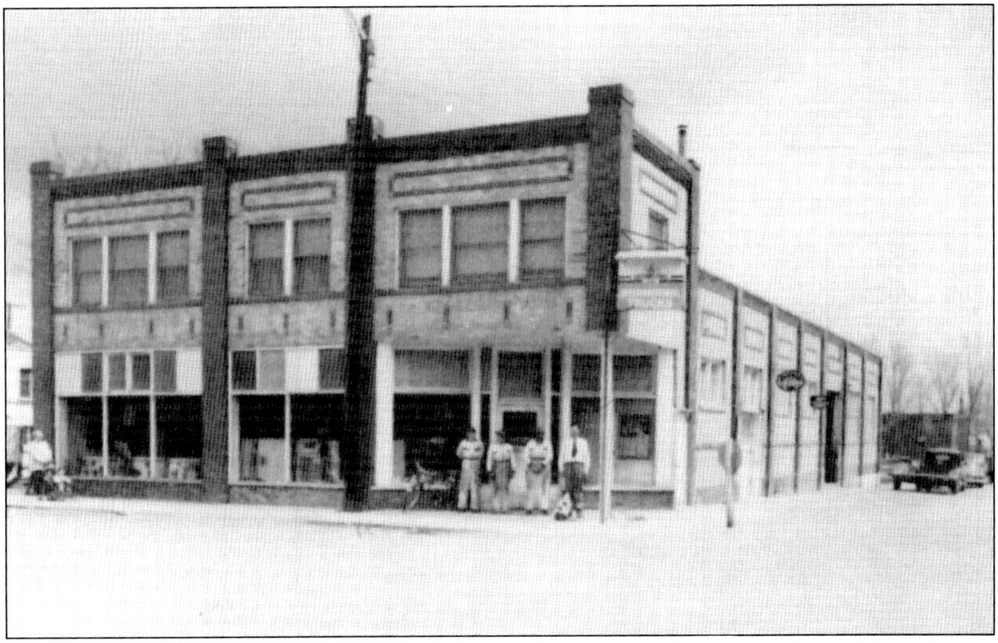

At first, garages and car dealerships were still housed in Goodwin's building. Clyde Miner Senior bought a 1936 Ford from Ern Hill. It even had a radio in it. In 1948, International Harvester maintained a supply store there. They sold mostly farm equipment such as beet harvesters, harvester threshers, and grain binders. The building burned down in 1997.

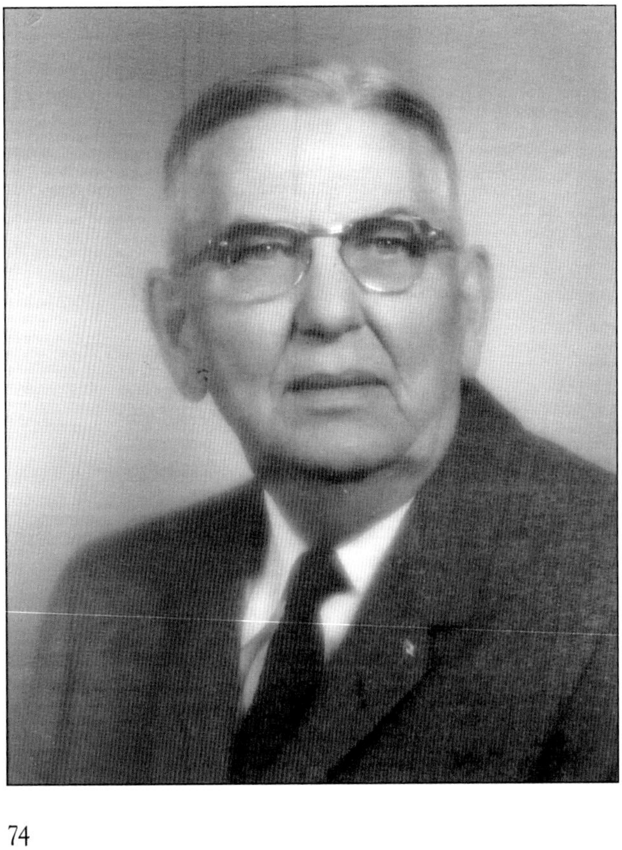

After becoming a doctor, Glenn A. Jones looked for a place to practice medicine. His search led him to Dr. Haskell in Windsor, who told him about the town of Johnstown, 10 miles away. Since there was no transportation service, Dr. Jones walked. When he reached the top of the hill north of town, he looked upon a beautiful valley and to the west, a panoramic view of the Rockies. (GHM.)

When Dr. Jones reached what he called "God's spot," he rented two rooms upstairs in the Eureka Building, constructed in 1907. He bought his supplies and furnished his office and began his practice in fall 1920. His car could often be seen parked in front of his office, as in this photograph. He married the love of his life, Dorothy, in 1922. (GHM.)

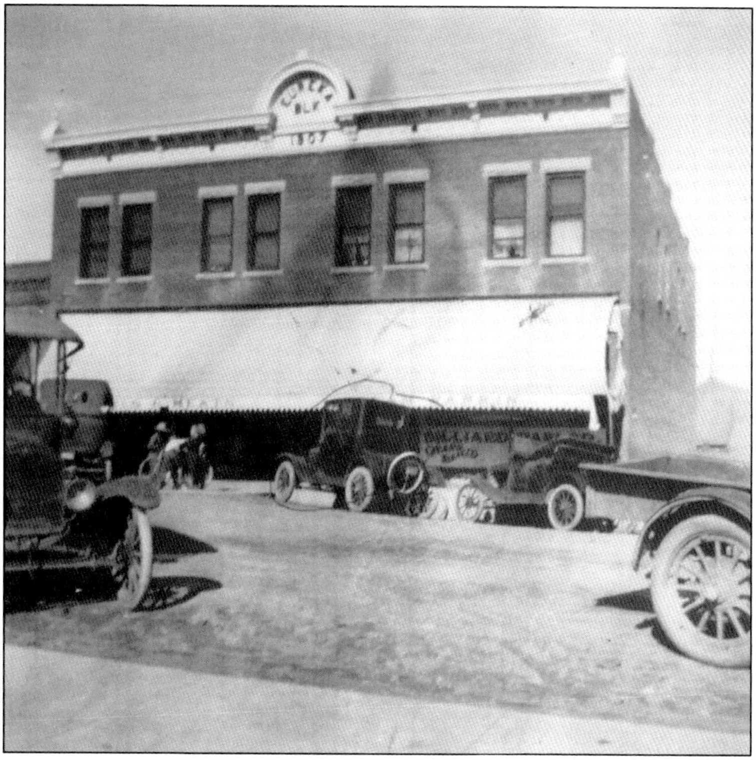

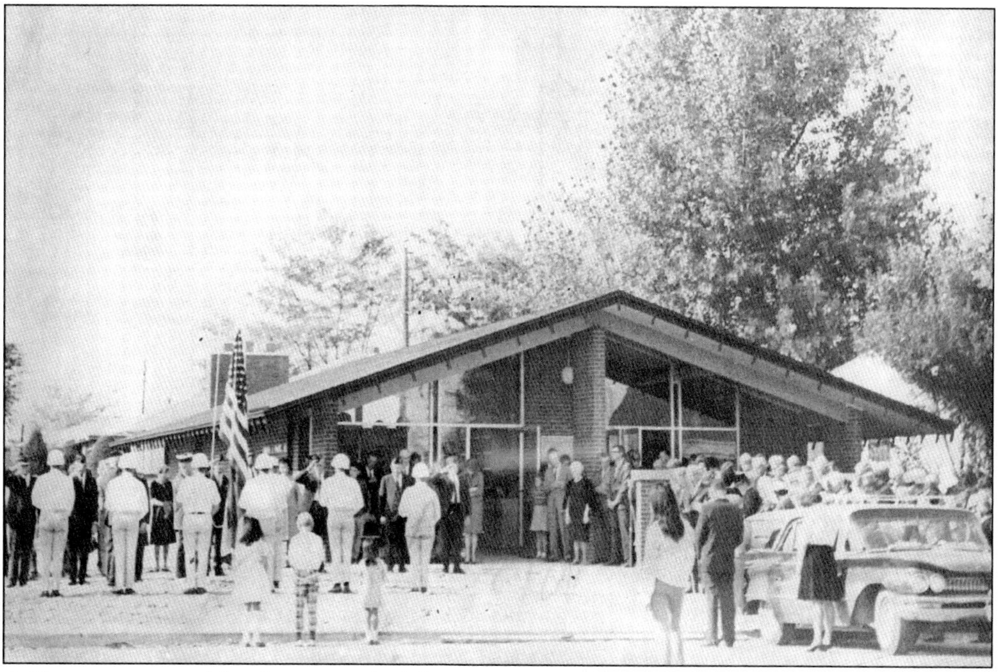

A library, sponsored by the women's club, was in operation in the town in 1916 and had 1,550 volumes. The first full-fledged library did not arrive until October 1967, when the Glenn A. Jones, M. D. Memorial Library was completed and dedicated. Much of the money for construction was donated by Dorothy Jones as a memorial to her husband, who had been an avid reader. (GHM.)

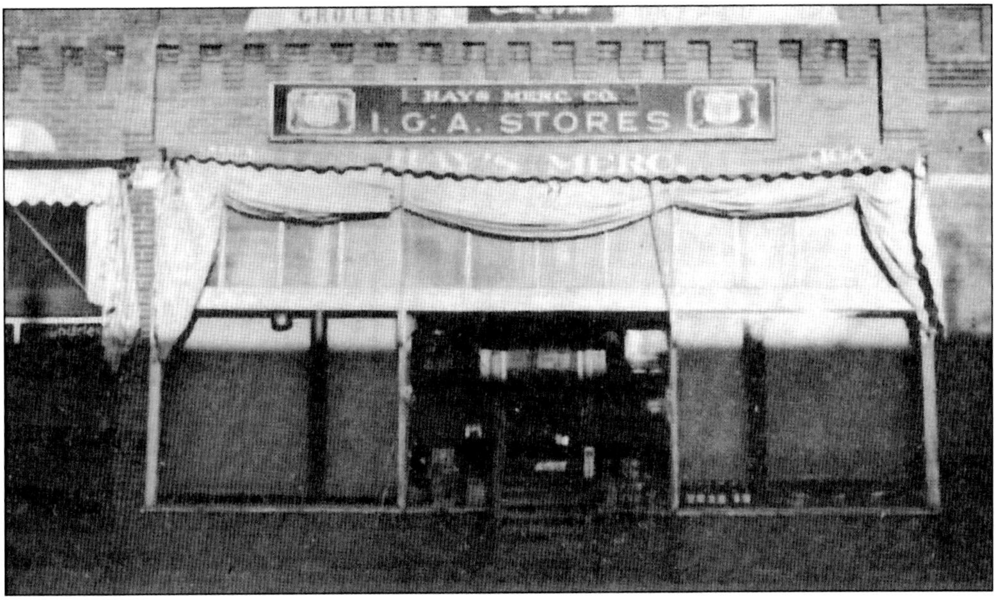

Thurman and Louisa Hays moved west to Johnstown in 1928, due to a daughter's poor health. They bought the remaining stock of McCormick Mercantile when it was sold in 1929 and started Hays Mercantile. It carried everything from horse collars to dry goods. After two years, the store was relocated to a larger building, shown in this photograph.

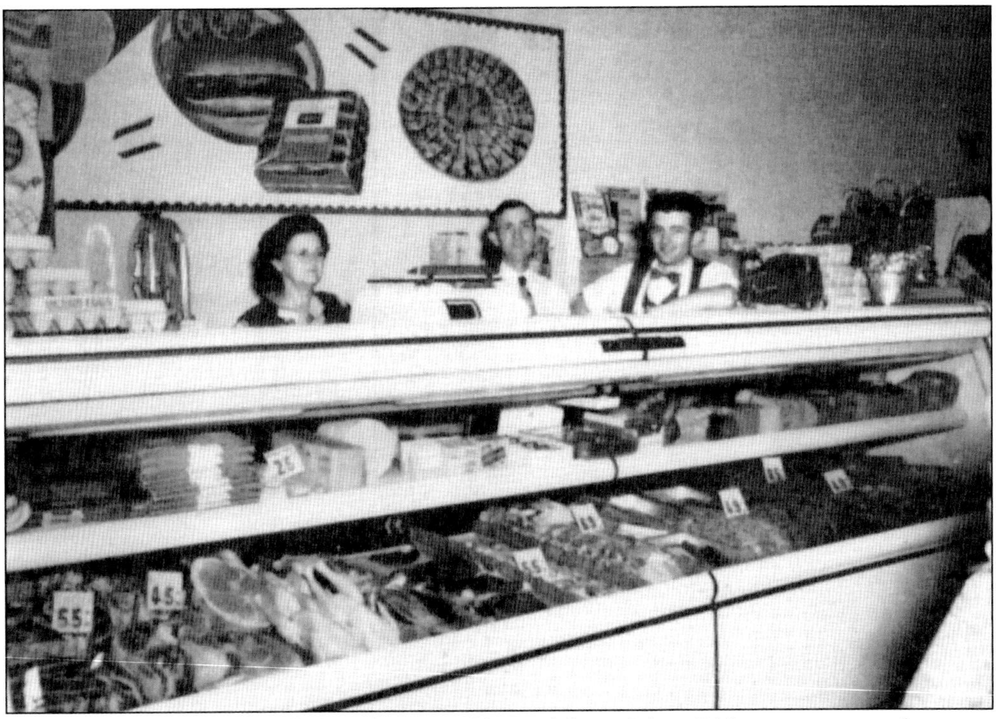

In 1953, the Hays family, including their son, Chet, celebrated their 24th anniversary in business. Five years later, they opened Hays Market next to the Eureka Building. It moved to its present location in 1996. After 80 years, Hays Market is still a family business and is in its fourth generation. It is still a gathering place and has qualities that people hold dear about a small town.

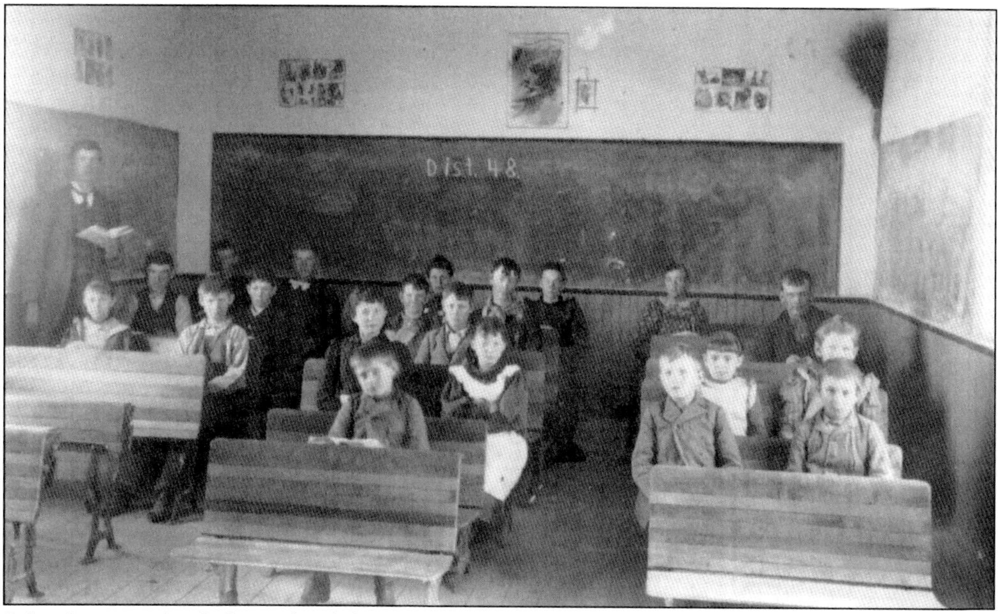

Schools created a feeling of stability in the new town. Whatever the name, each rural school was considered to be an important part of the community. The Smith School, shown in this photograph, was named for Winton Smith. It was built on the Little Thompson River and was the root of the present school system. (GHM.)

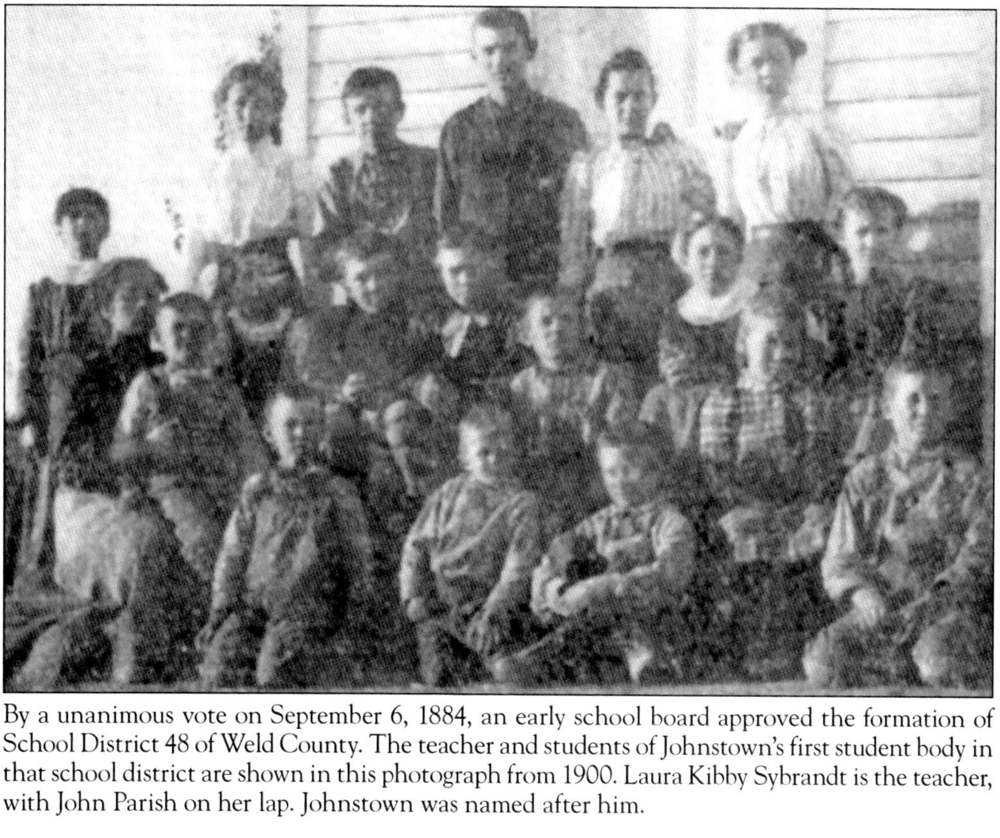

By a unanimous vote on September 6, 1884, an early school board approved the formation of School District 48 of Weld County. The teacher and students of Johnstown's first student body in that school district are shown in this photograph from 1900. Laura Kibby Sybrandt is the teacher, with John Parish on her lap. Johnstown was named after him.

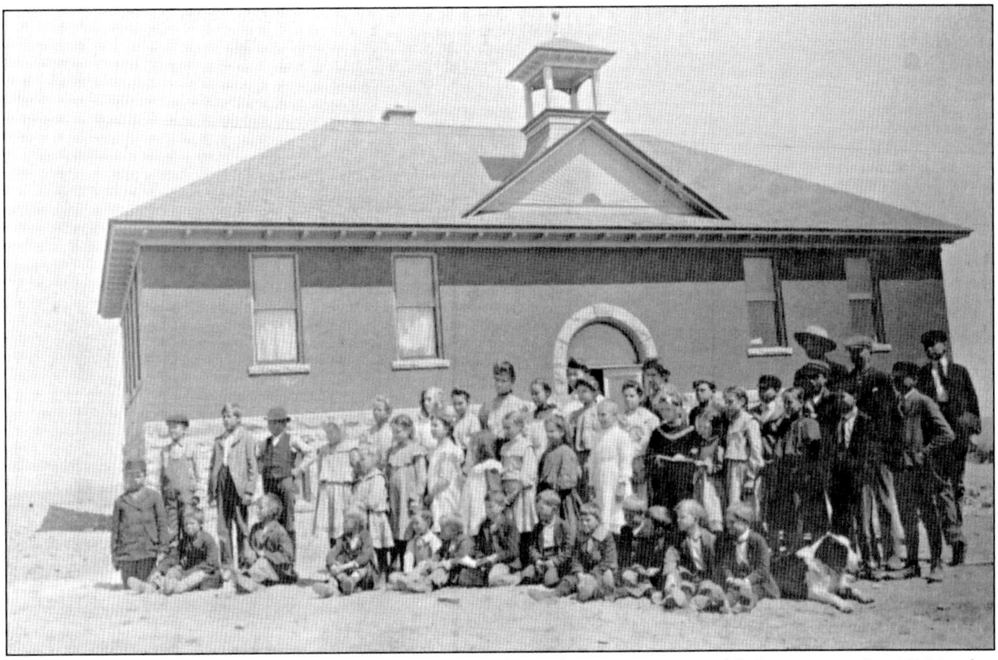

In 1903, the Smith School building was moved to the new town of Johnstown. In 1904, the grade school pupils moved into their new building, as seen in this photograph. Grace Mansfield (Mrs. Forbes Coates) was the teacher. She taught in the Johnstown schools from 1904–1906. Her daughter, Zola Coates, was a district teacher for 42 years. (GHM.)

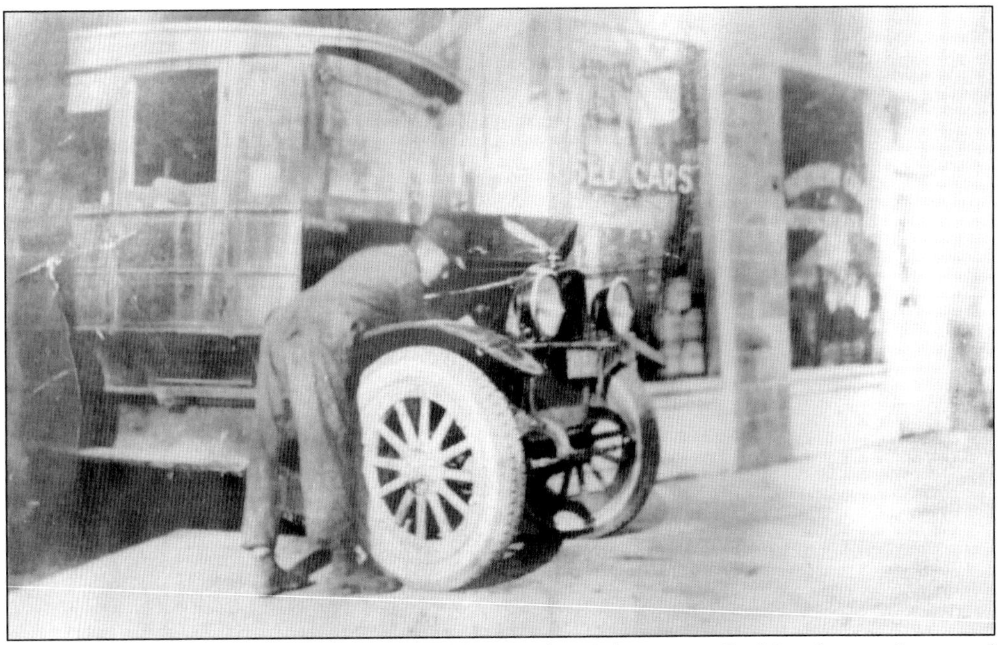

This photograph shows the first motorized bus used in Johnstown. Carl Lindstrom drove and serviced the bus. Before this, wagons were used to transport children to school. Each wagon had a seat running the entire length of the wagon bed on each side. The sides and back were enclosed by curtains in case of inclement weather.

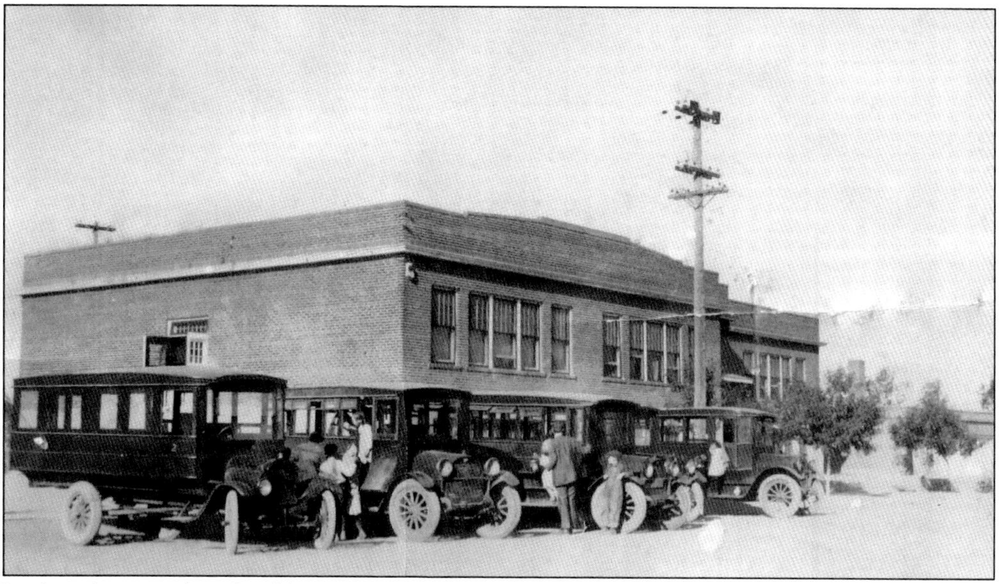

In this photograph, school buses are parked in front of the old Union High School, after it had been remodeled and made into the grade school building. It was dissolved in 1920 and was replaced by Johnstown High School. A new building was constructed in 1922.

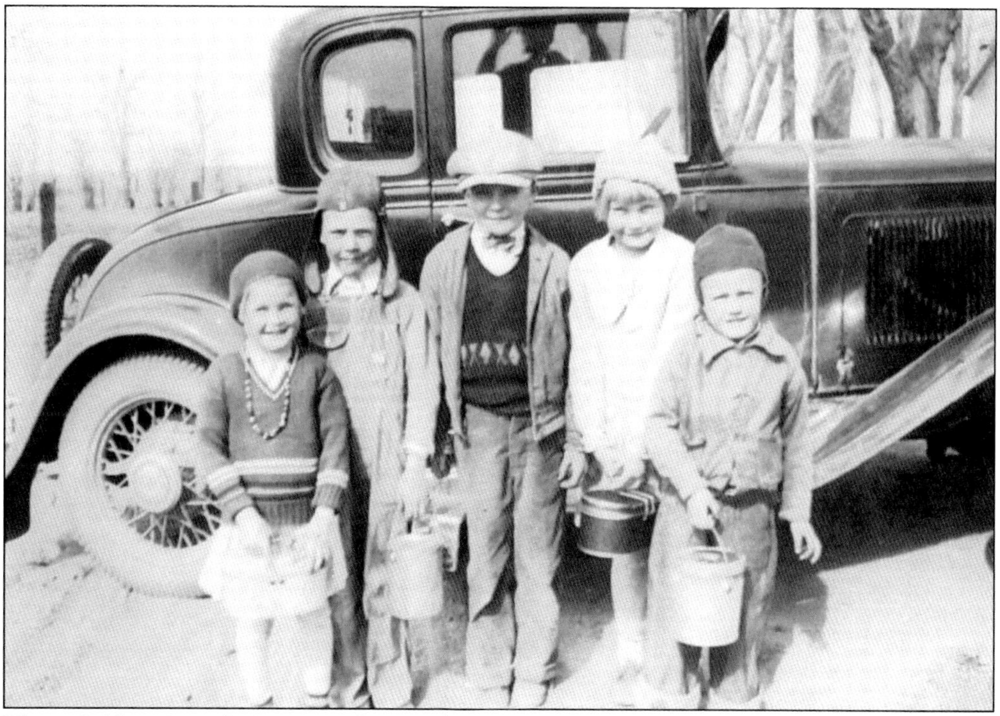

These children from the Lammers farm in the 1930s did not have to worry about walking to school 20 miles each way uphill in snowstorms. They were able to catch a bus that waited for them at the end of the drive. Notice the lard buckets and other items used for lunch pails.

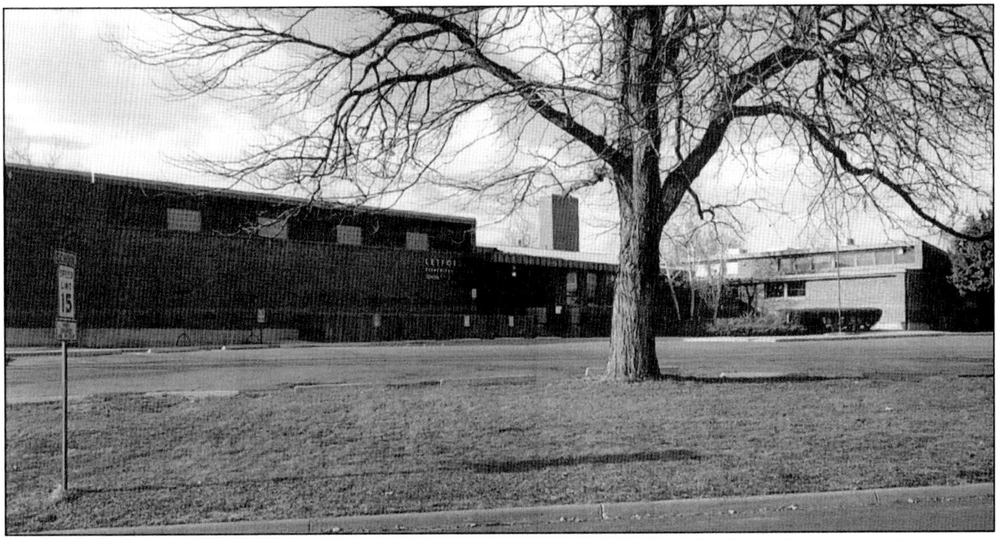

There are two elementary schools presently in Johnstown, including Letford Elementary. In March 1952, local electors approved a bond issue for the construction of the elementary school. It was named in honor of W. E. Letford and was built on land that had formerly been Letford Park.

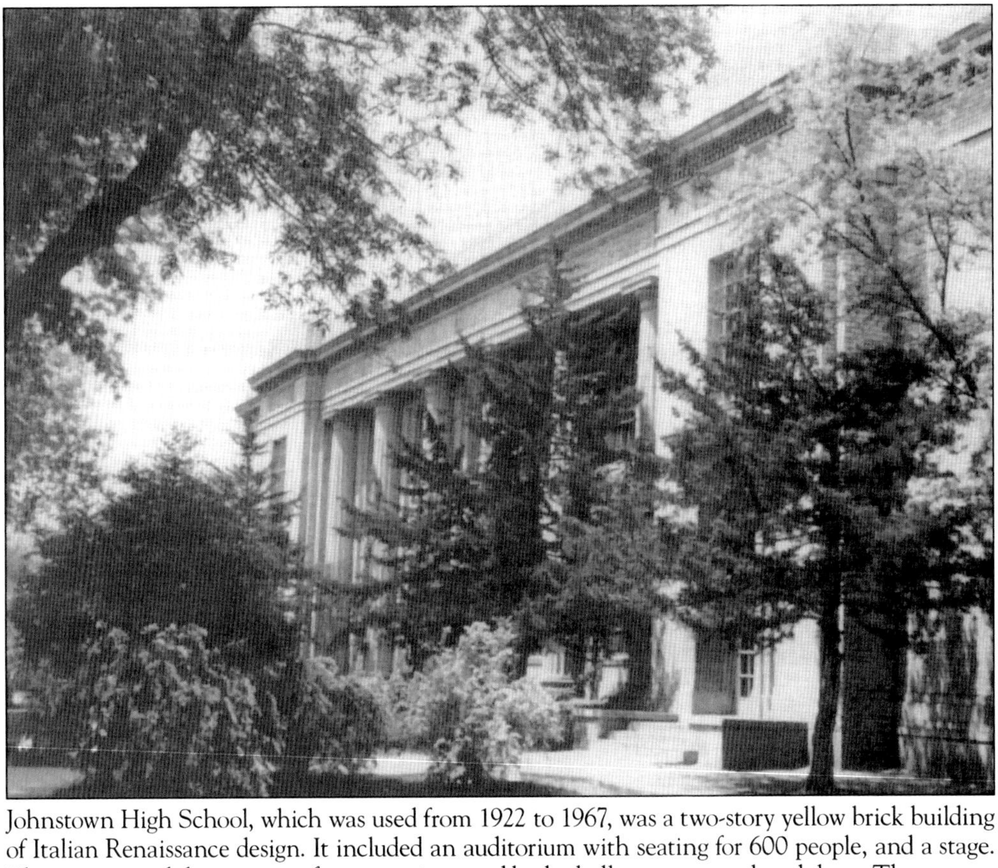

Johnstown High School, which was used from 1922 to 1967, was a two-story yellow brick building of Italian Renaissance design. It included an auditorium with seating for 600 people, and a stage. The stage served the purpose of a gymnasium, and basketball games were played there. The current high school is called Roosevelt High School, and the school's mascot is the Rough Rider.

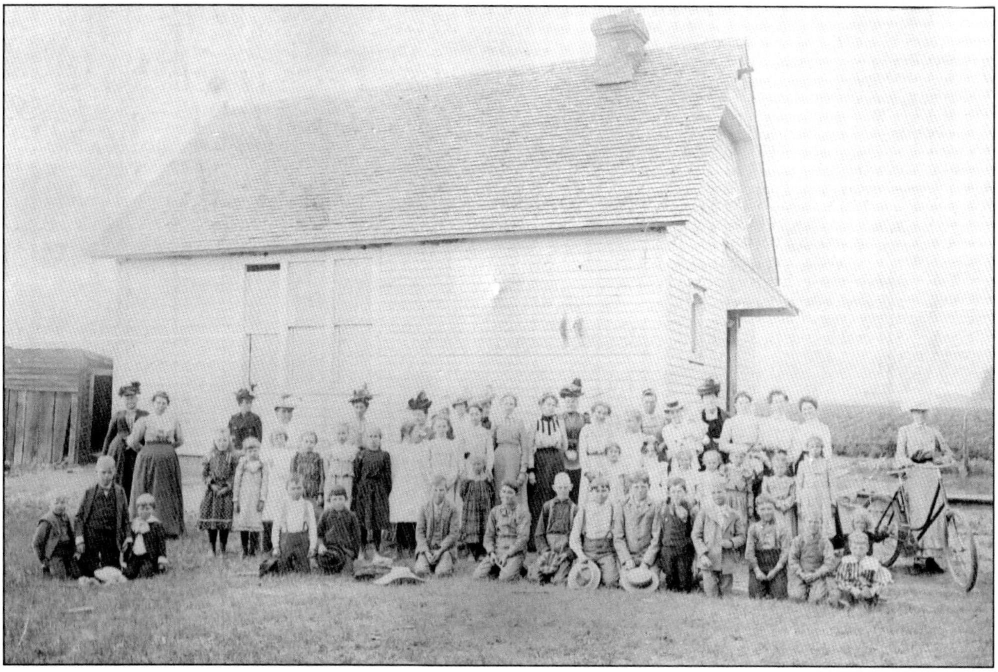

Churches added respectability to new towns in the early 20th century. The immediate need for churches was met by using space in other buildings, until construction of a new church building could be finished. In Johnstown's case, the first church services were held in the homes or at schools, like White Hall, pictured here.

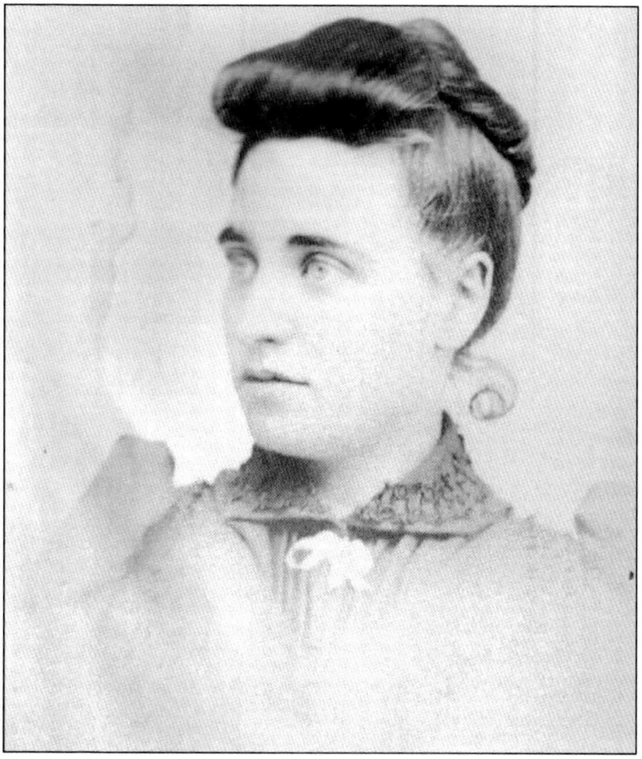

The early congregations were served by circuit riders. Rev. Cora Elwell Dilley was one of these early preachers. She traveled in a horse and buggy back and forth between the churches she served. She inspired her congregation to form a religious community and build a church west of present-day Johnstown.

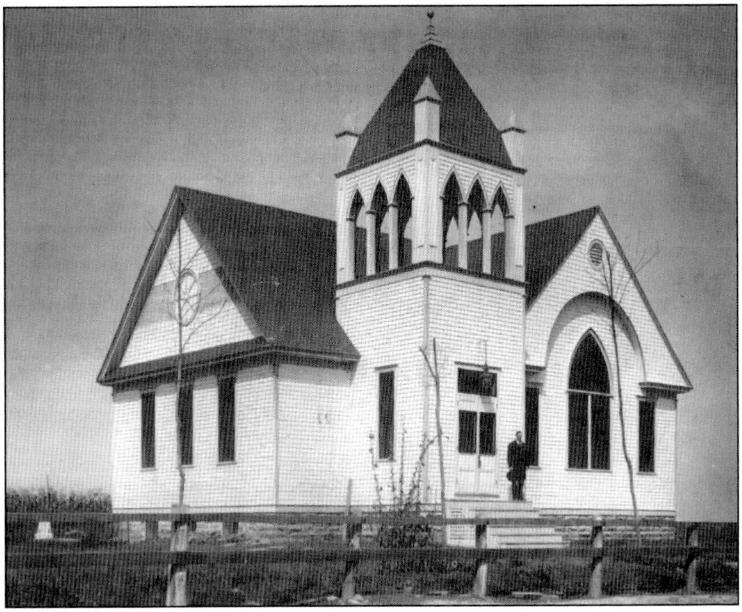

When the church was completed, it was named Dilley Chapel in honor of Reverend Dilley. She died at age 30 in 1898 and was buried beside the chapel, shown in this photograph. A few years later, the original church was destroyed by fire. The new church stood at the same location until spring 1927, when it was decided to move the church into Johnstown. (GHM.)

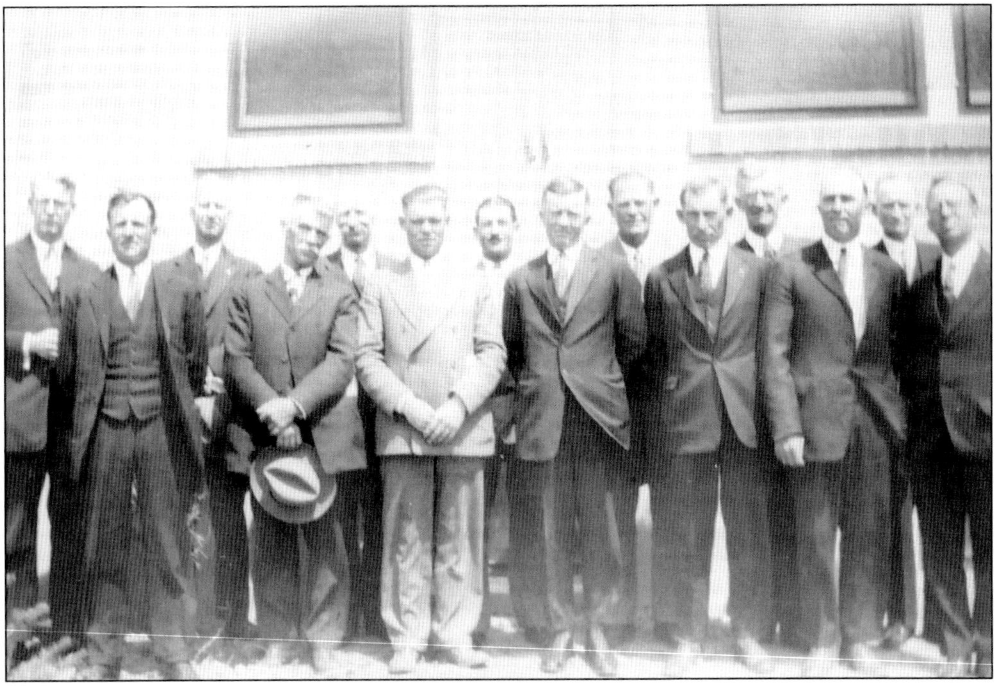

These are the men of the United Brethren in Christ Church in Elwell. John Sloan, fifth from the left, donated the land for Dilley Chapel and the cemetery at Elwell. He and his wife Armenda came to a farm west of Johnstown in 1892. When he died, he was buried in a plot that was originally part of his farm.

There were two churches in the town limits of Johnstown in 1908, the Methodist Episcopal and the Baptist church. In the early days of Johnstown, it was common for a man to be a minister and do other work too. Such was the case of A. R. Morrison, who was the minister of the Methodist church in 1917 and also the town's blacksmith.

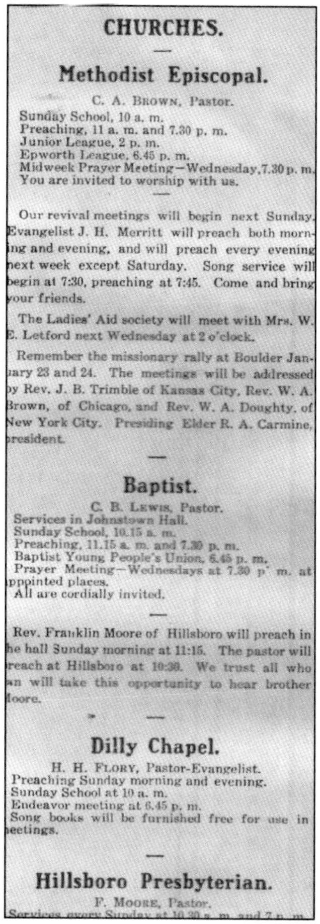

CHURCHES.

Methodist Episcopal.

C. A. Brown, Pastor.
Sunday School, 10 a. m.
Preaching, 11 a. m. and 7.30 p. m.
Junior League, 2 p. m.
Epworth League, 6.45 p. m.
Midweek Prayer Meeting—Wednesday, 7.30 p. m.
You are invited to worship with us.

Our revival meetings will begin next Sunday. Evangelist J. H. Merritt will preach both morning and evening, and will preach every evening next week except Saturday. Song service will begin at 7:30, preaching at 7:45. Come and bring your friends.

The Ladies' Aid society will meet with Mrs. W. E. Letford next Wednesday at 2 o'clock.

Remember the missionary rally at Boulder January 23 and 24. The meetings will be addressed by Rev. J. B. Trimble of Kansas City, Rev. W. A. Brown, of Chicago, and Rev. W. A. Doughty, of New York City. Presiding Elder R. A. Carmine, president.

Baptist.

C. B. Lewis, Pastor.
Services in Johnstown Hall.
Sunday School, 10.15 a. m.
Preaching, 11.15 a. m. and 7.30 p. m.
Baptist Young People's Union, 6.45 p. m.
Prayer Meeting—Wednesdays at 7.30 p. m. at appointed places.
All are cordially invited.

Rev. Franklin Moore of Hillsboro will preach in the hall Sunday morning at 11:15. The pastor will preach at Hillsboro at 10:30. We trust all who can will take this opportunity to hear brother Moore.

Dilly Chapel.

H. H. Flory, Pastor-Evangelist.
Preaching Sunday morning and evening.
Sunday School at 10 a. m.
Endeavor meeting at 6.45 p. m.
Song books will be furnished free for use in meetings.

Hillsboro Presbyterian.

F. Moore, Pastor.

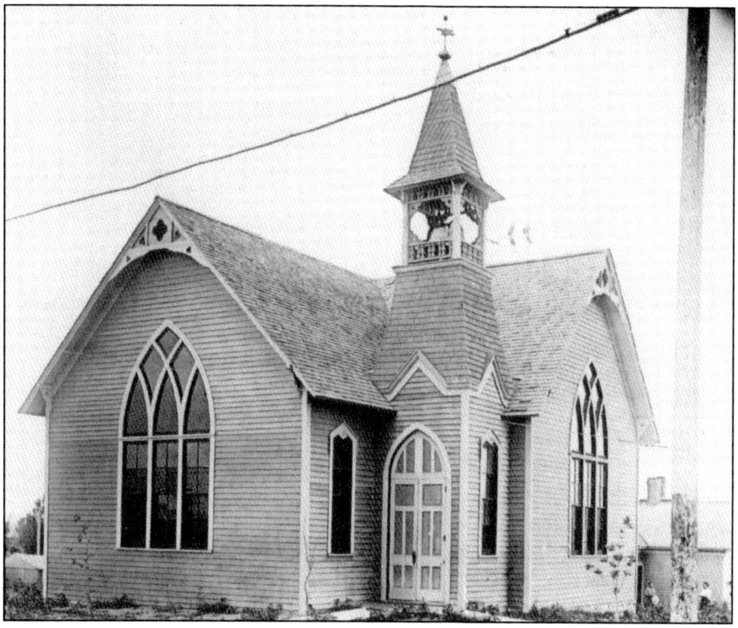

The Methodist Episcopal Church was the first church in the town of Johnstown. Early in 1903, a meeting was held in the Smith School and the Methodist Society was organized under Morrison's leadership. The new church was completed in September 1904. In 1932, this church building was destroyed by fire, and a new one was built in its place. (GHM.)

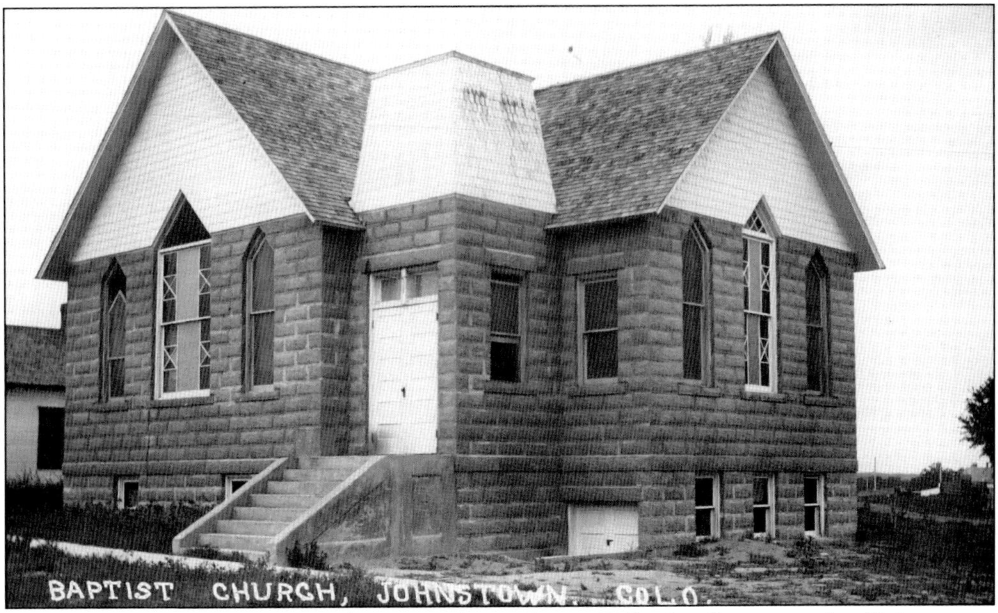

The First Baptist Church originally met at the Welcome Hill schoolhouse north of Johnstown. Reverend Pulliam came from Loveland to conduct these services. The membership started to construct the church building in 1907. Prior to completion of the building, the congregation met in the Johnstown Hall, and members were baptized in the Little Thompson River north of town. (GHM.)

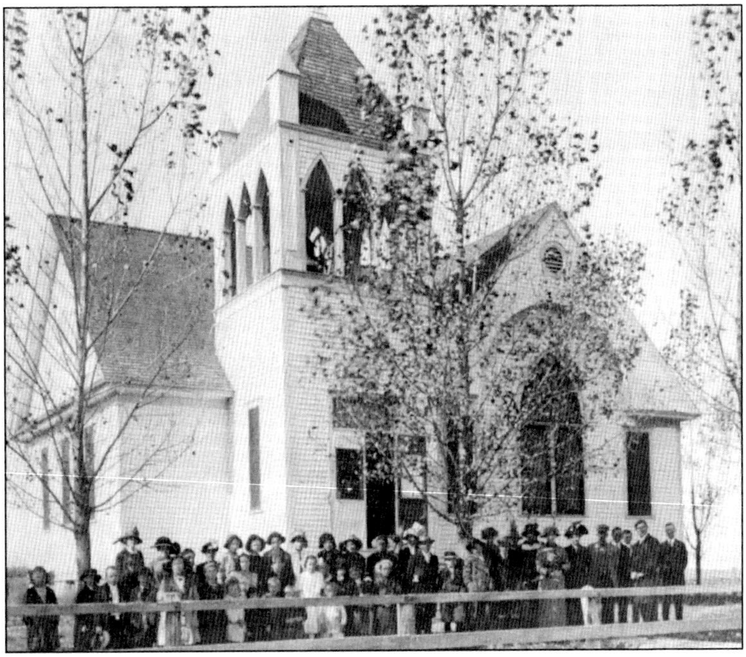

Dilley Chapel was moved from Elwell to Johnstown in 1927. The basement was dug while the ground was still frozen, so dynamite was used to loosen the ground. Since 1975, the chapel has belonged to the St. John the Baptist Catholic Church. The Catholic church was originally built in the Johnstown Colony, using plain benches for seating and handmade Stations of the Cross.

Five

Alcohol and Prohibition

The use or nonuse of alcohol played a large role in the establishment of towns in northern Colorado and continued well into the 20th century. The lawless miners and cowboys gave way to farmers and families. The new settlers became the town founders, taking advantage of the opportunity to establish new communities however they wished. Concerned with the morality of their citizens, these town founders and religious leaders alike intended to ensure a positive, law-abiding beginning to each community.

After the town was incorporated in 1906, Johnstown held its first municipal election in July of the next year. Harvey Jay Parish, who founded the town, was elected the first mayor. The liquor question was voted on by separate ballot, and the town went "wet" by a vote of 47 to 15—more than three to one. The town of Johnstown would allow alcohol to be sold. No other community in the area had allowed saloons. The outrage and ridicule of Johnstown was enormous, with people saying that Johnstown would gain notoriety as the saloon town of northern Colorado. The surrounding towns said the repercussions of allowing alcohol to be sold within the town's city limits would result in increased crime and make Johnstown a magnet for incorrigibles. A Berthoud man reported seeing 15 drunks within a few hours time while visiting Johnstown. Another reported discovering two men who appeared dead on the road from Denver. They were not dead, just "dead drunk."

Shortly after this, Parish endeavored to take matters in his own hands. Because he could not change the decision of the municipal election and because he wanted to salvage the town's reputation, Parish ensured that at least part of Johnstown remained liquor-free. He did this by inserting a clause into the deeds of all property he sold in Johnstown that stated, "No intoxicating liquor [may be] sold or manufactured in any place of public resort on this lot." The Parish side of town remained "dry."

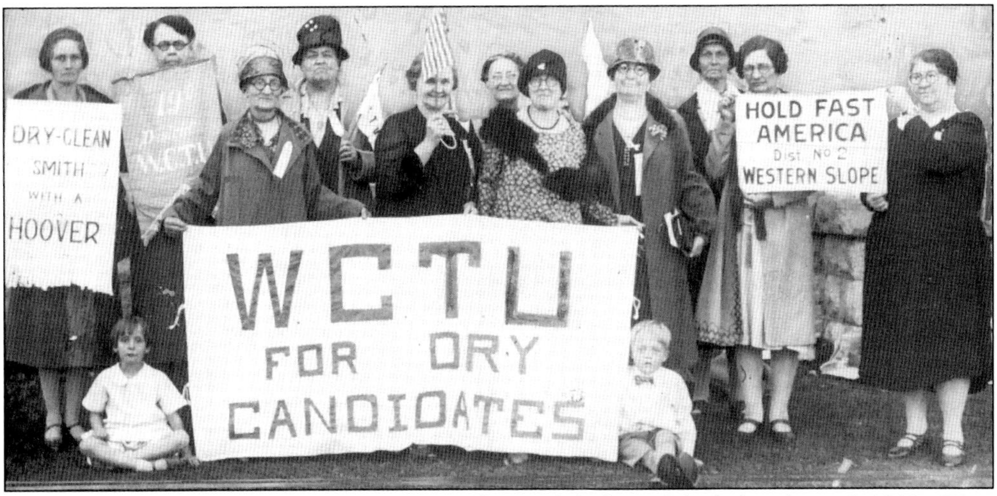

The Women's Christian Temperance Union influenced the ban of alcohol in the early 1900s. They worked to pass a local option bill in 1907 that allowed towns to ban alcohol in their communities. This created a controversy throughout the state, and 20 towns went dry. Prohibition became a state law in Colorado in January 1916, four years before the nationwide ban of alcohol. (DPL.)

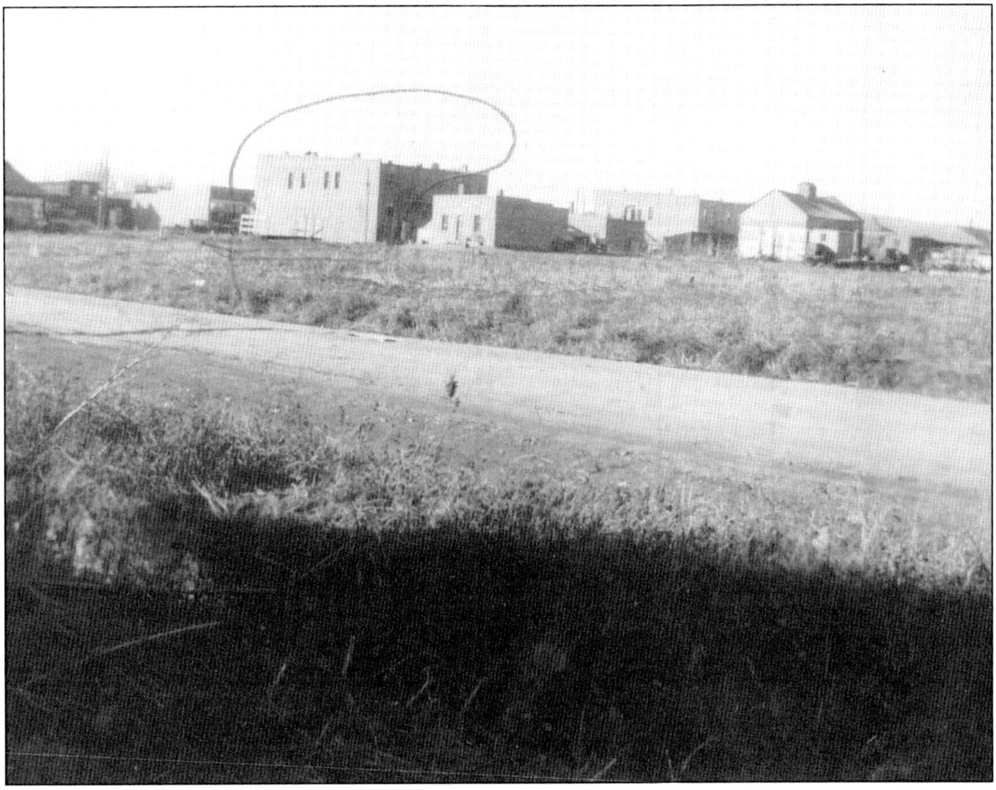

This photograph was taken of Johnstown about the time the town became one of the few communities in the area to allow alcohol. For example, Greeley, the Weld County seat, was originally founded as a utopian community, meaning a perfect town, where religion, temperance, and cooperative farming were cornerstones. The ban against alcohol in the city of Greeley was not lifted until 1969. (GHM.)

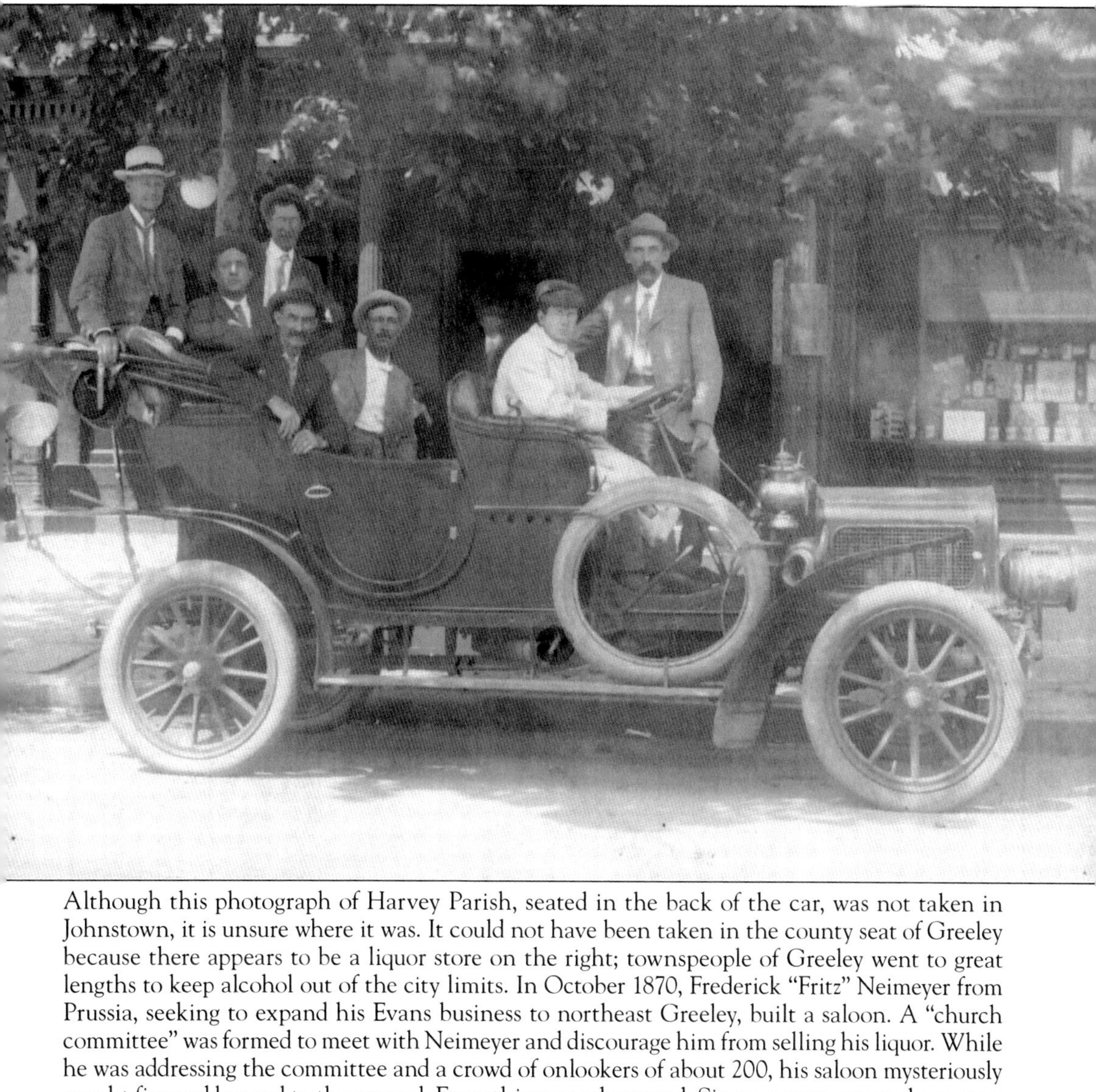

Although this photograph of Harvey Parish, seated in the back of the car, was not taken in Johnstown, it is unsure where it was. It could not have been taken in the county seat of Greeley because there appears to be a liquor store on the right; townspeople of Greeley went to great lengths to keep alcohol out of the city limits. In October 1870, Frederick "Fritz" Neimeyer from Prussia, seeking to expand his Evans business to northeast Greeley, built a saloon. A "church committee" was formed to meet with Neimeyer and discourage him from selling his liquor. While he was addressing the committee and a crowd of onlookers of about 200, his saloon mysteriously caught fire and burned to the ground. Everything was destroyed. Six men were arrested on arson and riot charges, including the son of Greeley's founder Nathan Meeker. None of them were ever convicted. Neimeyer returned to his home in Evans, never to attempt expanding his business again. (GHM.)

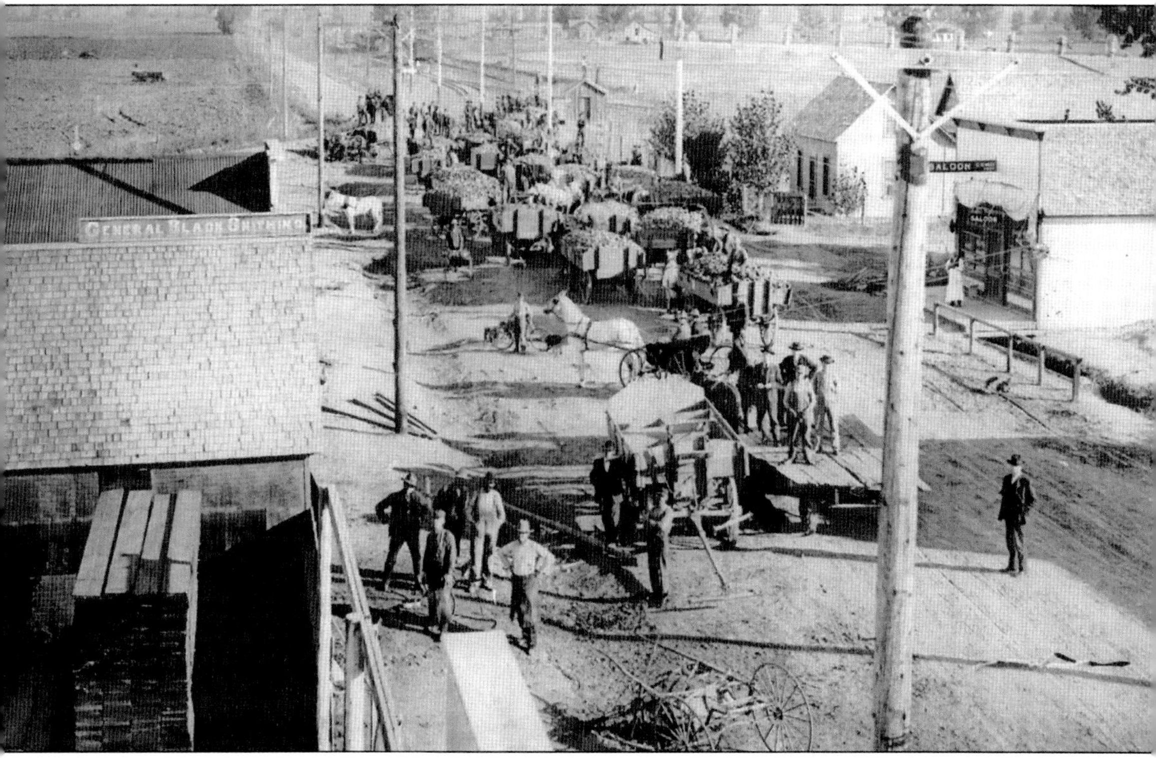

When Harvey Parish inserted a "no alcohol" clause into the deeds of all the property he sold in Johnstown, he was endeavoring to salvage the town's reputation. He once owned the entire west side of Parish Avenue, and that part of downtown remained liquor-free. He did not allow liquor on "his side of the street." However, J. J. Becker, who owned land on the east side of Parish Avenue, held no sentiments concerning liquor sales. He allowed liquor stores and saloons to buy his property. This caused Parish Avenue to become the dividing line between two sides of Johnstown—the "dry" side and the "wet" side. Nevertheless, local residents sometimes came up with ways to circumvent Parish's restrictions. During the beet harvest of 1910, an ingenious entrepreneur rigged a pulley from a saloon on the east side to haul buckets of beer to thirsty workers on the west side, as seen in this photograph.

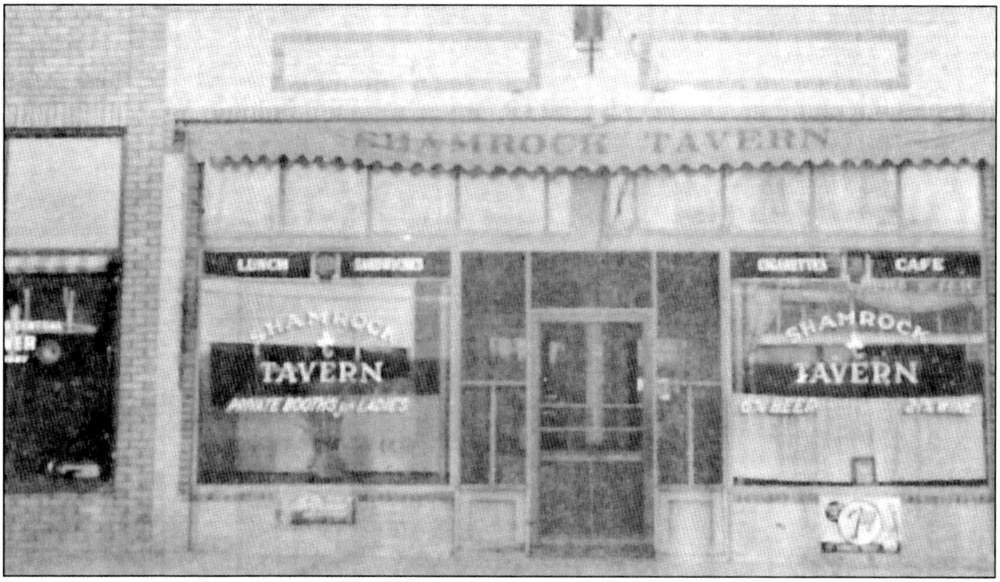

This is a photograph of Art Palmeteer's Shamrock Tavern in 1933 on the east side of the street. Liquor had been allowed on the east side of the street, except during the time of Prohibition. Interestingly enough, this tavern shared the same building with the John Parish Tire Shoppe, owned by the son of Harvey Parish.

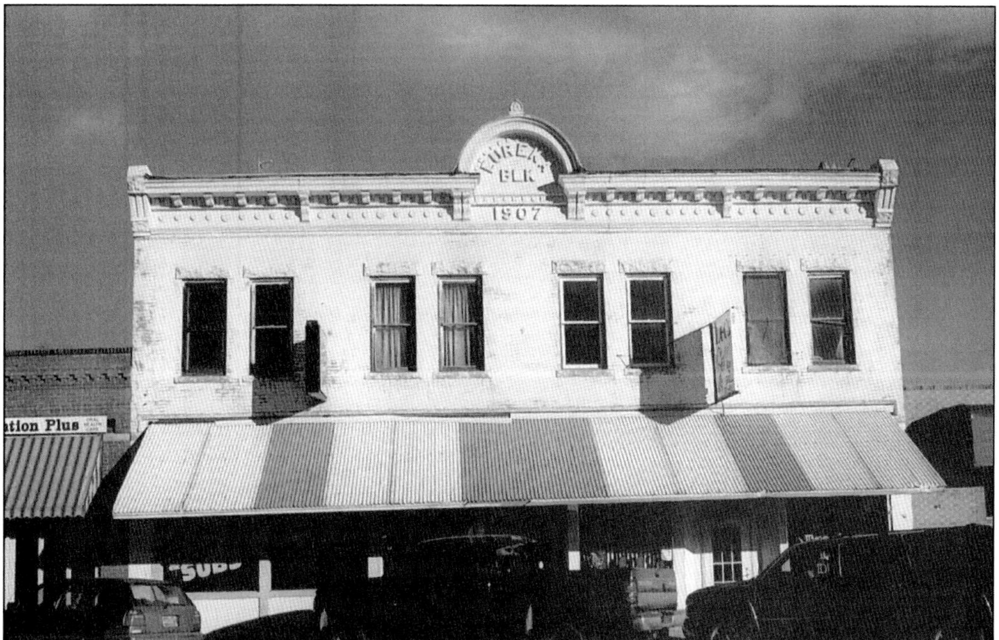

To this day, all stores and bars selling liquor in Johnstown are on the east side of the street. The Parish side of the street remains dry. This more recent photograph shows the Eureka building, which now houses the pool hall, with a liquor store next to it.

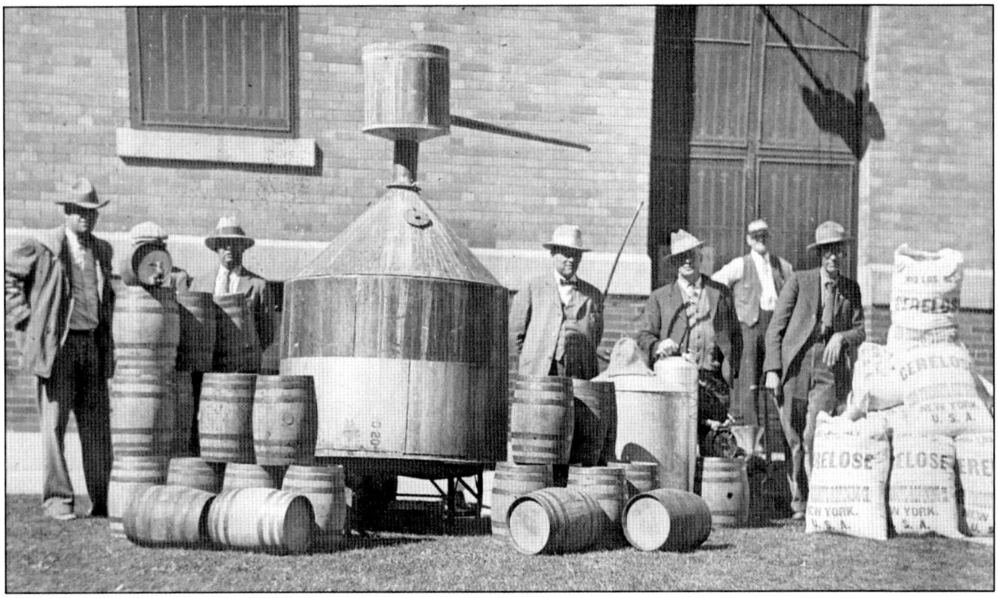

The Women's Christian Temperance Union greatly influenced the communities of the area, especially before and after the passage of the 18th Amendment. After the passage of prohibition, agents were sent to seize illegal alcohol and the means of making it, like the still pictured here. At WCTU meetings throughout northern Colorado, women met to extend their influence throughout the world. (GHM.)

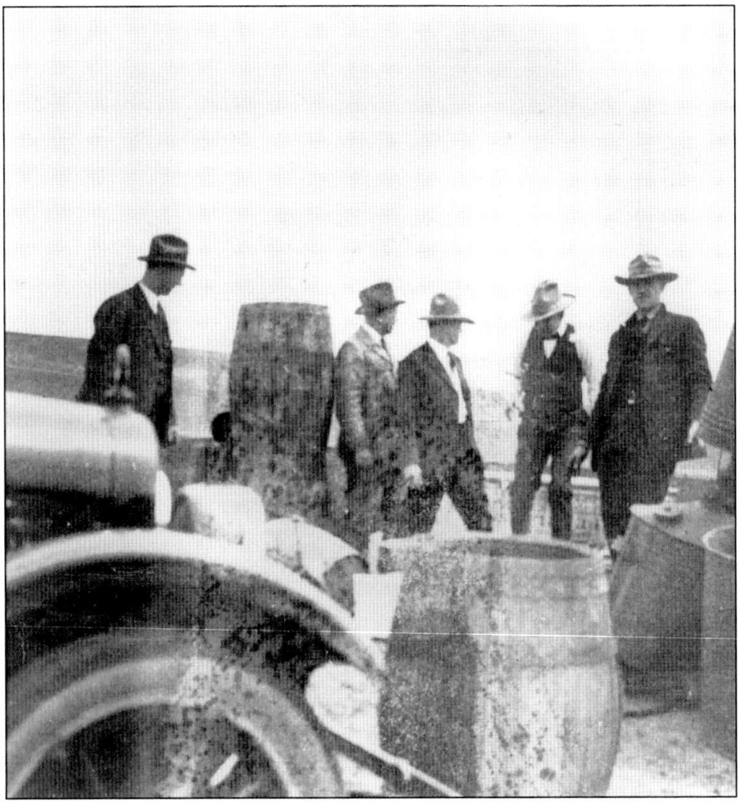

When law enforcement officers seized liquor, events could turn violent. A story was told of a man driving a truck load of alcohol near Johnstown being killed by officers. The story went on to say that the body was taken to Greeley, hastily embalmed with alcohol obtained from the "booze room" of the courthouse, and shipped to the man's home in Denver. (GHM.)

Six

JOHNSTOWN'S INDUSTRIES

The industry of Johnstown has been traditionally and continues to be agriculturally based. The earliest industries processed the raw farm products, providing jobs not only for the factory workers, but also for the suppliers such as sugar beet farmers, dairy farmers, and laborers. In 1930, Johnstown had a payroll from its factories of $500,000 and employed 350 men.

Willard E. Letford knew that industry was the lifeblood of any beginning town. He was instrumental in starting the first milk condensery, the Great Western Factory, the First National Bank, and was a power behind the school system.

Letford spent many days traveling around the area making people aware that a canned milk processing plant was planned for the Johnstown area. Dairy cattle were shipped to local farmers from Wisconsin and Minnesota. One of the largest condensed milk factories of the Colorado Condensed Milk Company operated in Johnstown from 1910 to 1978.

The largest industrial plant in the immediate area was opened in 1925. The barium-process sugar refinery of the Great Western Sugar Company operated 24 hours every day of the year manufacturing sugar and other products from the waste products of other sugar beet factories of the company. It was the only sugar factory of its kind in the United States. Again W. E. Letford was credited with convincing W. D. "Bill" Lippitt, then Great Western president, to build the refinery in Johnstown.

Following World War II, the use of monosodium glutamate became popular in America. It could be made from many sources, one being sugar beet molasses. Letford was a factor in making it possible for Johnstown to be the home of the MSG plant. The combination of this plant and the barium-molasses refinery made Johnstown even more unique in the sugar world.

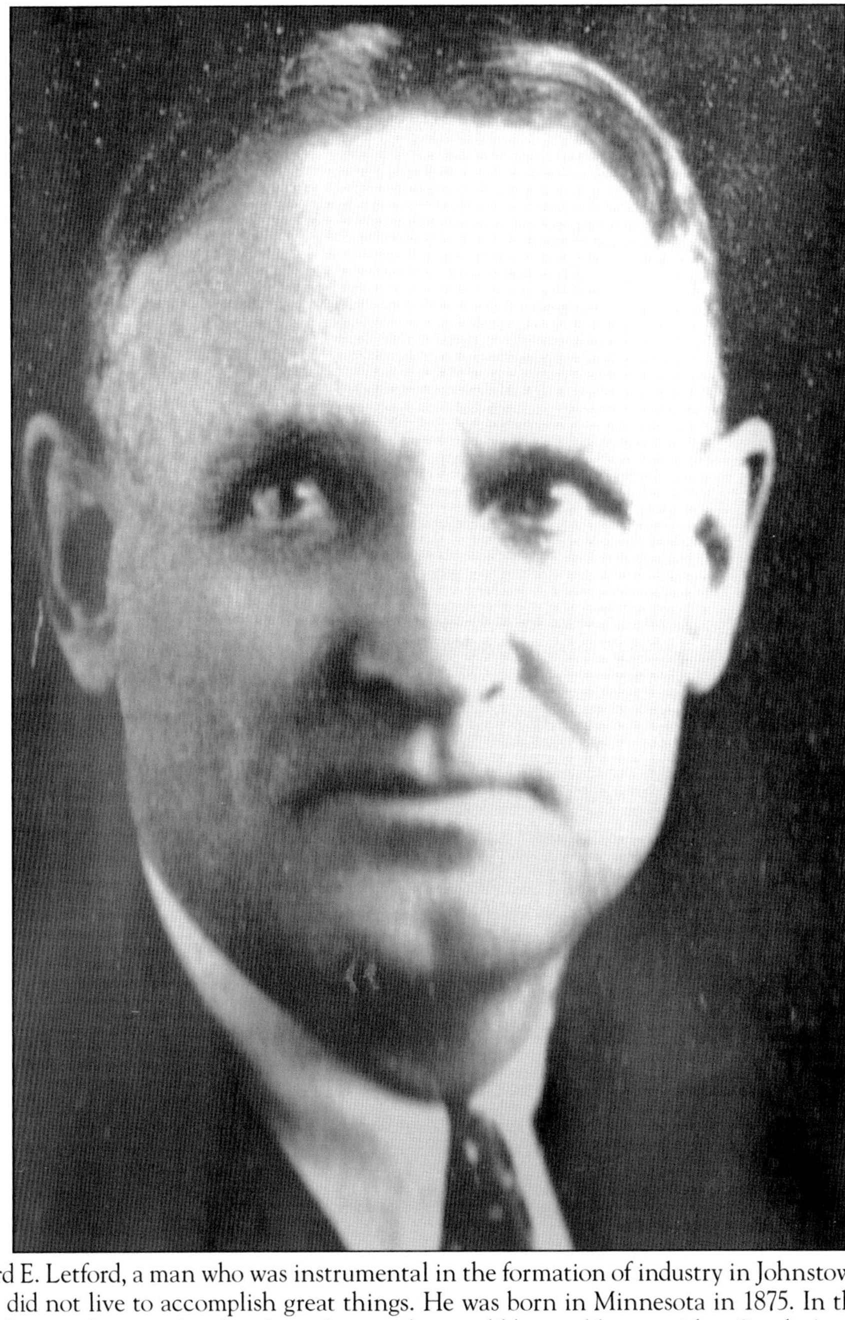

Willard E. Letford, a man who was instrumental in the formation of industry in Johnstown, very nearly did not live to accomplish great things. He was born in Minnesota in 1875. In the early 1890s, he was diagnosed with tuberculosis and was told he could go to either South America or Colorado. In any event, he was told he did not have long to live. First Letford came to Longmont, where he worked in several banks and married Leona Kitely. In 1904, Letford and his wife came to Johnstown, where he and T. M. Callahan started a private bank. He was instrumental in bringing the dairy industry to Johnstown and in locating a Great Western Sugar factory there. Before his death, Letford Elementary School was built and named in his honor. Willard E. Letford, the man who was not supposed to live to see his 21st birthday, lived to realize the dream of helping build Johnstown and died in 1959 at the age of 84.

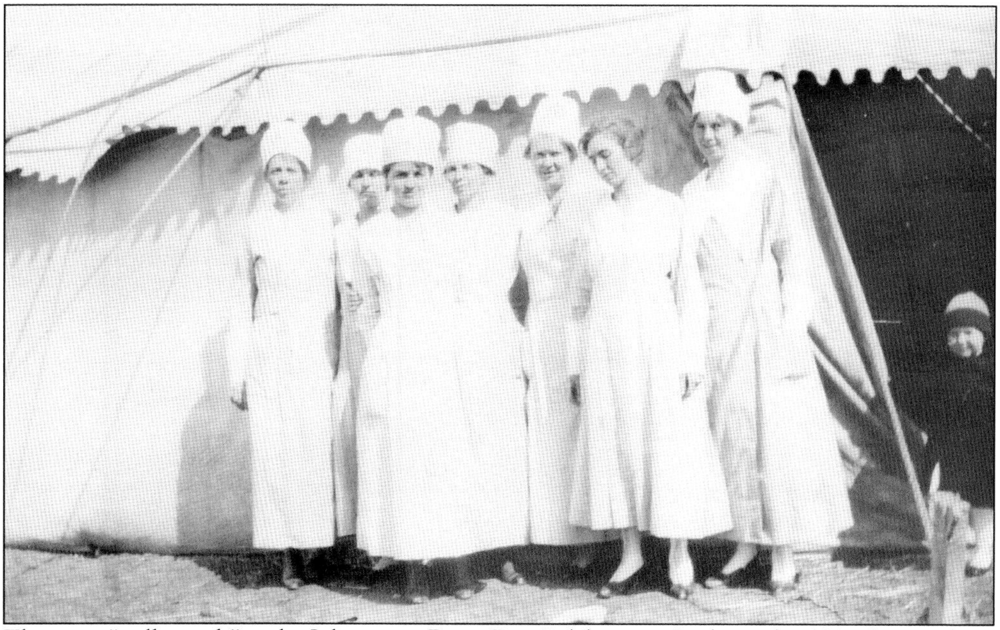

These are "milk maids" at the Johnstown Dairy Day Celebration. In the early 1900s, farmers from Colorado and the surrounding states brought their stock here to be exhibited and judged. Other events included carnival rides, food and game booths, and entertainment. Circus-like tents were erected to house the events. Johnstown now celebrates Barbecue Day annually with a parade, games, booths, and a barbeque.

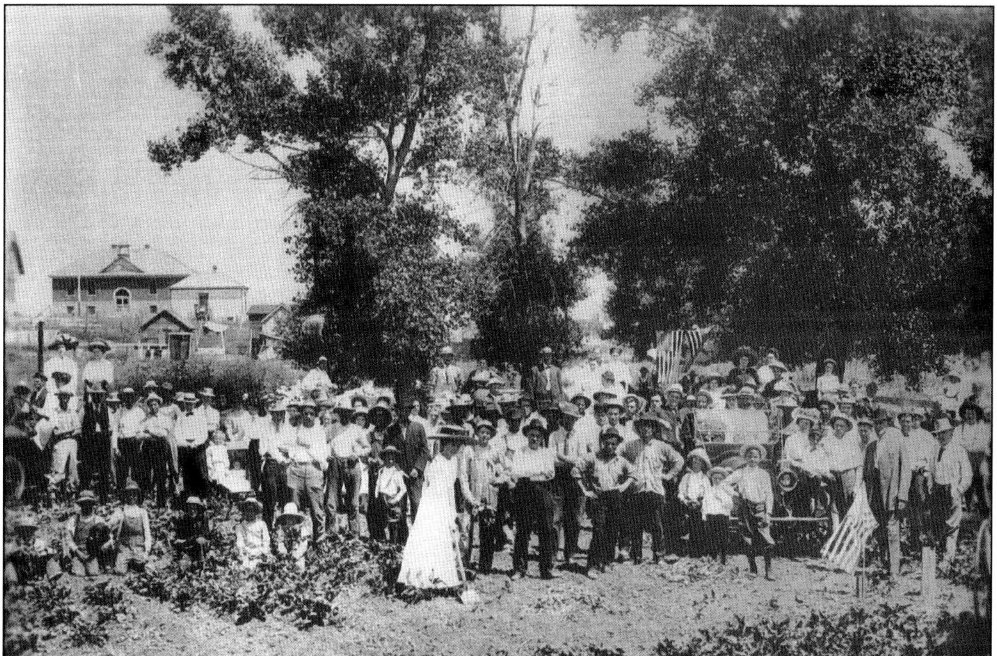

In 1910, a milk condensing plant was added to the area. In this photograph, Lottie Parish, daughter of Harvey Parish, the town founder, breaks ground for the factory. As more milk was brought in from greater distances, the plant was enlarged and more types of products were produced.

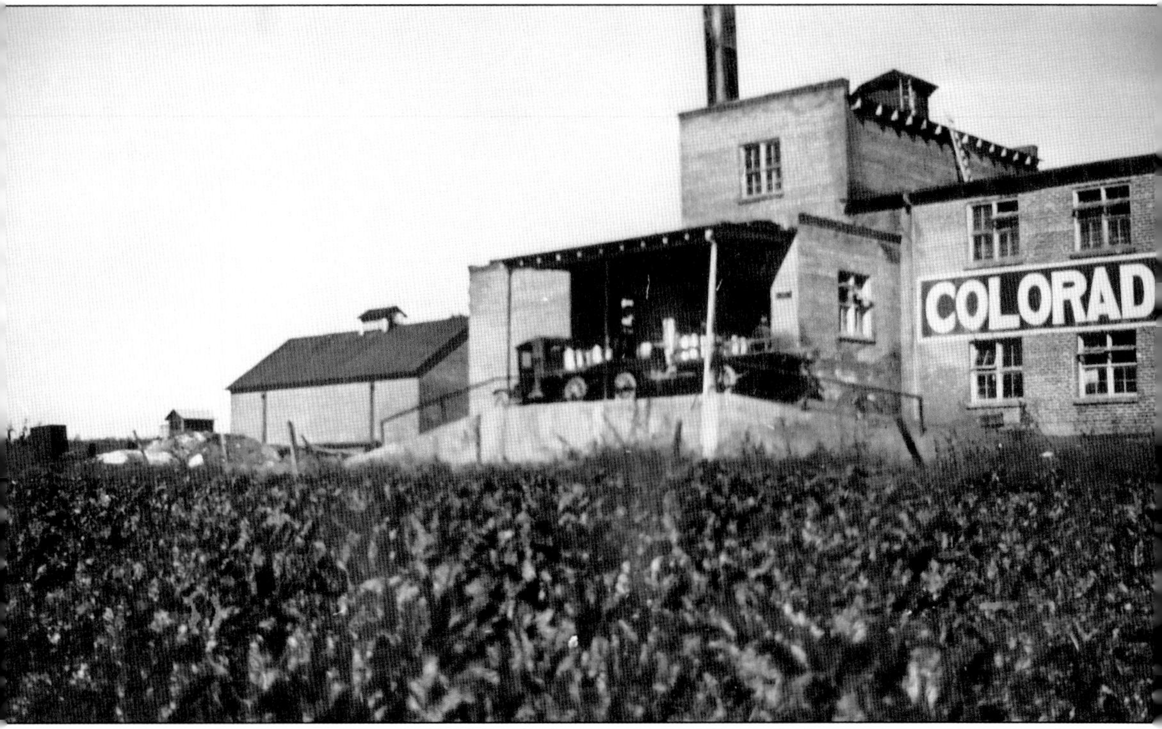

Realizing that industry was the lifeblood of any town, W. E. Letford spent many days traveling around the area signing up people for dairy farming, lending money to establish herds, and in general, making people aware that a canned milk processing plant was planned for the Johnstown area. Area businessmen set an agreement with Mohawk Condensed Milk Company that they would take over the operation when a prescribed volume of milk was delivered to the plant each day. Large numbers of dairy cows were shipped to local farmers from Wisconsin and Minnesota. Before long, the prescribed volume had been reached. The Mohawk Company called the operation "Colorado Condensed Milk Company." It was operated as such until 1921 when Carnation Company bought out Mohawk here, as well as their plants in the East. The Carnation Company closed its evaporated milk plant in Johnstown in 1978.

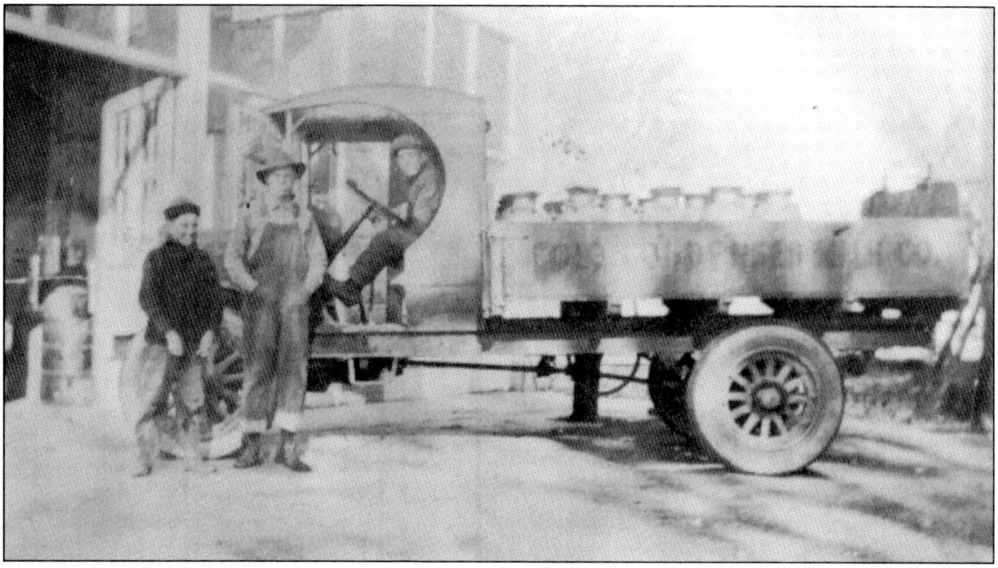

Milk was collected from about 250 farmers. Joseph Charles Becker hauled the first milk to the new condensery. Some of the milk was hauled in 10-gallon cans by truck from the farms in the surrounding area. Shown is driver Carl Lindstrom in the first milk truck. The finished product was sold to wholesale grocers.

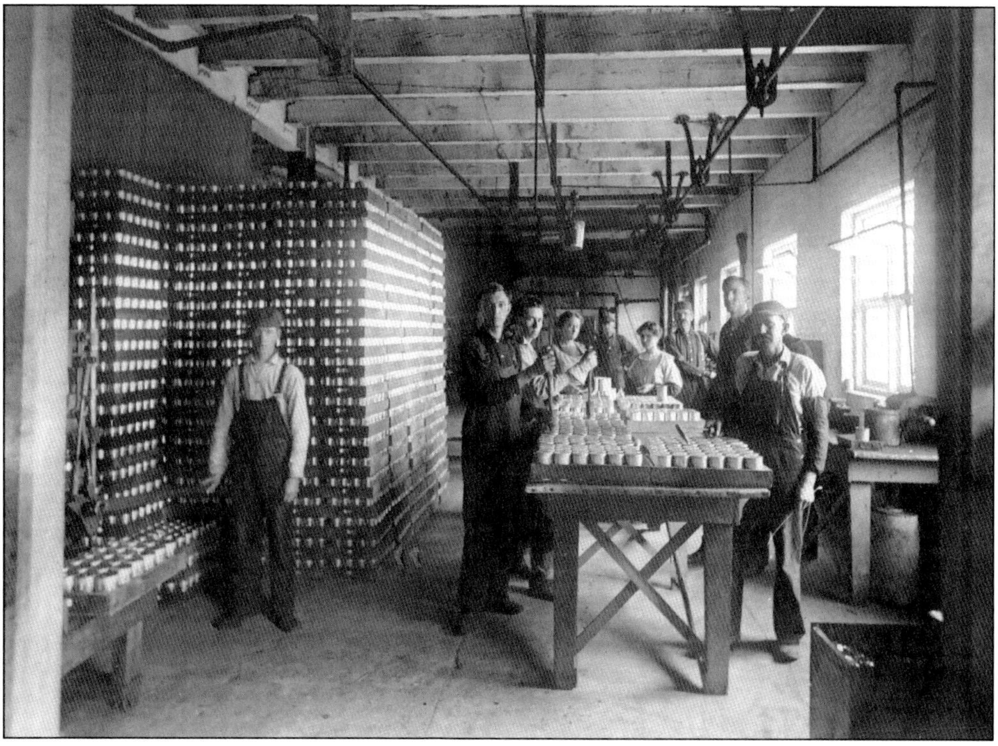

The milk condensing plant made about 200,000 cans of evaporated milk a day. When they got the milk from the cow, it was about 85 percent water. About half of the water was removed and the milk was homogenized. It was put through another process, which broke it down more. Then it was put into cans, sealed, labeled, and shipped.

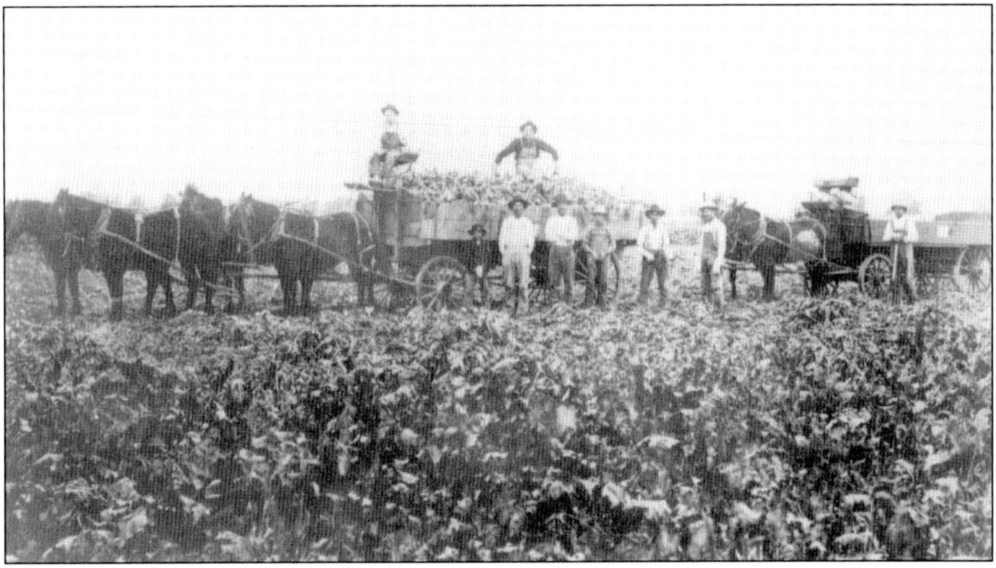

Charles Boettcher, a wealthy Denver investor, became interested in sugar beets on a trip to Germany. He brought back seeds and distributed them to farmers, who successfully proved that they would grow along the Platte Valley. The growth of the sugar beet industry in Colorado exploded in the early 20th century. Arthur Kibby, shown in this photograph, hauled the first load of beets to the Johnstown beet dump. (GHM.)

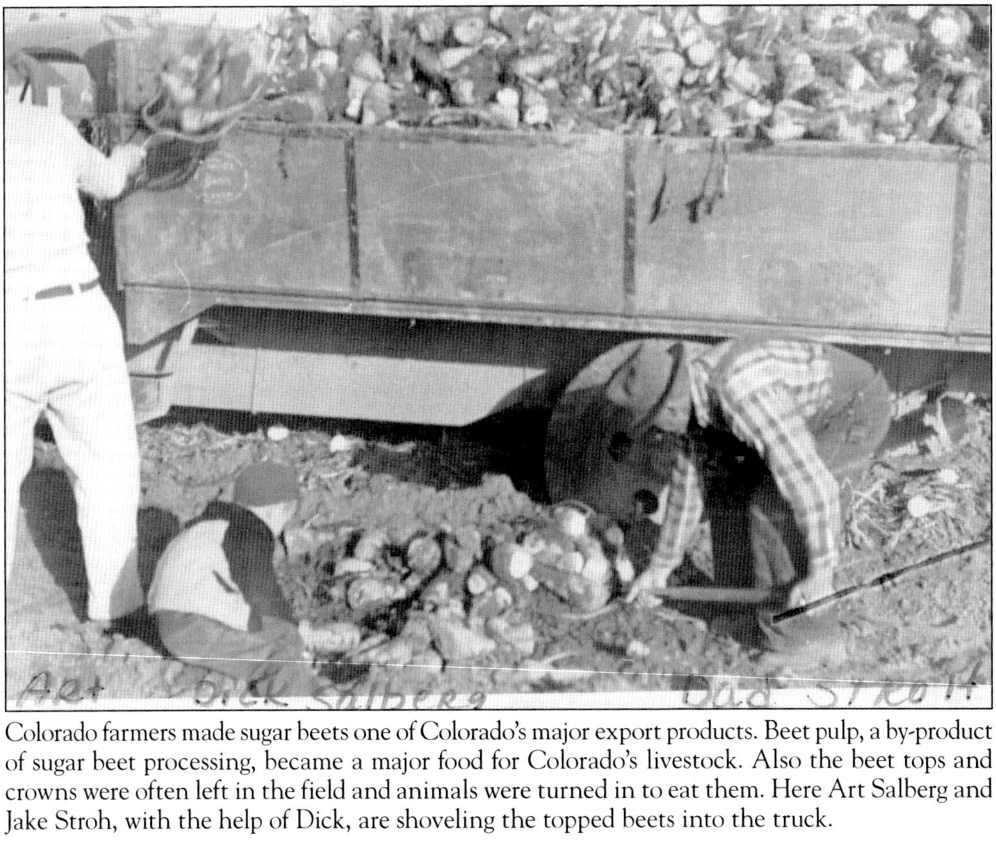

Colorado farmers made sugar beets one of Colorado's major export products. Beet pulp, a by-product of sugar beet processing, became a major food for Colorado's livestock. Also the beet tops and crowns were often left in the field and animals were turned in to eat them. Here Art Salberg and Jake Stroh, with the help of Dick, are shoveling the topped beets into the truck.

After the beets were loaded into the wagon or truck, they were taken to the beet dump. In this early Johnstown photograph, Joseph J. Becker is shown bringing his beets into town. In the background is the first building in town, the Parish Fairbairn Lumber Yard. Joseph's son, Joseph Charles Becker, donated the land for what was to become Becker Beet Dump.

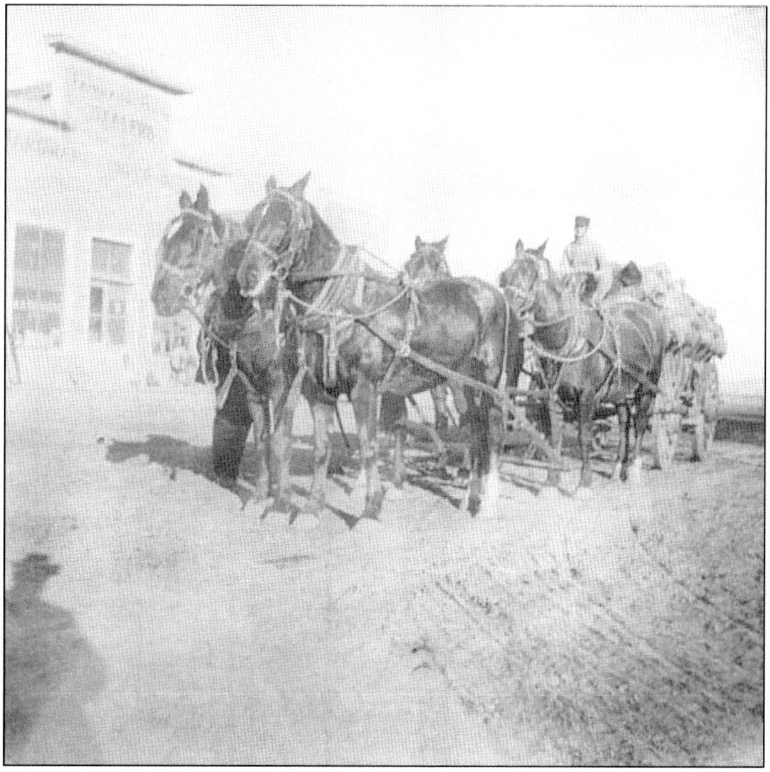

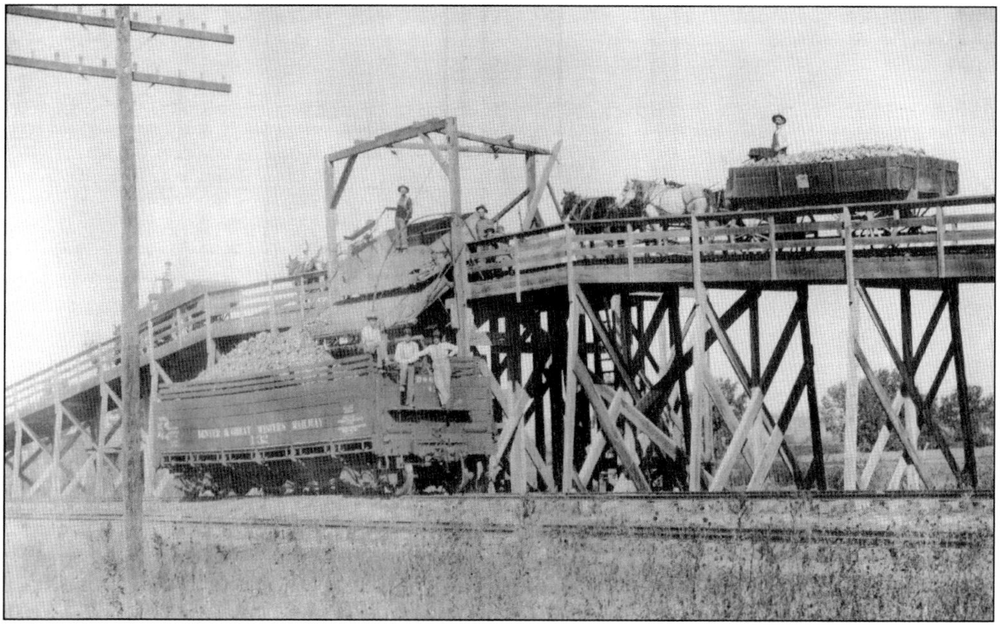

Great Western Railway was constructed in 1902 to carry beets to the sugar factory in Loveland. Rather than hauling sugar beets a long distance by wagon to the factory, farmers needed only to deliver the beets to the nearest beet dump. In 1933, four area beet dumps were combined into one big station on the Johnstown factory grounds. Becker dump was one of the dumps that was discontinued. (GHM.)

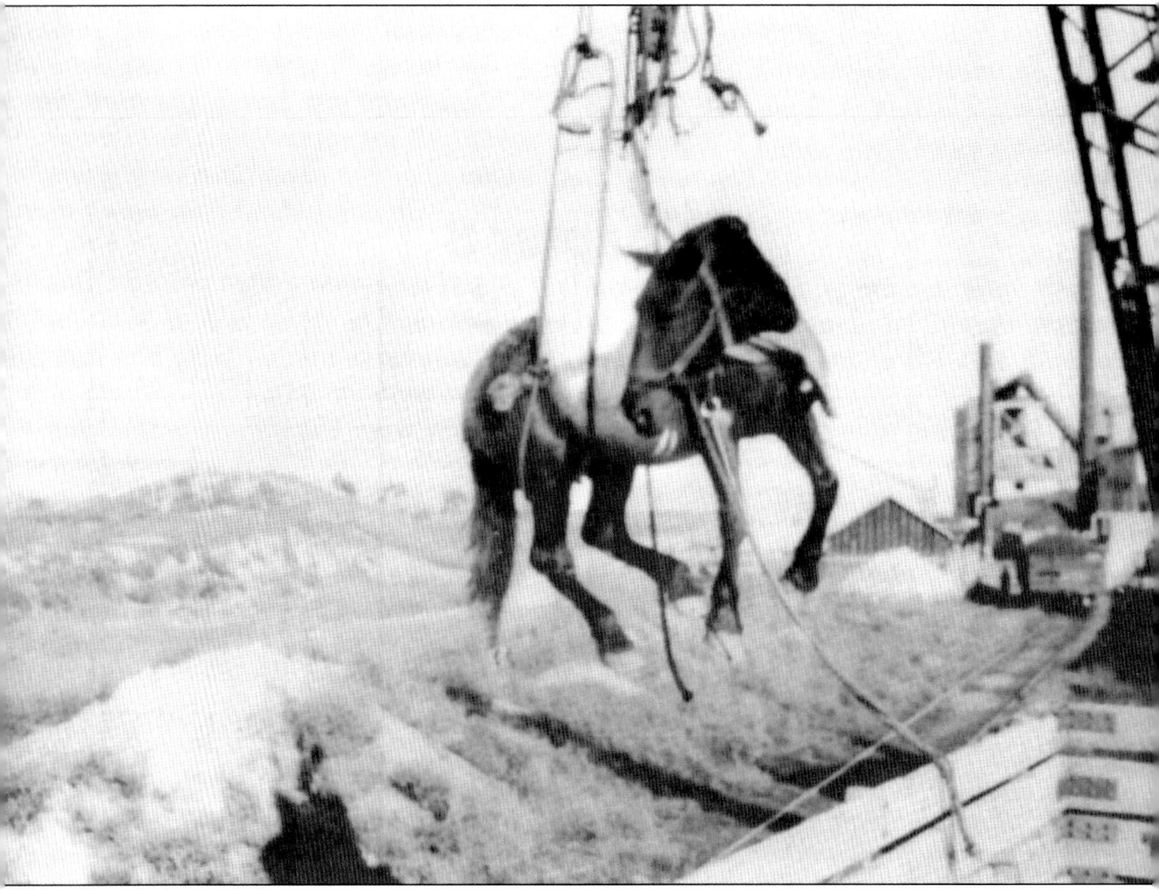

On June 23, 1929, the Johnstown Sugar factory received a "50-50" shipment; a shipment that was half horse and half beets. The mixed cargo was the result of an accident during loading at the Bunyan dump, south of Johnstown. As a team of horses, belonging to W. M. and J. C. Sellers, was being driven over the dump, the horse standing near the edge of the runway lost its balance when the wagon was dumped. The harness broke, and the horse somersaulted into the railroad beet car. Although the horse was uninjured, all attempts to get it out of the car failed. The train was sent to town with the mixed cargo. At the factory, a hoisting sling was improvised from filter cloth and the animal was lifted safely to the ground.

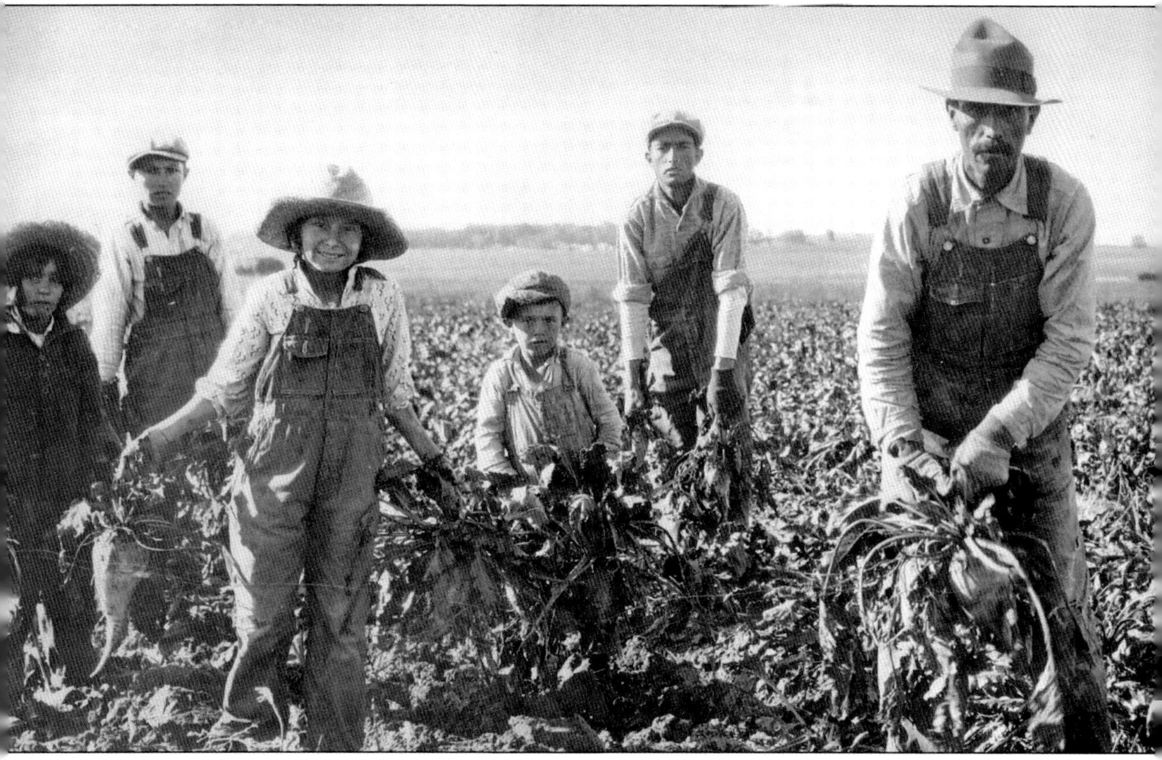

Sugar beet farming was labor intensive and often involved more work than the family on the farm could manage. Recent German immigrants who came from the Volga River valley in Russia were the first to be hired in Weld County. The German laborers soon purchased farms of their own, and Japanese laborers were then brought in to work the beets. They, too, soon were farm owners. Another source of labor was sought. Great Western turned southward and began recruiting seasonal workers from Mexico and the southern United States. Many of these workers gained citizenship and also bought farms. Some returned south for the winter. After spending about $360,000 a year in transportation costs to support this program, the Great Western Sugar Company realized it would be more effective and economical to retain experienced workers in this region by establishing permanent settlements near the sugar beet fields. Great Western established worker colonies by providing land and materials for workers to build their own dwellings. By 1927, Spanish-speaking workers comprised 60 percent of the labor in Colorado sugar beet fields. (DPL.)

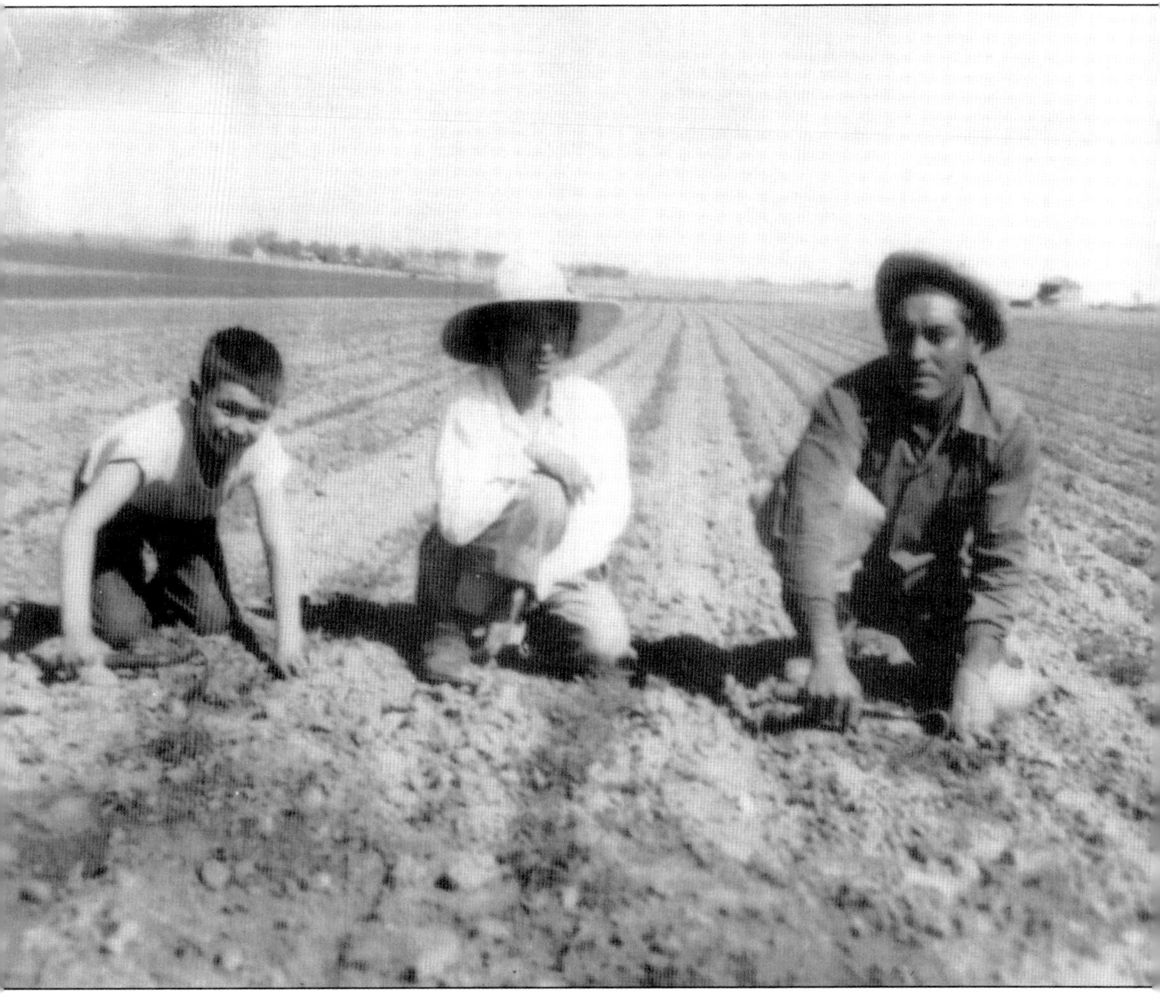

This photograph shows Charlie Solano, age seven, with his parents in the 1940s. They are using a short-handled hoe to block and thin the beets. In planting sugar beets, it was necessary to overplant, putting in many times the seeds necessary to produce a sugar beet to offset the high losses to the growing plants. If all the seeds were allowed to mature, they would be so crowded that none would have the space to produce a usable beet. The farmer needed to chop away many of the plants, and leave only one strong plant. This was called blocking and thinning. It was tedious work because it required a person to move slowly over the entire field, hour after hour, hacking away at the unwanted plants. At the end of the day it was impossible to stand up straight. The farmers required the workers to use the short hoe to make fewer mistakes. Later the use of the short handled hoe was ruled illegal because of the injuries sustained by workers.

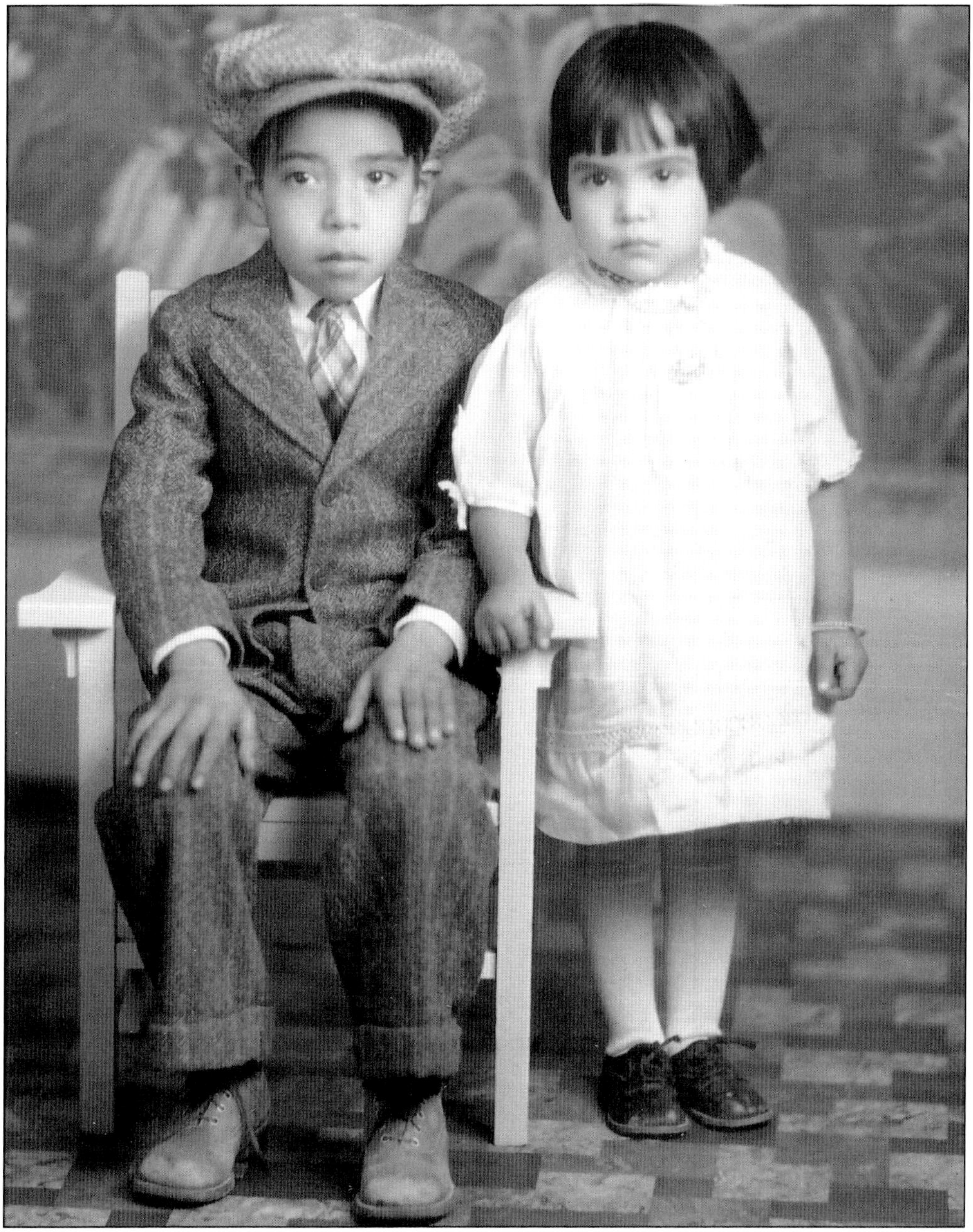

German and Japanese workers were hired to work year round. This was not true for the Mexican nationals or Mexican Americans. They were not allowed to plow, cultivate, or transport sugar beets. They were only allowed to work in the fields at backbreaking labor. Mexican men often needed their families to thin and harvest beets. This photograph shows Paul and Annie Meza, who came with their family to the Johnstown area. Paul stayed in the area and raised a family of his own. When sugar beets were ready to harvest, a grower would loosen the ground around the beets with a mechanical lifter while members of the family walked behind and lifted the 3- to 5-pound beets from the soil with the sharp point at the end of the beet knives. The beet would then be held between the workers' knees when they "topped" the beet with an 18-inch knife. It was very dangerous.

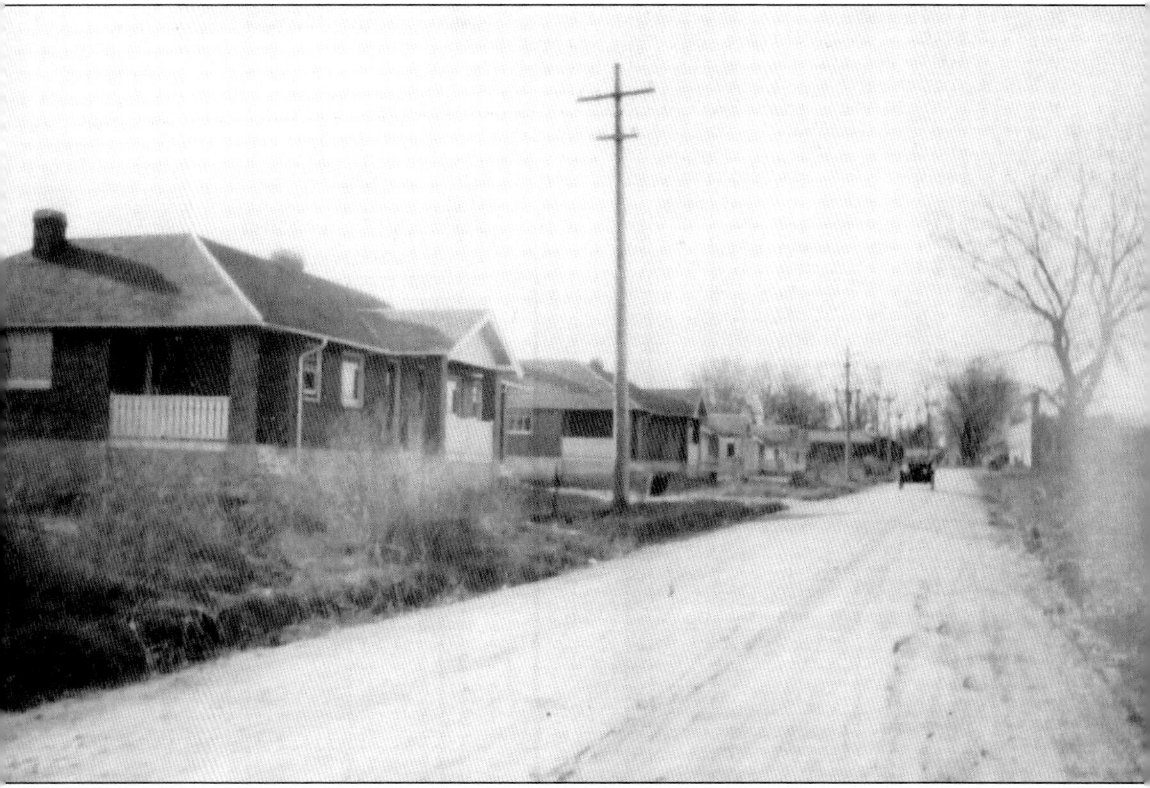

The buildings in this photograph were constructed by the Great Western Sugar Company for company supervisors. These homes were not made available for seasonal workers such as the Hispanic workers. A neighborhood with a distinctly Hispanic flavor still can be seen in Johnstown, and at times is referred to as "the Colony." Underneath the siding on most of the houses is evidence of the original adobe construction. Most of the original homes consisted of two rooms with no plumbing or electricity. Many did not receive these utilities until the 1960s when the town paved Maestas Street and put in city water and electricity. The Colony was annexed into Johnstown in 1992. (GHM.)

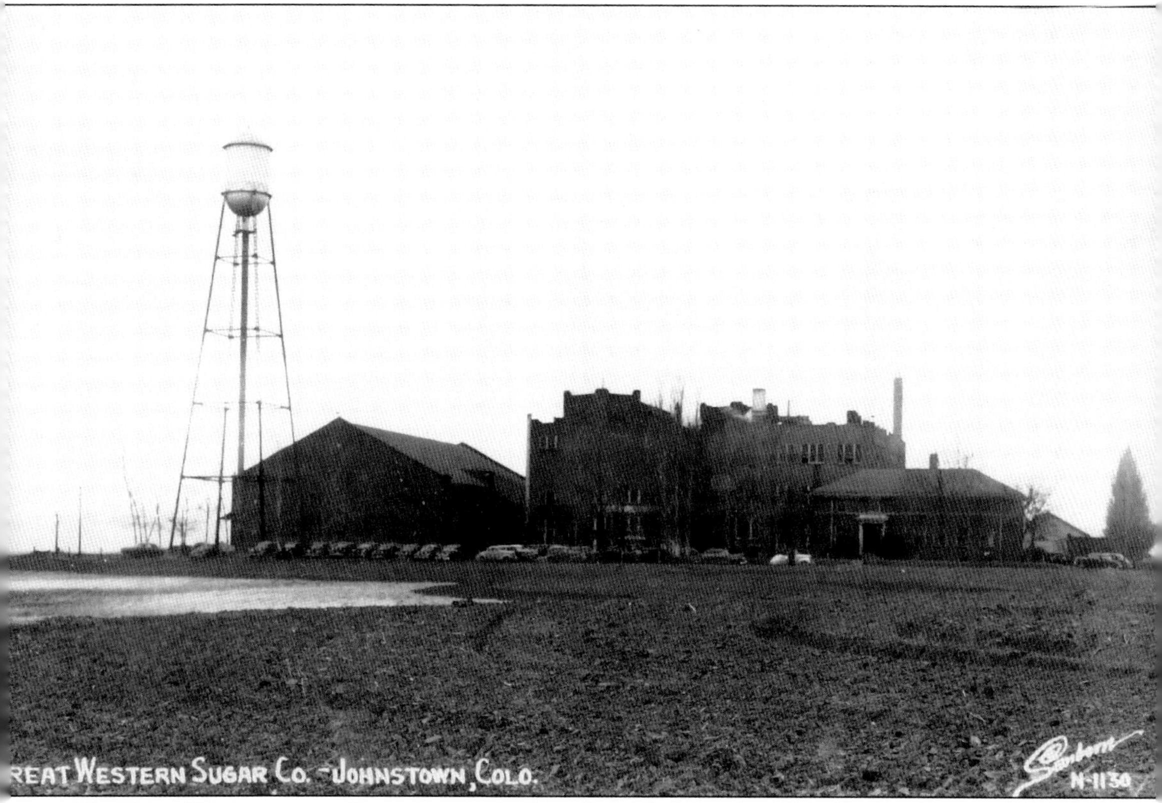

The Great Western Sugar Company was built and was dedicated on October 28, 1926. Opening day was quite a celebration with 1,800 visitors. To honor the founders of the factory, it was arranged that both Letford and Lippet push a button with their thumbs on one another. This button was supposed to open the steam valve to the turbine on the other side of the factory. As they pressed the button, the turbine started and operations officially commenced. But the starting was really a fake. It was impractical to push a button to start the turbines from that far away, so it was arranged that several men would signal each other when the founders pushed the button, and the engineer at the end made sure to start the turbines at the same time. The founders were none the wiser.

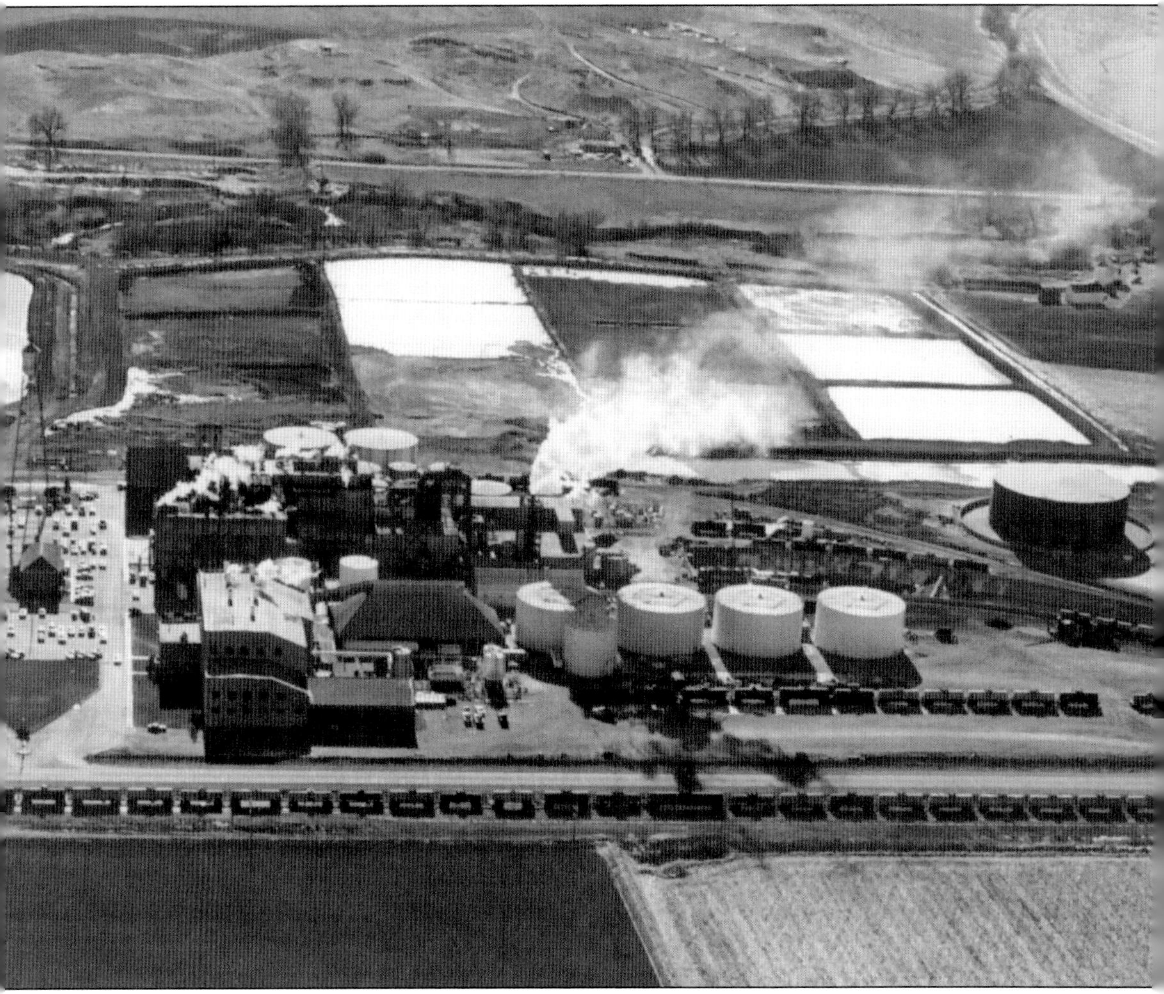

The Johnstown Sugar Factory had an impact not only on the immediate area, but also on the entire sugar beet industry. It was built as a one-of-a-kind refinery to extract sugar from molasses and was the only successful plant of its kind in the world. The round molasses tanks are shown in this photograph. Molasses was a necessary byproduct of refining beet sugar. It became such a drag on the market that the company was unable to even give the molasses away. Great Western was forced to build a molasses barium refinery. This process had been tried in several places in orthodox factories around the world with no economical success. After years of research and experimentation, the company felt they were ready to build a refinery that would be able to extract the large part of the sugar that was always remaining in beet molasses. The refinery was built in Johnstown. It was the only one of its kind in the world. (GHM.)

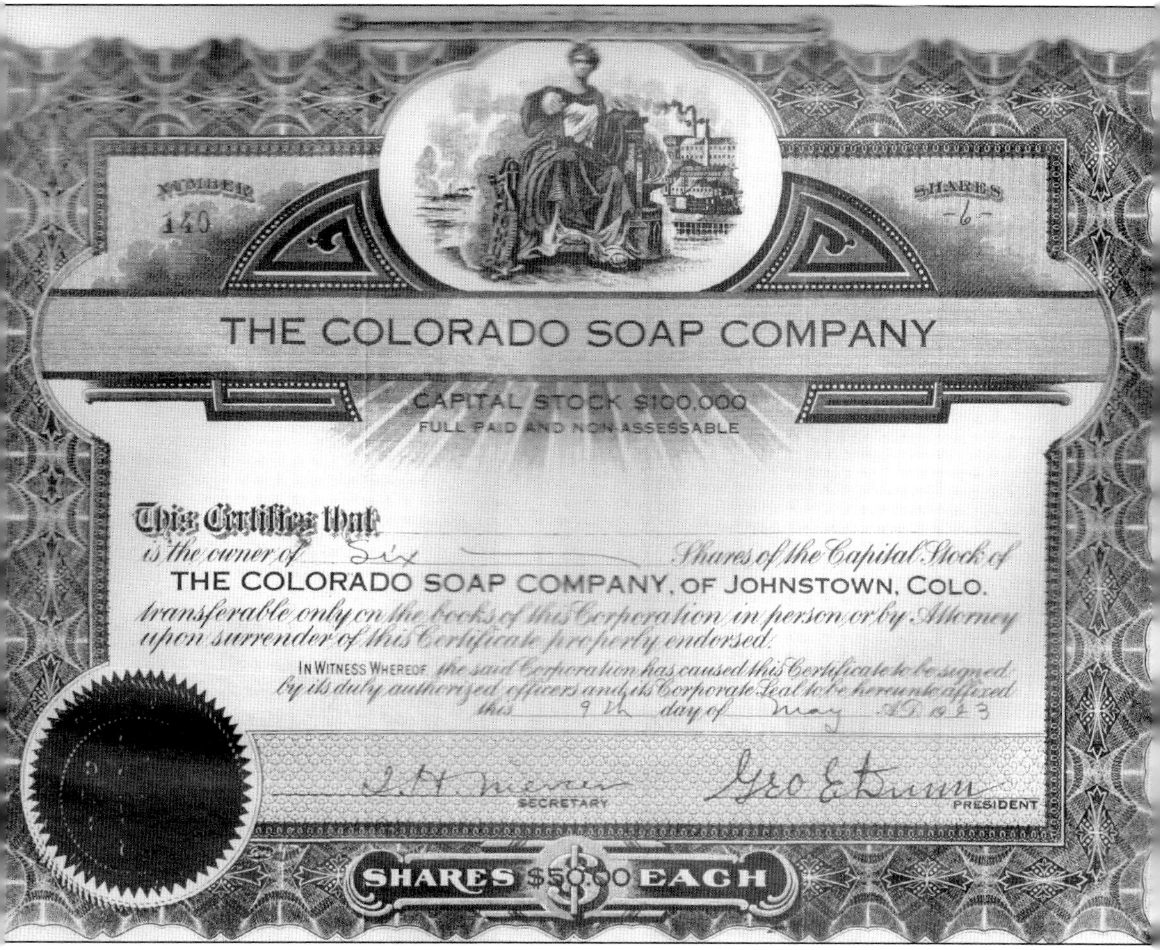
NUMBER 140

SHARES -6-

THE COLORADO SOAP COMPANY

CAPITAL STOCK $100,000

FULL PAID AND NON-ASSESSABLE

This Certifies that

is the owner of Six Shares of the Capital Stock of

THE COLORADO SOAP COMPANY, OF JOHNSTOWN, COLO.

transferable only on the books of this Corporation in person or by Attorney upon surrender of this Certificate properly endorsed.

IN WITNESS WHEREOF the said Corporation has caused this Certificate to be signed by its duly authorized officers and its Corporate Seal to be hereunto affixed this 9th day of May A.D. 1923

SECRETARY

Geo E Dunn PRESIDENT

SHARES $50.00 EACH

The October 12, 1922, issue of the *Johnstown Breeze* announced a new industry, the Colorado Soap Company, was moving to Johnstown. And indeed the factory did come, much to the painful memory of many who invested in the company. The over 7,000 feet of floor space in the factory provided room for the most modern, labor-saving machinery to mix and box the soap that was supposed to arrive soon. The factory promoters promised the Johnstown people a beautiful financial dream for a small investment. Many people jumped at the chance, and these stock certificates were issued. One night, however, the promoters left town, and the investors were left "holding the bag." They received no money and no soap. The promoters were never located and no money was ever returned.

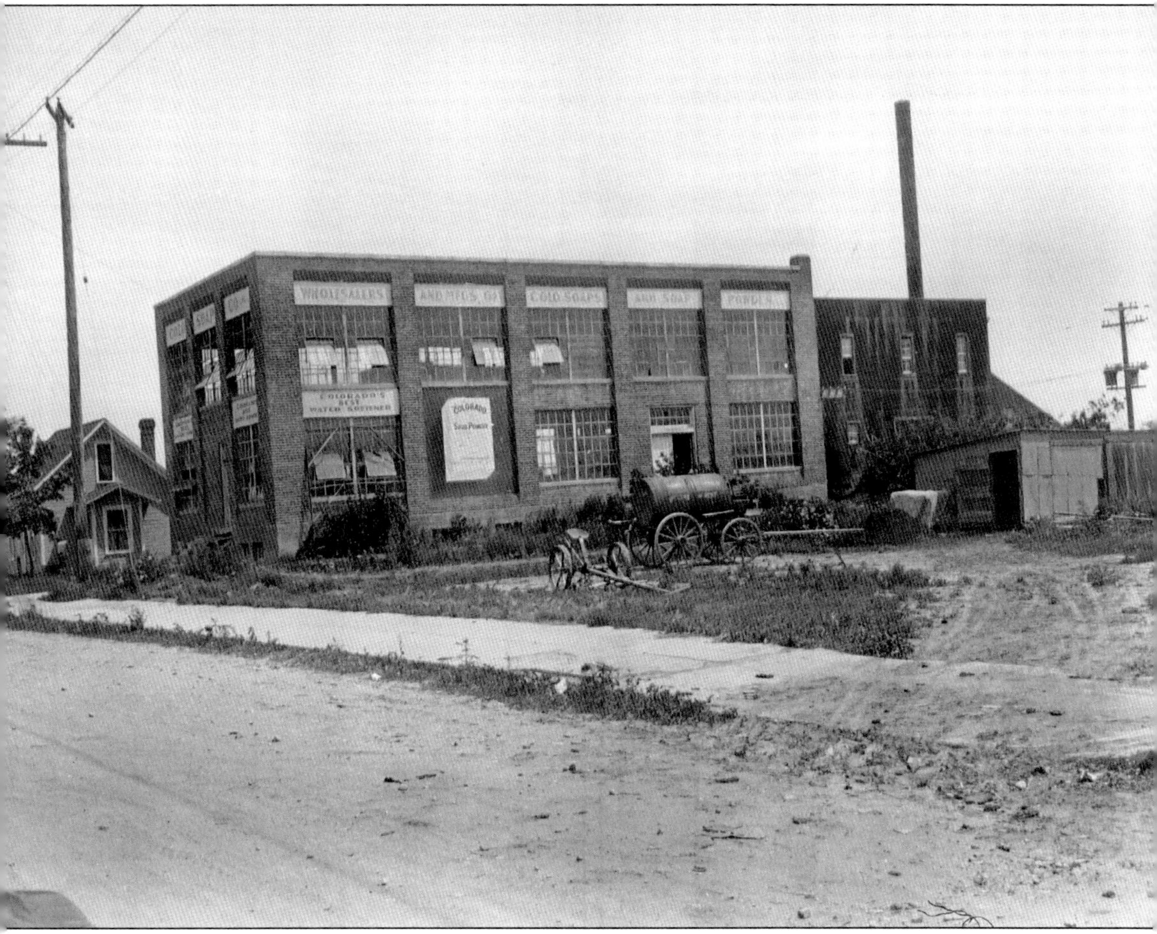

The Colorado Soap Factory building, located on North Parish Street, was the very latest in factory construction. It was conveniently arranged, well lighted, and steam heat was installed. The soap factory was a scam, but the building remained. In the late 1920s, a group of promoters from Denver took over the abandoned building. They made the necessary changes, brought in the required equipment, and started an operation to make denatured alcohol. Again it turned out to be just a promotion scheme. (DPL.)

Seven

Tidbits through Time

Although Johnstown shares much of the same history as other agricultural towns in Colorado, there are happenings in Johnstown that are unique to the area. This last chapter shows parts of Johnstown's history that would not be found in too many other places.

The 1920s may have been called the Roaring Twenties in Johnstown because of the natural disasters that occurred here. In that decade there were terrible snowstorms, a devastating tornado, and a meteorite that fell. Severe snowstorms do not occur as often as some might think. Tornadoes in this part of Colorado are very rare. The natural occurrence with the least probability, however, had to have been the meteorite of 1924. Scientists wanted to study this meteorite, in particular because it was retrieved immediately and was not contaminated. The biggest piece of the meteorite, a chunk weighing 37.47 pounds, is in the American Museum of Natural History in New York City. The Denver Museum has the next largest piece weighing 11.46 pounds.

Although nearly every town in Colorado had a baseball team in the early 1900s, none was like the Johnstown Juds. The Juds took their name from their manager, coach, and sponsor, Jud Martin, who adopted the team in the 1930s.

Another popular man in the 1930s was Verne Elliott. His bucking broncos provided entertainment for years at many rodeos in the area and throughout the world. He was inducted into the National Rodeo Hall of Fame, along with one of his most famous horses, Midnight.

When World War II started, many of Johnstown's finest signed up to serve their country. At home, area farmers took advantage of the labor in the fields from the nearby German prisoner of war camp.

The last part of the book is devoted to a connection from the past to the present. The Historic Parish House and Museum is featured.

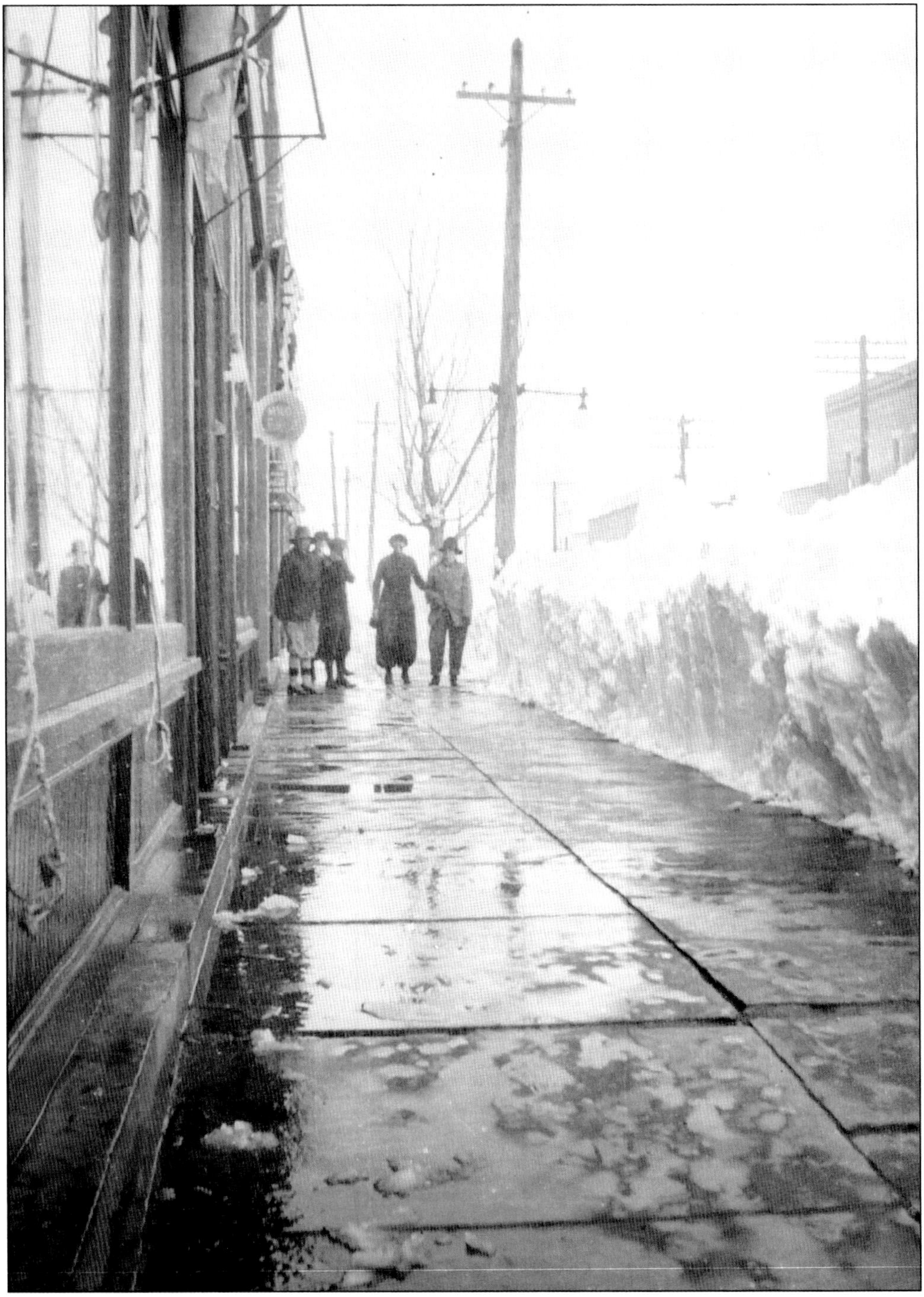

Snowstorms in Colorado were welcomed and hated at the same time. They were welcomed because of the much needed moisture. The snowstorm pictured here came in mid-April 1920. There was 2.85 inches of moisture, making the total precipitation for the month of April well over 4 inches. The value of the storm was especially appreciated because the total precipitation in Greeley for the entire year of 1919 was less than 9 inches.

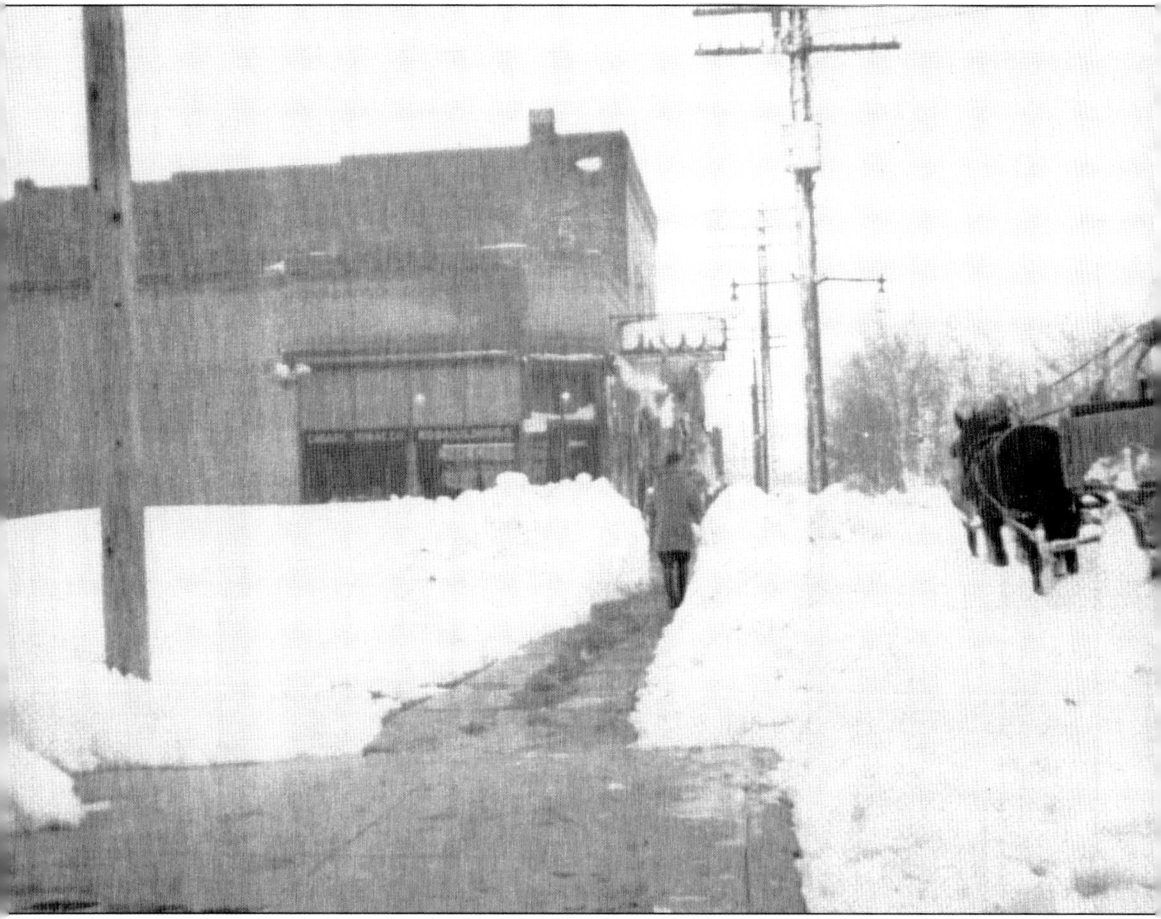

In this photograph, the walkway was cleared to the drugstore on the southeast corner of Charlotte Street and Parish Avenue, but the horses had to make a path of their own. The spring snowstorm of 1920 caused big damage to the area, and livestock was lost. A peculiar incident of the storm was related in connection with several colts that one farmer had turned out near some wagons. During the snowstorm, these colts disappeared, and the farmer searched for them for two days afterward. Finally he gave up and decided that the colts had climbed the drifts near the fences and taken off into the hills. Shortly after giving up, however, he heard a slight noise, and he saw something move beneath a cluster of wagons and machinery. He found all the colts down among this equipment, completely snowed under. They had taken refuge there and had found enough air space beneath the wagon to stay alive.

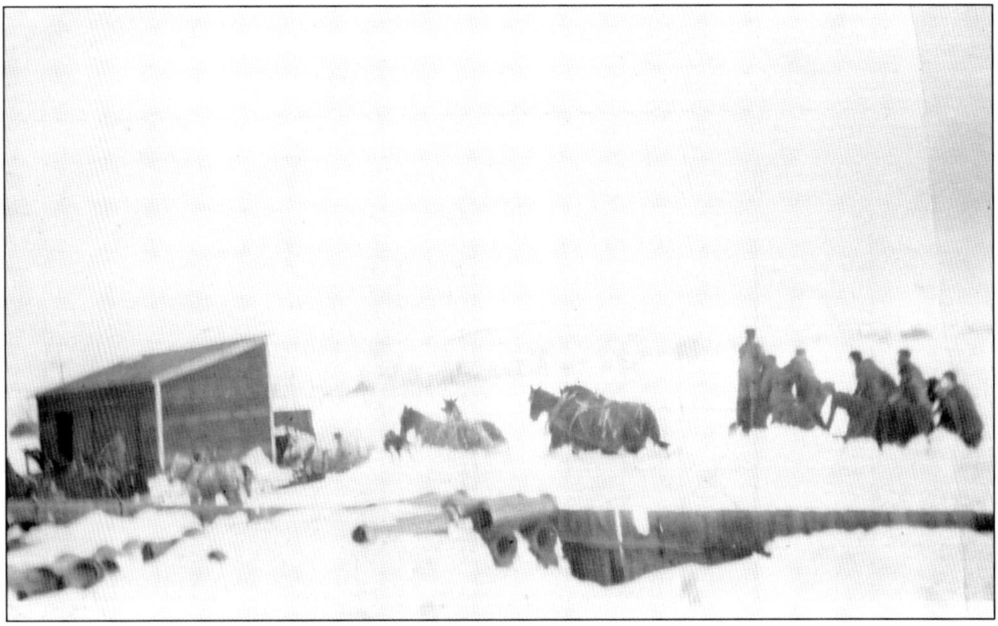

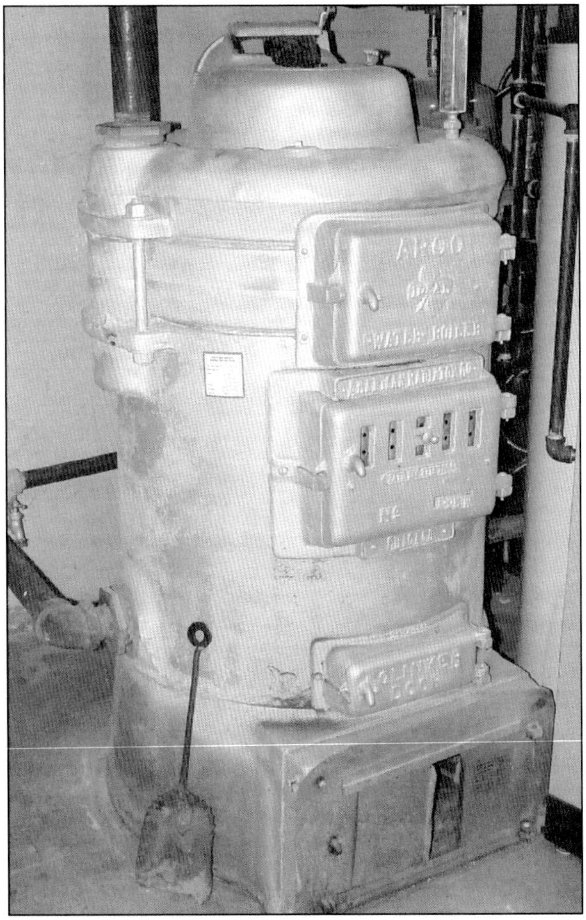

The town of Johnstown was paralyzed by the 1920 snowstorm. There were no mechanical means of clearing the roads, so the town depended on horse power. It was a common sight to see horses pulling automobiles out of snowdrifts and forging a path through places where roads did not exist. People were brought together with a single common purpose. In the first photograph, people are helping one another break through the snow to Peter Mintner's coal bin. The second photograph shows a coal furnace that is displayed in the Historic Parish House and Museum. Coal was first mined commercially in Weld County in 1872, and the county continued to rank high among coal-producing areas in the state until natural gas became the favorite domestic fuel.

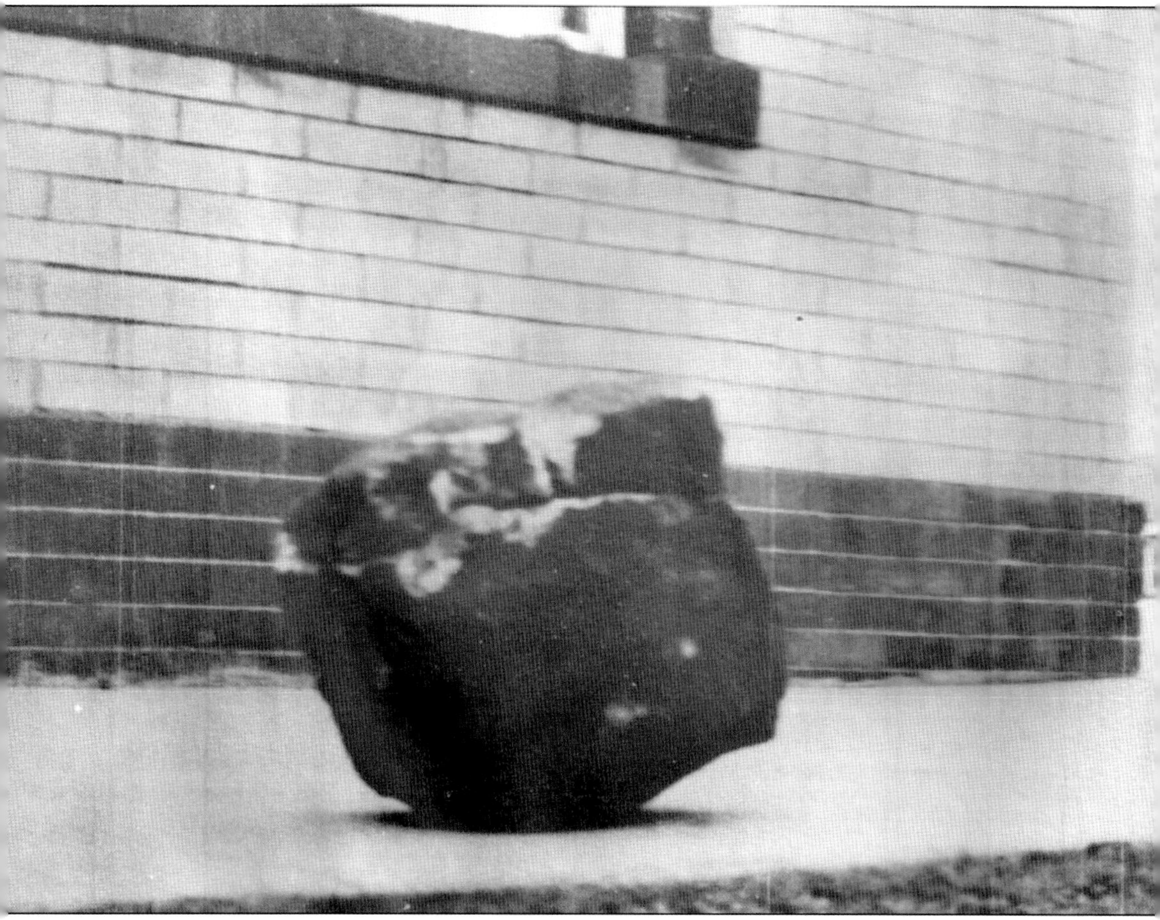

On a warm, clear day in the afternoon of July 6, 1924, a meteor fell to the earth. About 200 mourners were gathered in front of Dilley Chapel in Elwell for the service of John Moore at the time. There was a burst of sound, reportedly like the roaring of a jet engine today. Everyone's attention was drawn to a number of fireballs with smoke trails streaking across the sky. These were closely followed by four loud explosions. The explosions are now known to have resulted from the larger pieces of the meteor exceeding the speed of sound and creating sonic booms in the process. Henry Clingenpeel, the Johnstown undertaker who was directing the funeral, dug up the meteorite immediately with the shovel used at the gravesite. The meteorite was almost the size of a man's head, burned black on the outside. Inside lime-green crystals of pyroxene could be seen. Some 27 stones were recovered, the largest weighing 37.47 pounds.

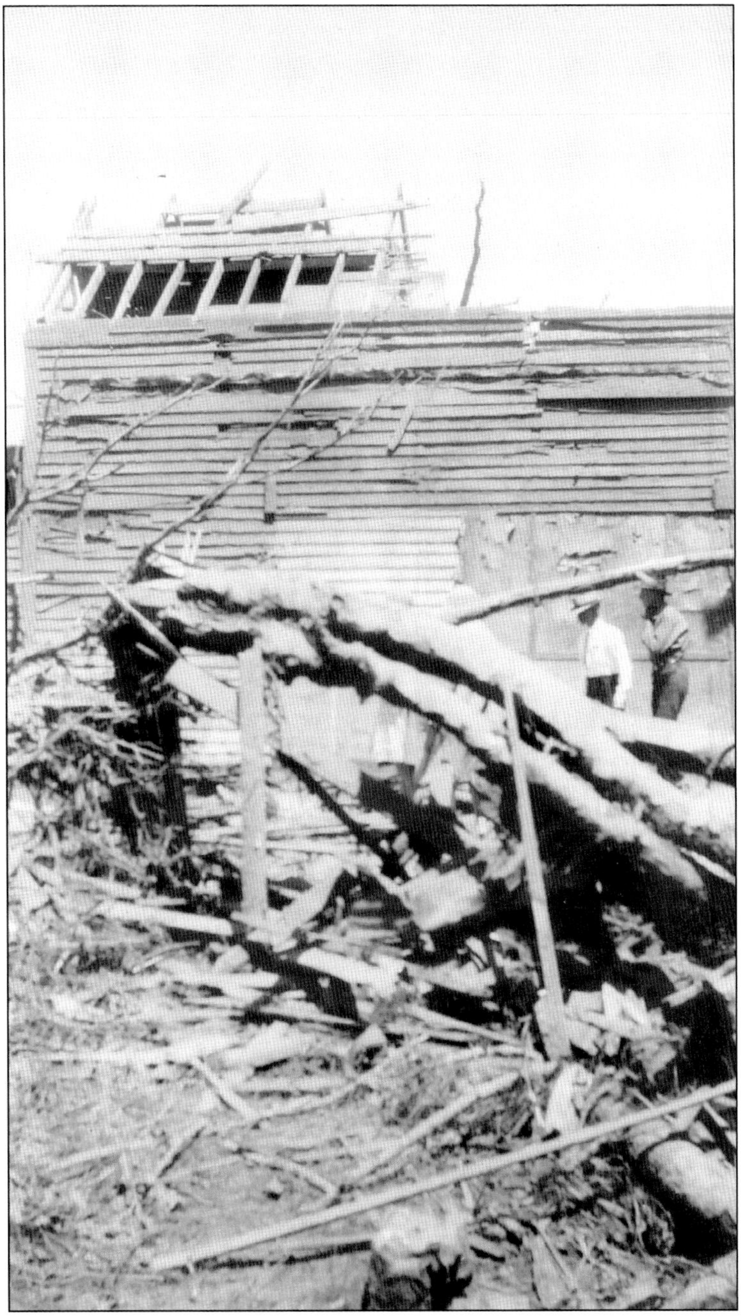

Black clouds began creeping in from the southwest about 11:00 a.m. on June 29, 1928, a hot, early summer day. The tornado hit about 12:00 p.m. Approximately 25 minutes later, the twister had injured several people and caused $100,000 worth of damage to buildings, equipment, and crops over 10 square miles of prime farmland west of Johnstown. The tornado initially touched down 4 miles south and 2.5 miles west of town, moving northeast. When it came to the Anderson home, Marie crouched against a wall in the kitchen and shielded her two children from the fury of the storm. When the storm had passed, it was discovered that although uninjured herself, she had held the weight of a wall and several pounds of debris on her back, and had saved her children as well.

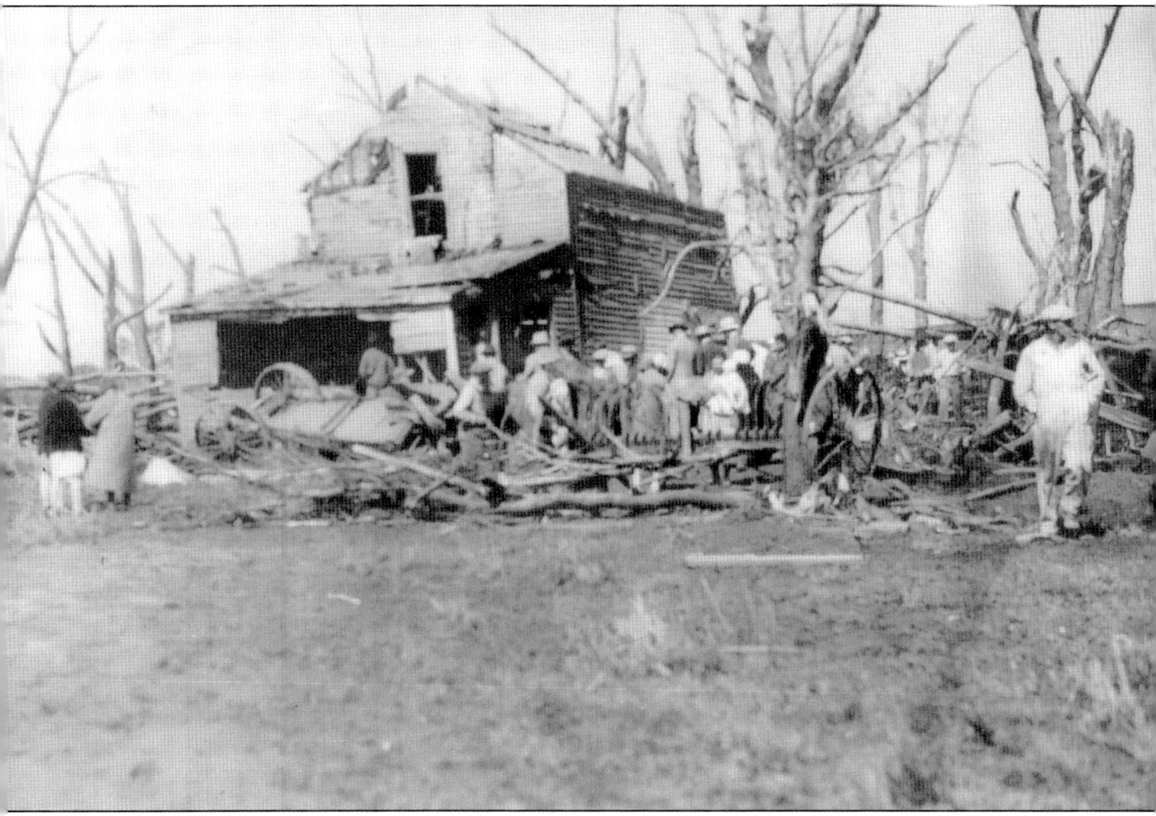

The McLaughlin farm was destroyed by the tornado, and Susie McLaughlin was killed. She and three others had gone into a clothes closet to shield themselves. Susie McLaughlin died of injuries received when a large tree limb, driven through the wall of the closet, punctured her left side. She suffered four fractured ribs and a ruptured kidney and spleen. Wayne Becker was at the McLaughlin farm and did not reach the house in time to escape the tornado. He crawled into an open cellar. He was badly frightened when a horse was blown in after him and was wedged in the cellar door. He was later able to crawl through the opening.

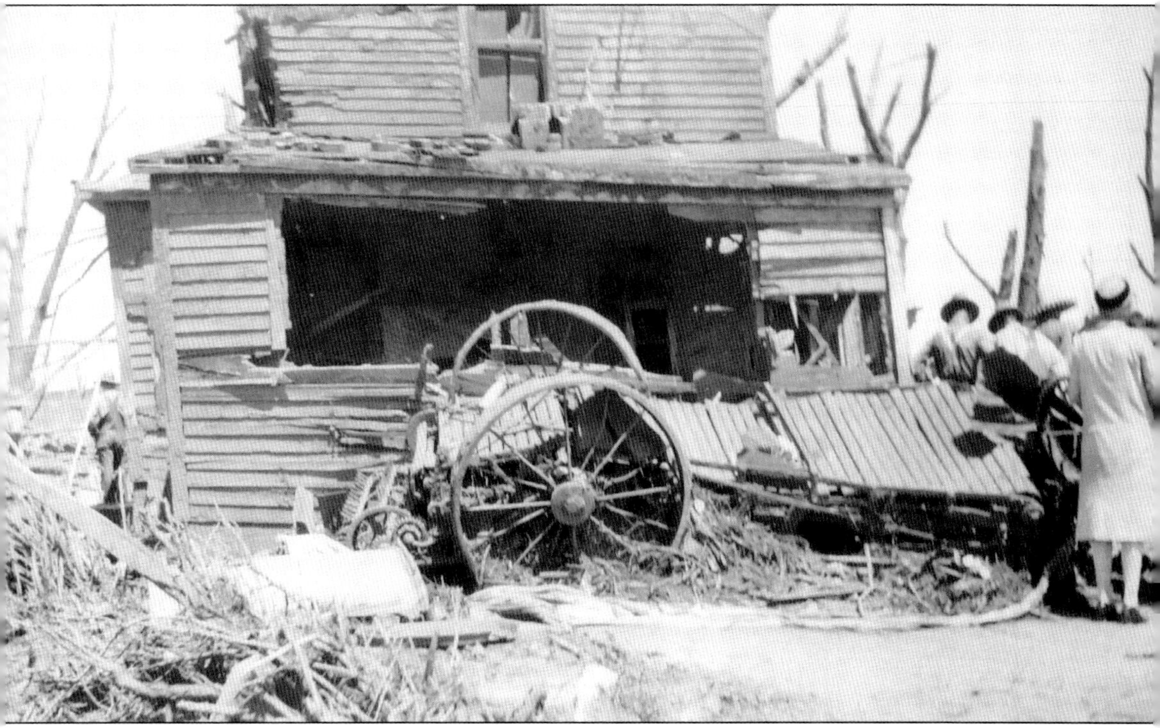

Adelina Montez, 17 years old, lived in a little cabin between the McLaughlin house and the river. Her home was blown from its foundation and into the Little Thompson River. Montez was either killed outright or was drowned. Her body was found floating amid splintered timber in the river. The third person killed by the storm was C. P. Johnston, age 50, who was seeking shelter under a bridge when a piece of timber pierced his hip. He died the day after the tornado in a Longmont Hospital. His death was attributed to the injury and loss of blood.

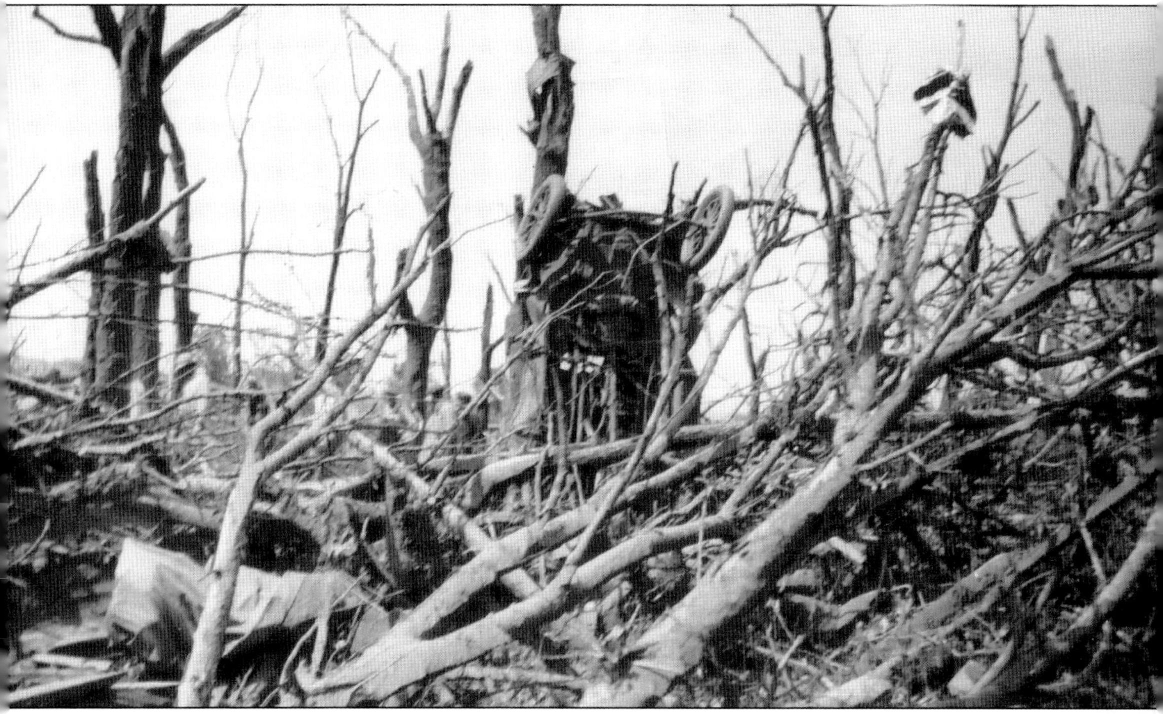

The funnel pulled apart and the tornado disappeared 20 minutes after it had begun. A large hailstorm that followed the twister also caused damage and injury. Although the tornado left much misery in its wake, it also left freak effects in its path. Chickens were plucked clean but not killed. Straws and pitchforks were driven into trees. Five children were huddled on the floor at the Ernest Hardesty home after the tornado lifted the roof off the house. Mrs. Hardesty and the baby she held in her arms were carried about 50 yards and dropped. All were unharmed. At the Sid Gray home, eight horses were tied in the barn when the storm struck. The barn was demolished, but the horses were found 200 yards away, still tied to the hitch rails of the stalls.

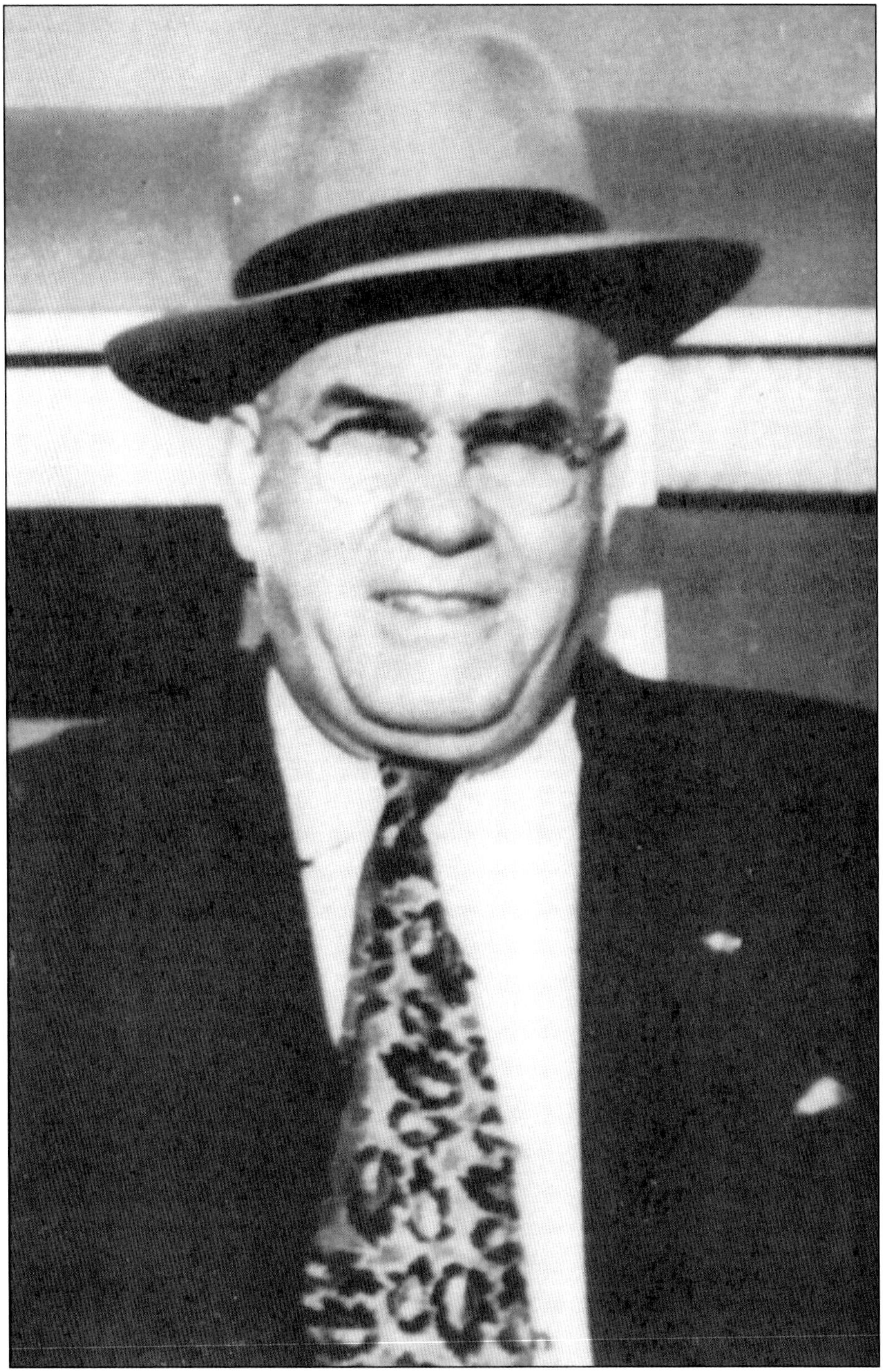

George Oliver "Jud" Martin came to Johnstown in 1920 and soon purchased and operated a pool hall. In 1928, he sold the pool hall and opened a confectionery and clothing store. Jud was a veteran of World War I, mayor of Johnstown for 12 years, and active in many community affairs. He never married nor had children of his own, so he "adopted" the town. Jud's place was popular with everyone, adults and children alike.

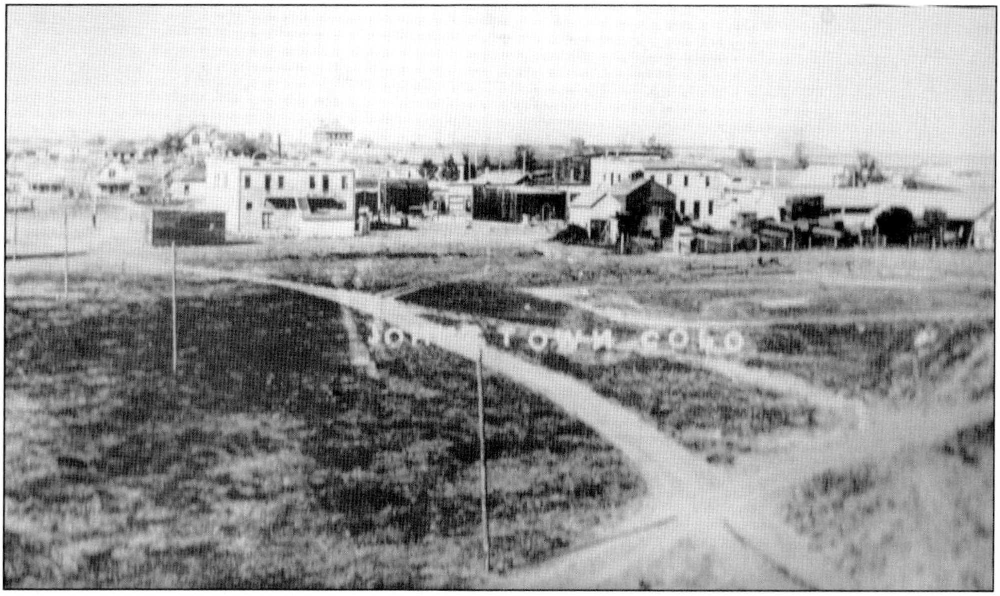

Baseball was firmly established as America's favorite pastime at the beginning of the 20th century. Nearly every town had a baseball team, including Johnstown. The baseball diamond in the foreground of this early photograph shows the popularity of baseball in Johnstown even then. Jud Martin was instrumental in the development of the first "real" baseball field in the 1930s. Colorado Central Power Company donated and installed poles and reflectors, so for the first time, the public could watch baseball games under the lights. The Juds softball team, shown below, was recognized wherever they went. They participated in town, city, district, state, and national leagues. They won state titles in 1938, 1950, and 1952.

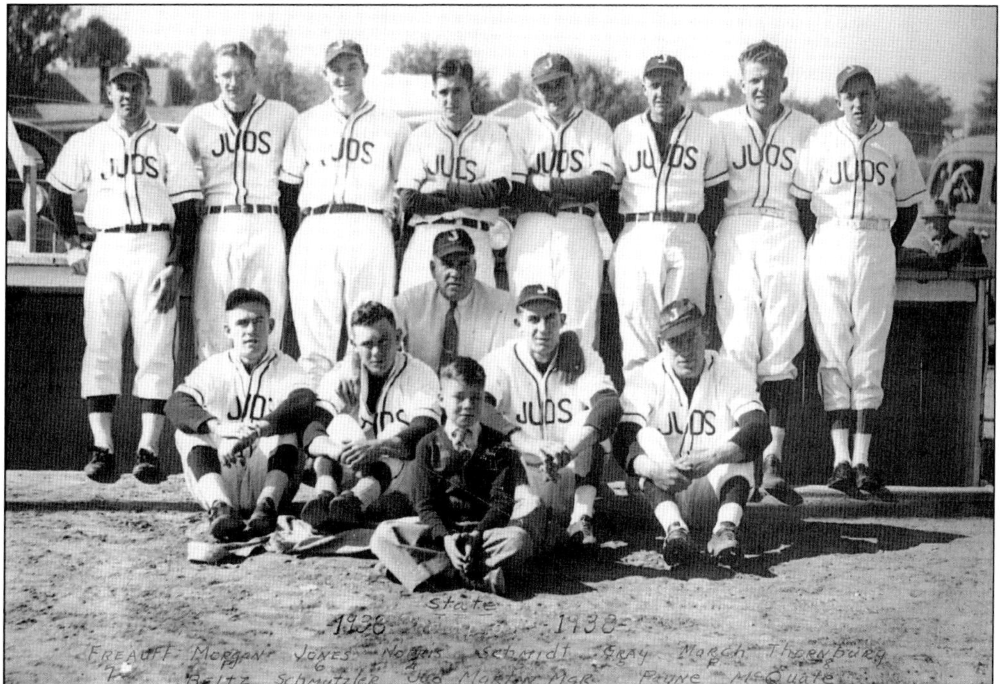

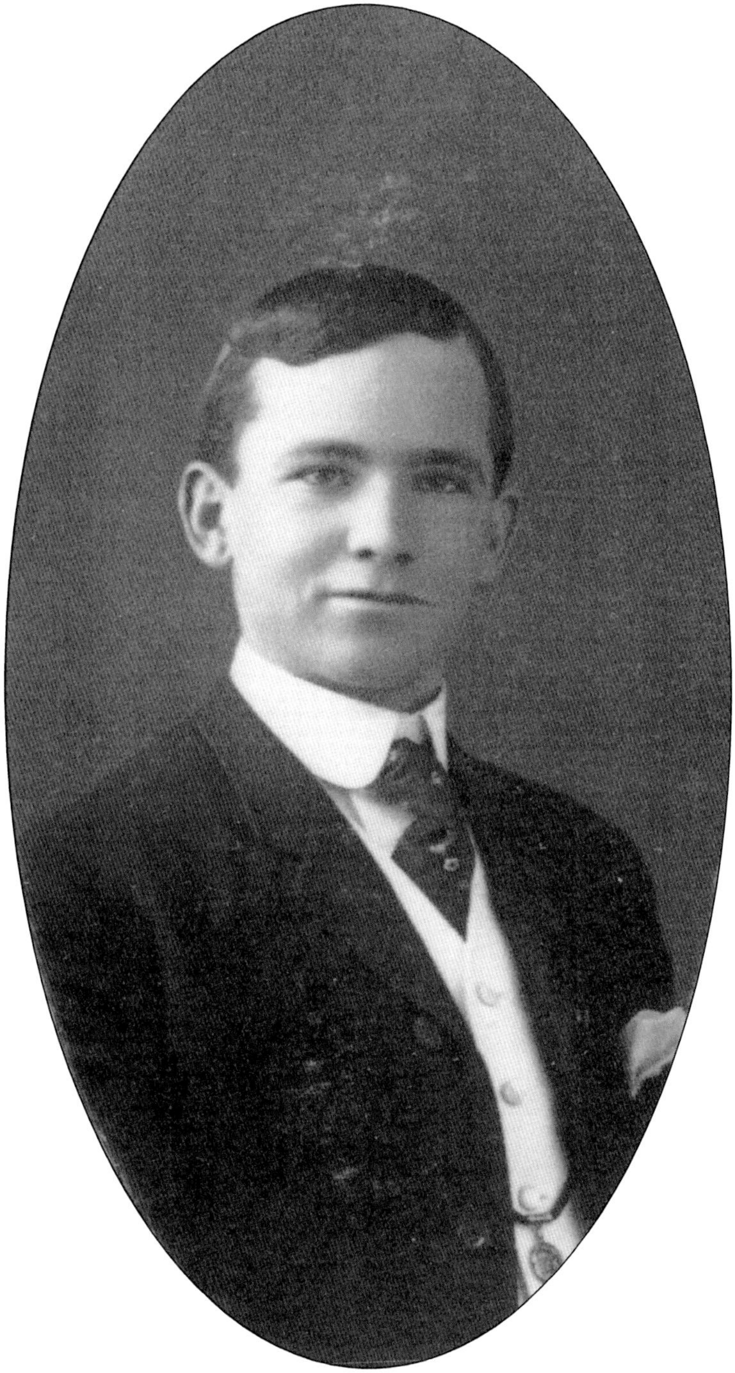

Verne Elliott was born on July 1, 1890, on the ranch between Johnstown and Platteville. The ranch, which was homesteaded by his grandfather, John Carl Elliott, began when John failed as a gold miner in 1859. It was said that John scrounged out a bag of gold dust and started back for his family in Illinois. He thought he could use the gold as money, but nobody would accept it. They thought it could be just brass filings, not gold. He walked all the way to St. Louis, where he finally found a buyer for his gold and was able to bring his family west. (GHM.)

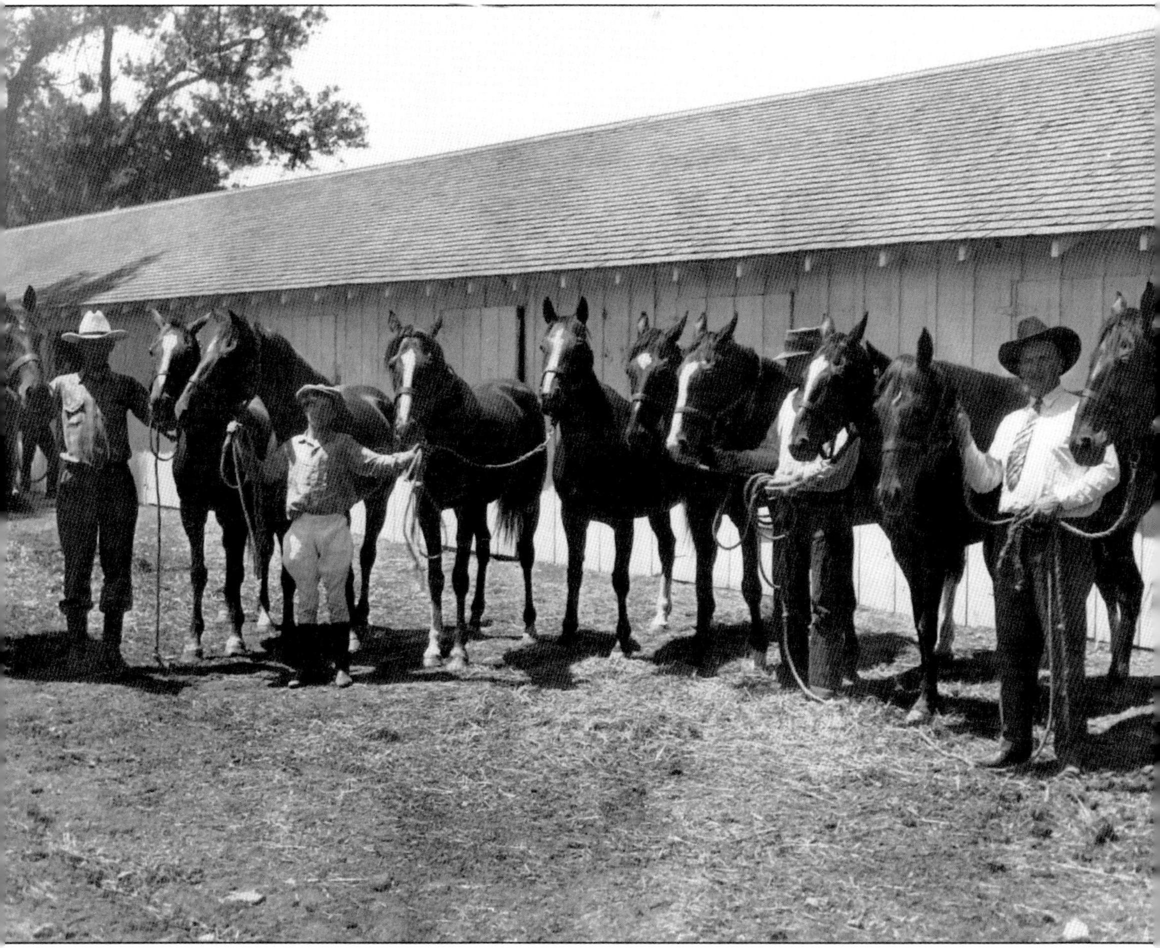

Verne Elliott had much to do with the development of rodeo. Inducted into the Professional Rodeo Hall of Fame in 1990, he produced or coproduced all of the top rodeos in the history of rodeo. At the peak of his career, he had a string of 500 horses and cattle. This photograph shows Elliott, on the right, with his racing stable for the pony express ride that was held at the Denver rodeo. One of his chief contributions to the sport became Brahma bullriding. He was also credited with creating many of rodeo's most colorful features, such as the mounted grand entry of flag-bearing contestants.

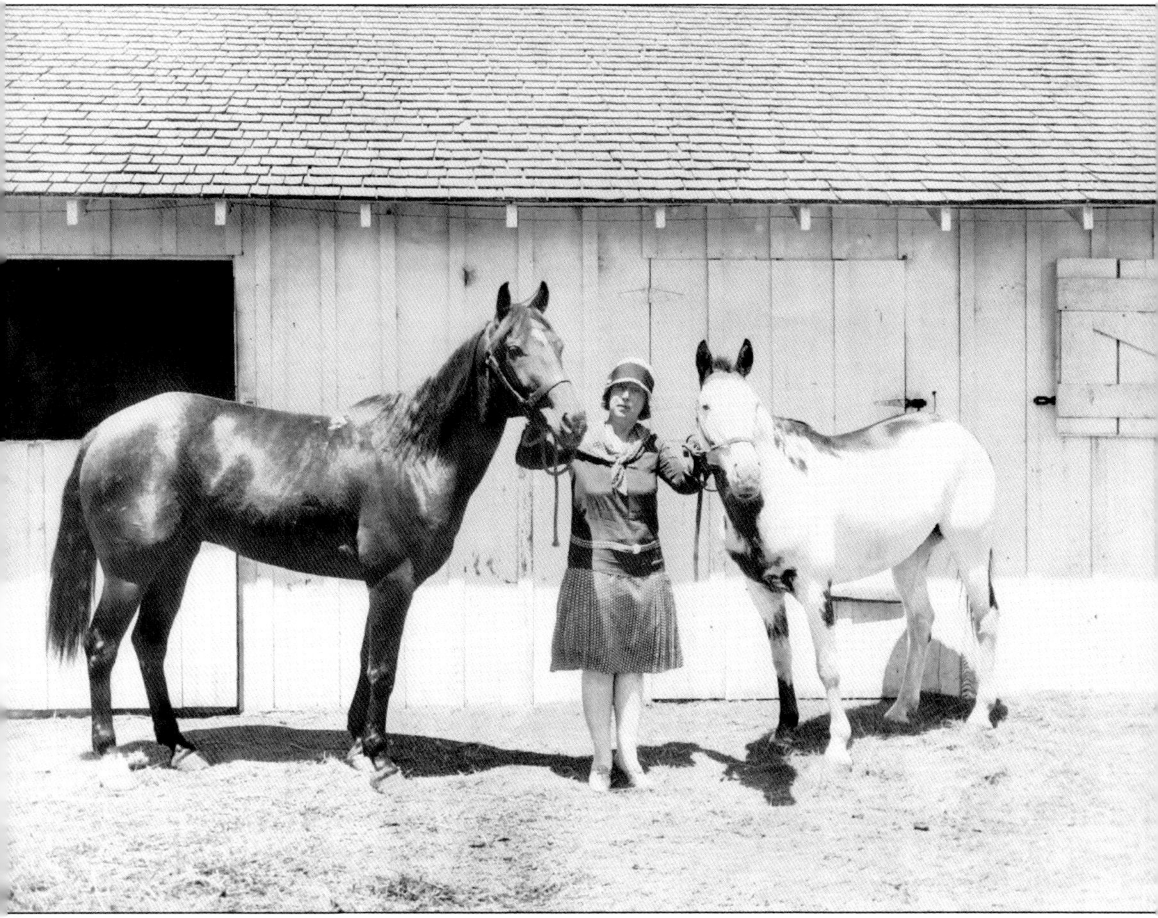

In this photograph, Verne Elliott's daughter Greta is shown with Broken Box, on the right, and perhaps the most famous bucking horse in the history of rodeo, Midnight, on the left. When Midnight died at the age of 26, nobody was reported to have ever ridden him. Verne Elliott helped to make Midnight into a legend. Elliott toured the United States and Europe with Midnight, hailing him as "the horse that can't be ridden." Elliott stated that a cowboy had to stay aboard the bronco for 10 seconds to qualify as a ride. The longest any rider stayed atop Midnight was seven seconds, and it must have seemed like seven years. In 1934, Midnight was bucked before King George V of England in a command performance.

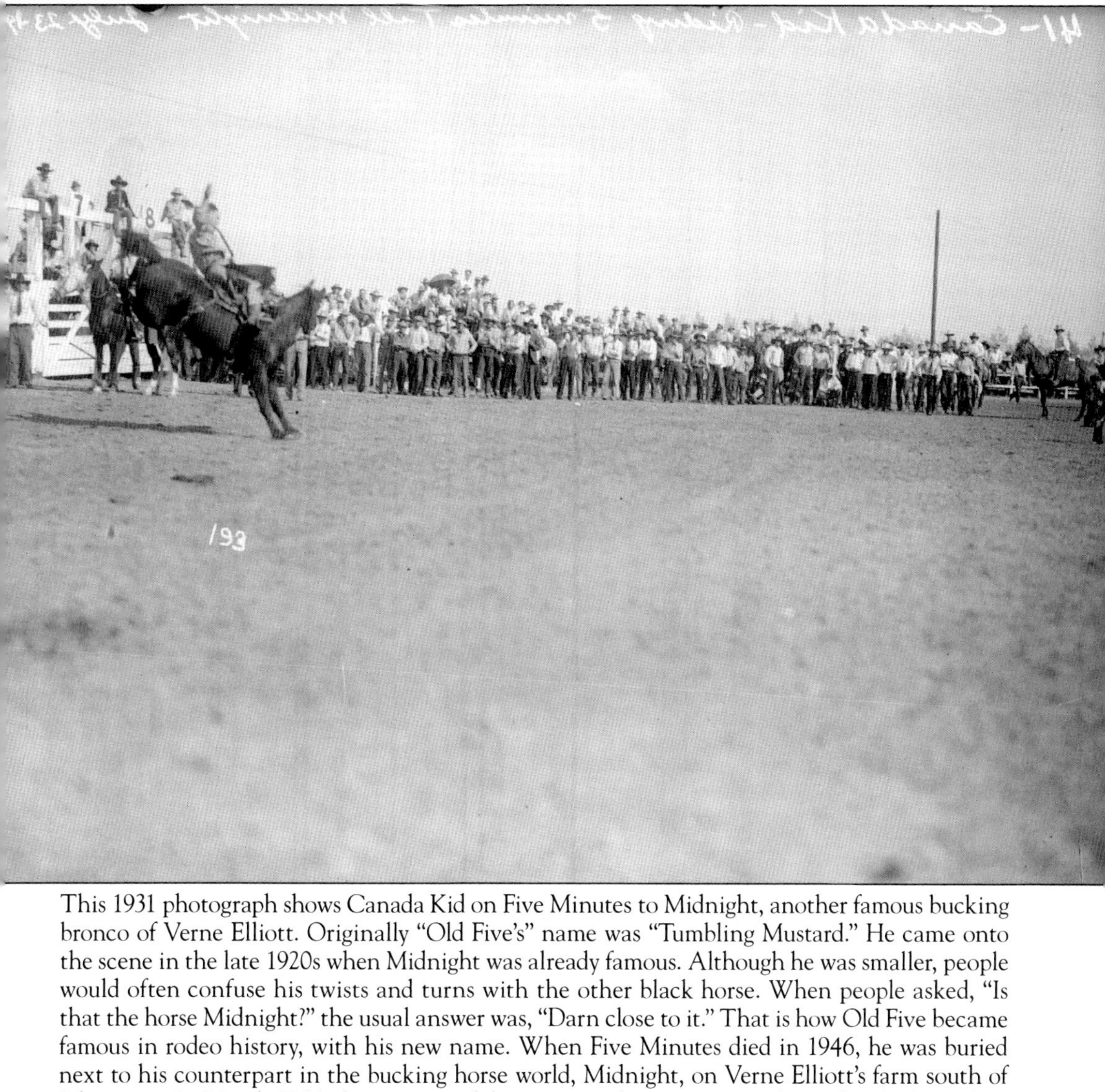

This 1931 photograph shows Canada Kid on Five Minutes to Midnight, another famous bucking bronco of Verne Elliott. Originally "Old Five's" name was "Tumbling Mustard." He came onto the scene in the late 1920s when Midnight was already famous. Although he was smaller, people would often confuse his twists and turns with the other black horse. When people asked, "Is that the horse Midnight?" the usual answer was, "Darn close to it." That is how Old Five became famous in rodeo history, with his new name. When Five Minutes died in 1946, he was buried next to his counterpart in the bucking horse world, Midnight, on Verne Elliott's farm south of Johnstown. In March 1966, the remains of the two great broncos were exhumed and reburied on the grounds of the National Cowboy Hall of Fame in Oklahoma City. (DPL.)

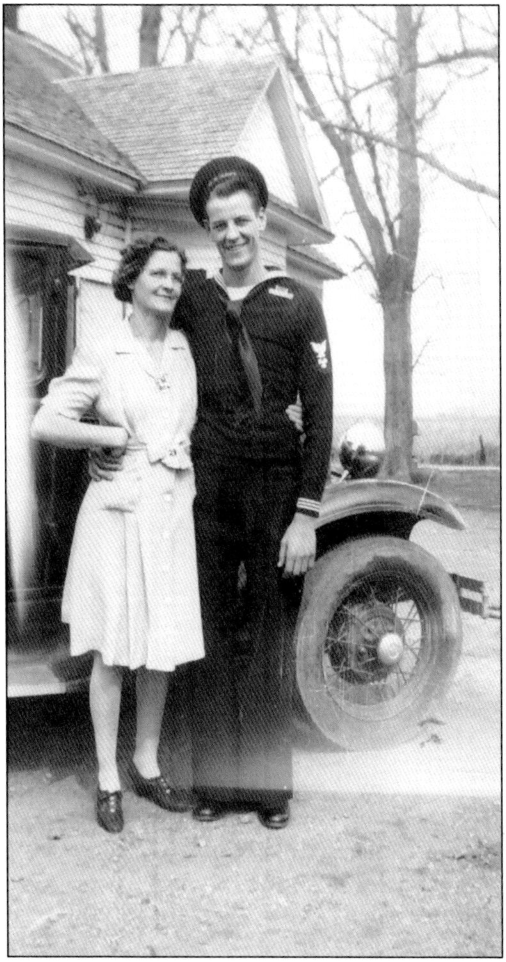

When the Japanese attacked Pearl Harbor on December 7, 1941, young men of Johnstown answered the call to serve their country. James Wailes is shown at left with his mother Irene. He joined the U.S. Navy shortly after his 18th birthday in 1943. The family had moved to Johnstown shortly before Jim's senior year in high school. He had not adjusted well. When Jim's report card came out in January, his grades were not good. When Jim told his father that he thought he might join the navy, his dad replied, "Well, with grades like these, you might as well." He served on the aircraft carrier *Saratoga*, and received his GED in the service. Calvin Schwalm is shown below in his army uniform getting ready to go to war.

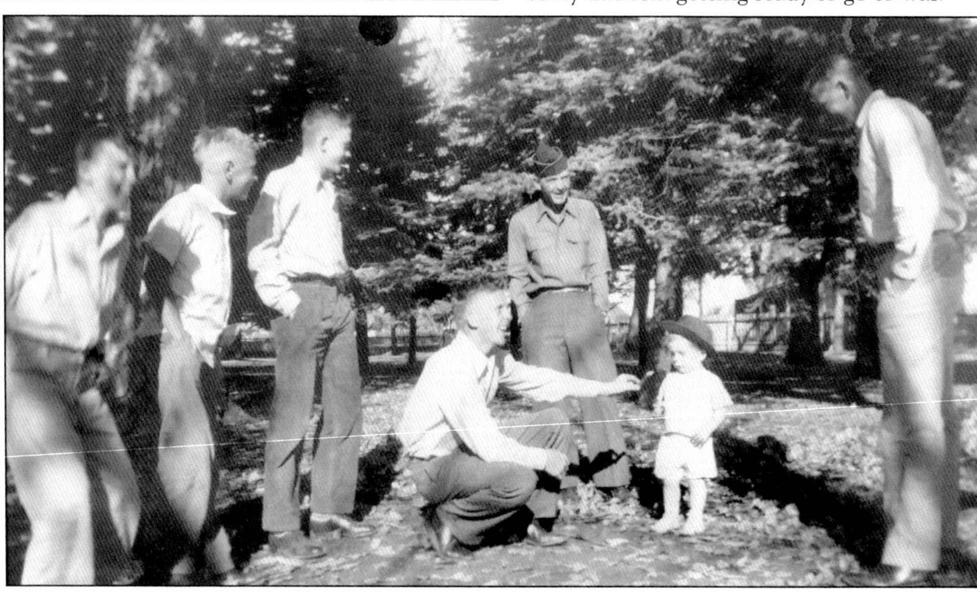

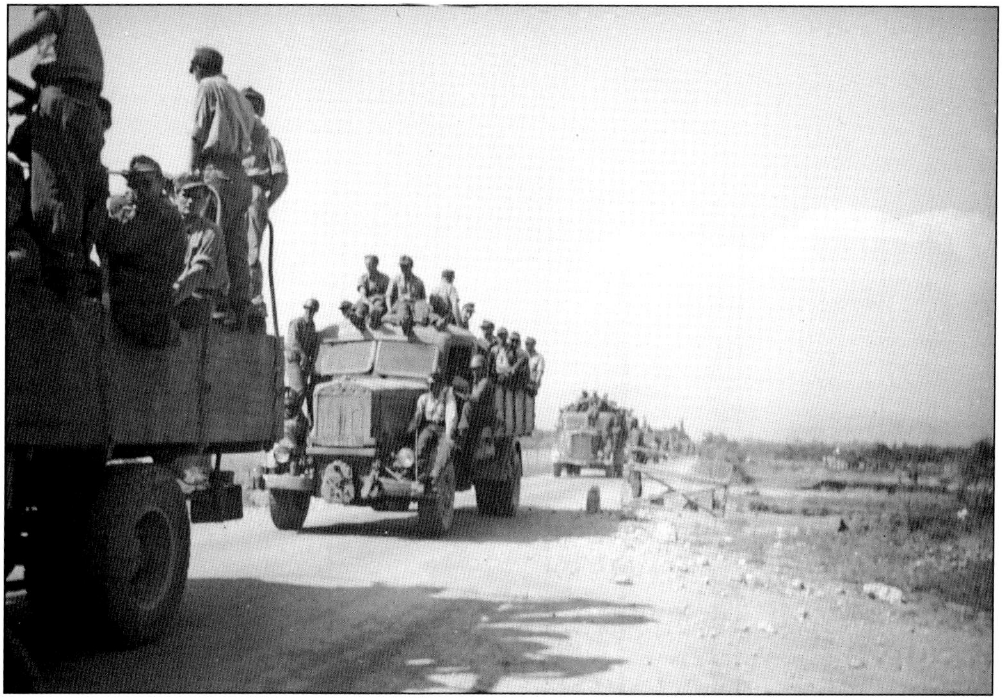

In the above photograph, members of the 10th Mountain Division of Colorado escort German prisoners of war in Italy during the Italian campaign of World War II. Some of these prisoners may have been transported to the German prisoner of war camp near Johnstown. The camp was constructed with a total capacity of 3,000 men. Prisoners were transported from the railroad to the camp by truck. The route for the trucks passed over about half a mile of U.S. Highway 34. While the trucks were on the state highway, traffic was halted both east and west of the camp so that no traffic passed the trucks filled with prisoners. (Above, DPL; below, GHM.)

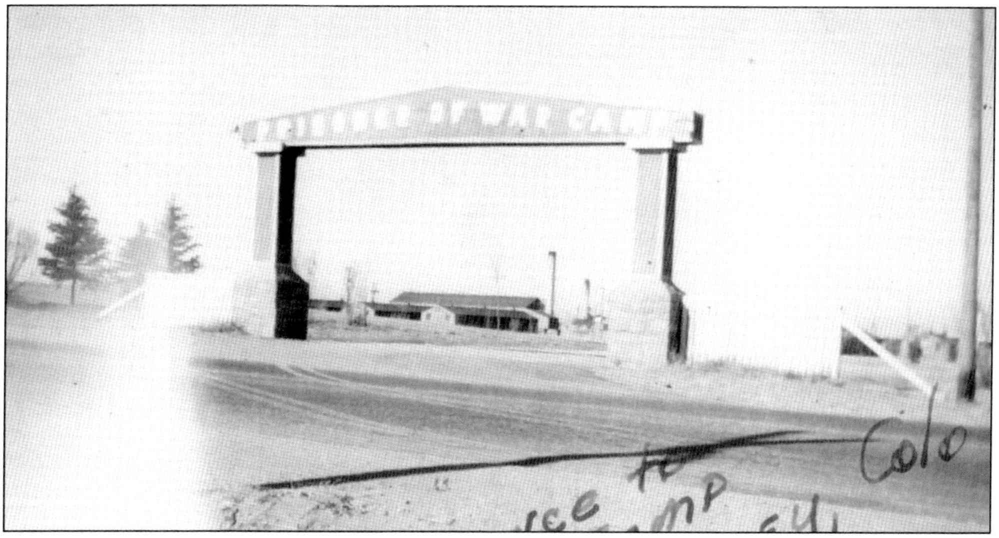

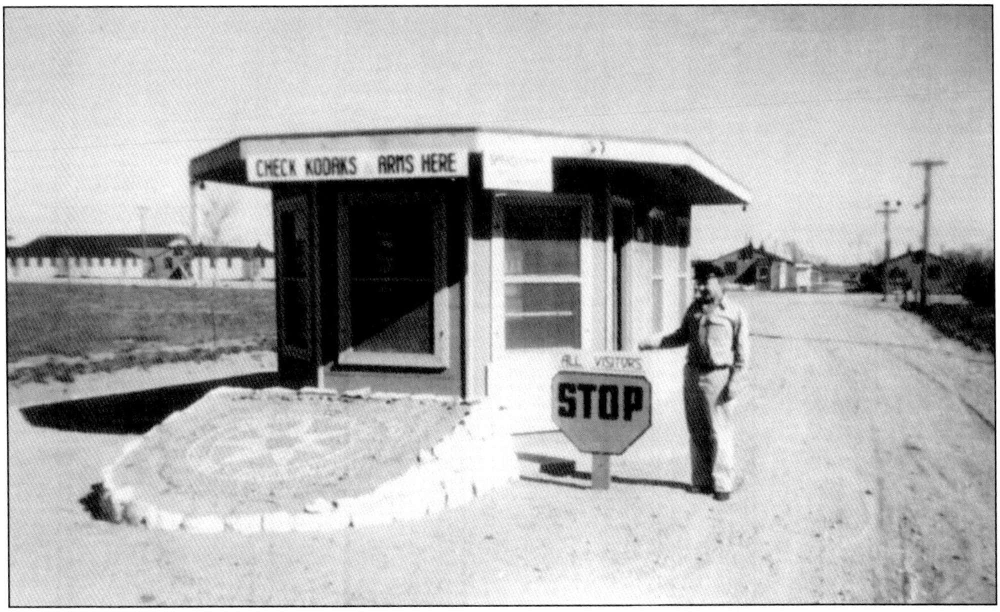

Above, a guard stands at the entrance of the prisoner of war camp on U.S. Highway 34, north of Johnstown. Interestingly enough, the request to leave Kodaks behind had a special meaning when years later, the Kodak Company built a plant a short distance away. Below, barbed wire fences can be seen. Most often escapes were not successful. Most of the men who tried to escape said that they just wanted to get away from confinement or being under guard for a little while to get the feeling of being free. None of them expressed any hope of reaching the coast or Mexico. (GHM.)

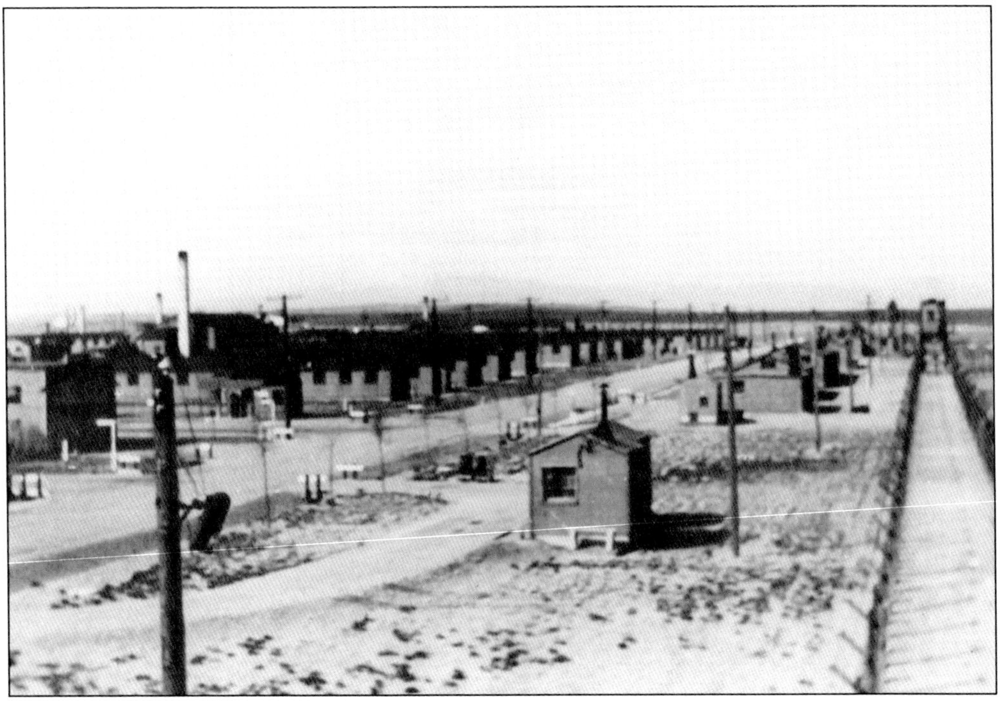

Because of the labor shortage due to many young American men serving in the war, labor camps were set up throughout northern Colorado. Some of the prisoners from POW Camp 202 were housed in the Great Western warehouse in downtown Johnstown. (GHM.)

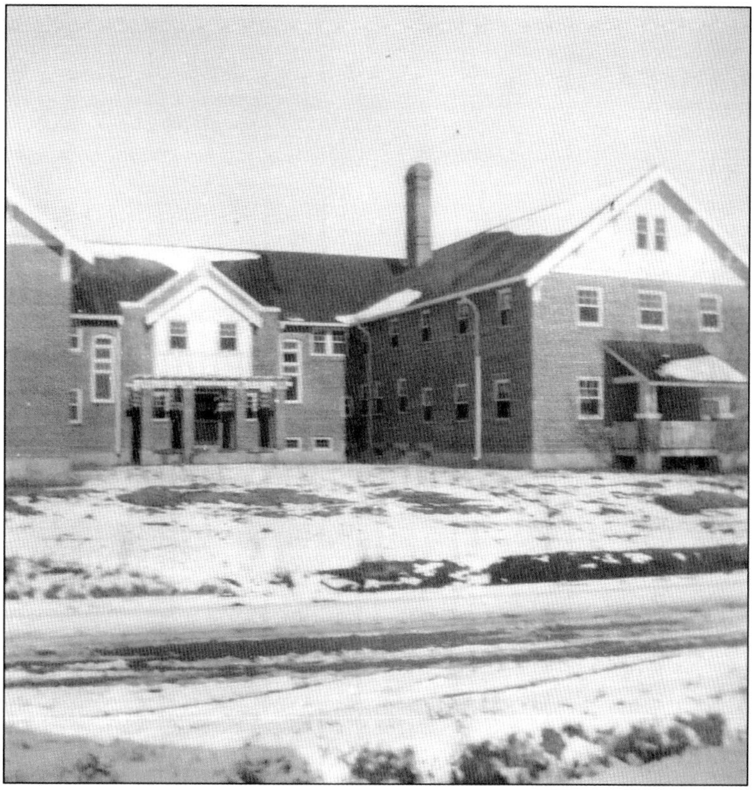

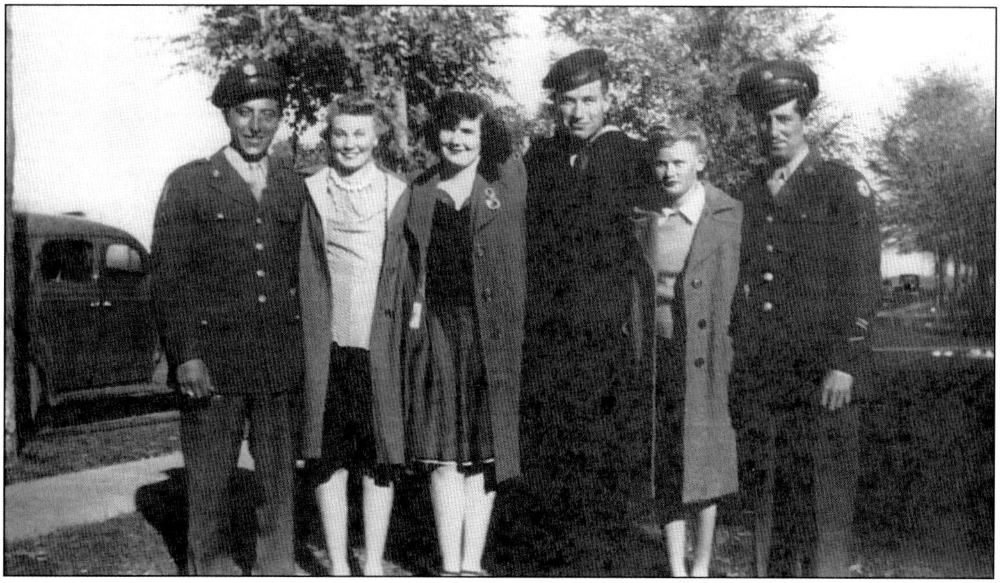

Most days, farmers picked up the prisoners in a truck and took them to work in the sugar beet fields. The men serving as guards at the side camp got acquainted with the local girls. One Italian guard named Tony, shown on the left of this photograph, fixed real Italian spaghetti at Elizabeth Teal's house, right across the street from the camp. Elizabeth returned the favor by cooking meals and bringing them to the guards when they were off duty.

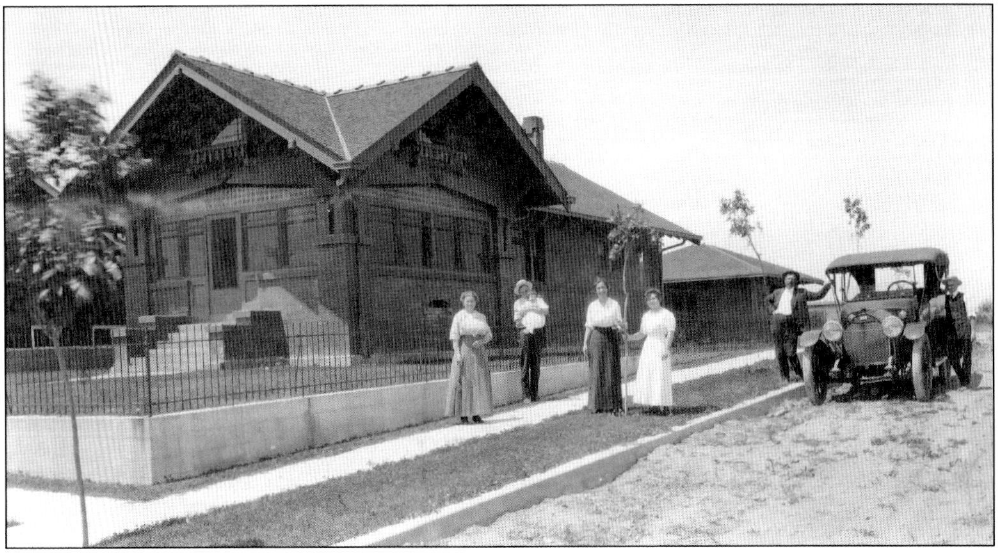

The house shown here was the last family home that Harvey and Mary Parish built. The Craftsman-style house was built in 1914 for $3,750. By this time, the children of the Parish family were all grown. Although Harvey died a few years later in 1923, the house remained in the family until the 1940s. The Johnstown Historical Society and the Town of Johnstown bought the home in 1998 and began a cooperative effort to create a museum. The museum is furnished with antiques to depict a home of the early 20th century, as well as displays to celebrate the history of Johnstown.

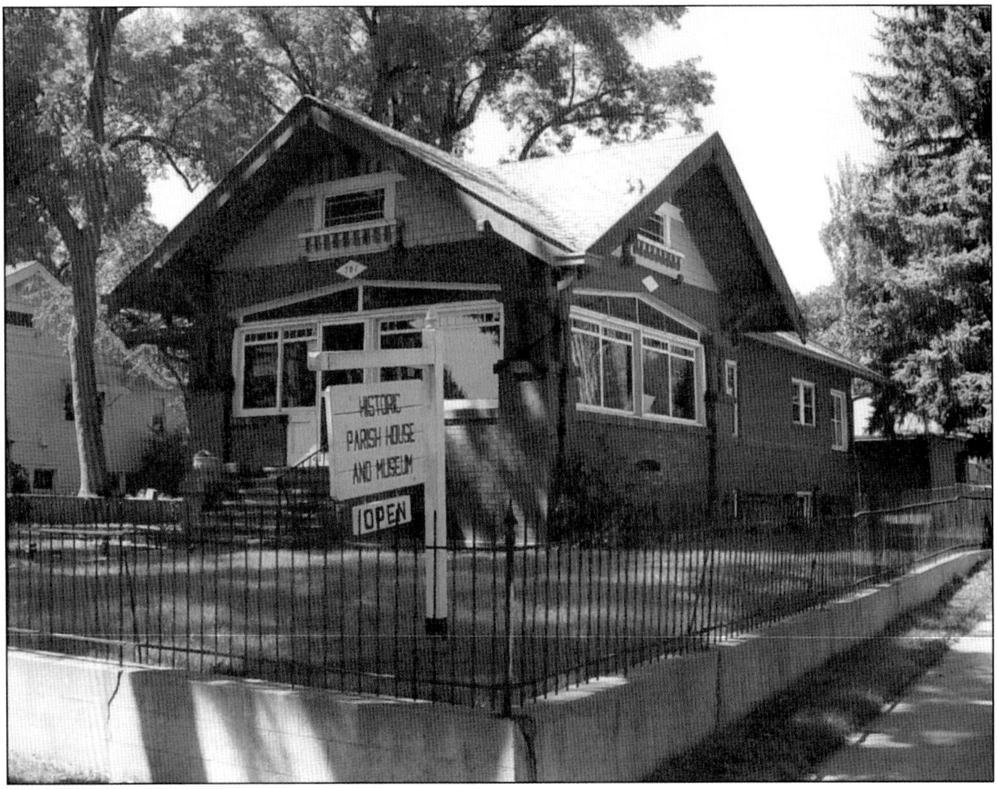

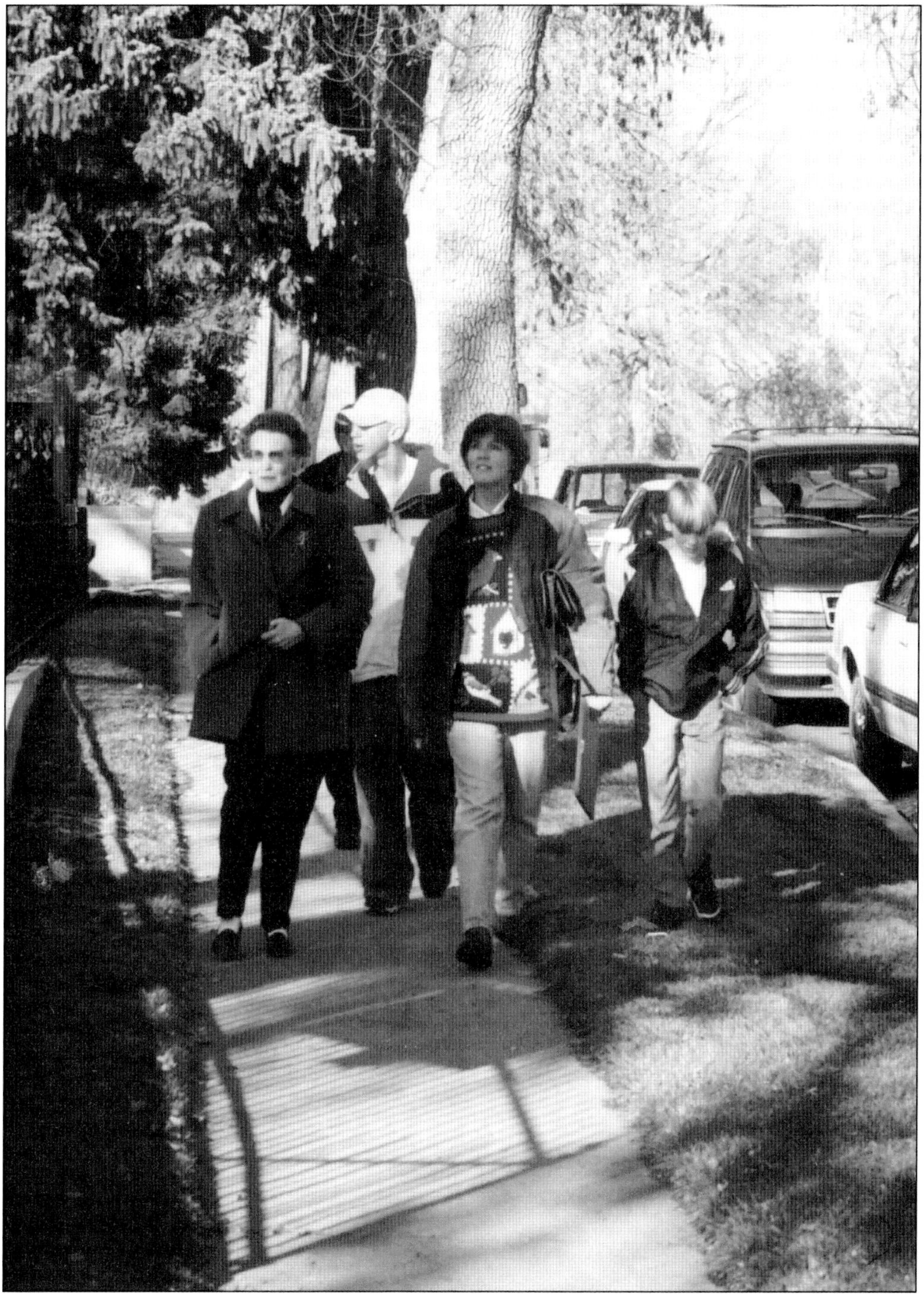

Three generations of the Parish family are represented in this photograph. Frances Lammers Wailes, Sandy Wailes Bennett, and Sandy's two sons, Brad and Randy, are shown on the walkway in front of the Historic Parish House and Museum on opening day. The Town of Johnstown started the purchase process at Thanksgiving time in 1998, and the historical society opened the doors for the first open house just a few weeks later.

www.arcadiapublishing.com

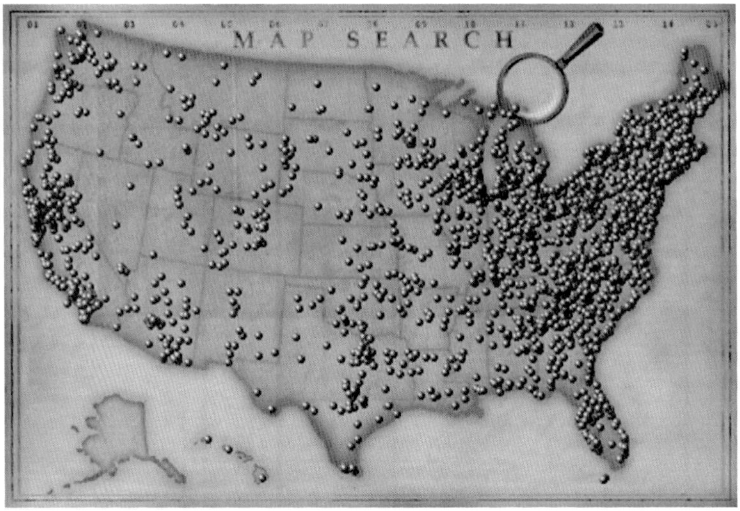

Discover books about the town where you grew up, the cities where your friends and families live, the town where your parents met, or even that retirement spot you've been dreaming about. Our Web site provides history lovers with exclusive deals, advanced notification about new titles, e-mail alerts of author events, and much more.

MADE IN THE USA

Arcadia Publishing, the leading local history publisher in the United States, is committed to making history accessible and meaningful through publishing books that celebrate and preserve the heritage of America's people and places. Consistent with our mission to preserve history on a local level, this book was printed in South Carolina on American-made paper and manufactured entirely in the United States.

This book carries the accredited Forest Stewardship Council (FSC) label and is printed on 100 percent FSC-certified paper. Products carrying the FSC label are independently certified to assure consumers that they come from forests that are managed to meet the social, economic, and ecological needs of present and future generations.

FSC
Mixed Sources
Product group from well-managed forests and other controlled sources
Cert no. SW-COC-001530
www.fsc.org

Find *Your* Place in History.